# Uncovering The Devil's Hiding-places

# Uncovering The Devil's Hiding-places

The devil having many **fooler-faces**, he can **hide** in many **unsuspected places**. Big **surprises** await those ignorant of his many **devious disguises**.

By

Ron Craig

Pastor of

Living Way Fellowship

Copyright © 2019 by Ron Craig.

Library of Congress Control Number: 2019906209
ISBN: Hardcover 978-1-7960-3123-2
Softcover 978-1-7960-3122-5
eBook 978-1-7960-3121-8

All rights reserved. No part of this book may be reproduced or transmitted in any form or by any means, electronic or mechanical, including photocopying, recording, or by any information storage and retrieval system, without permission in writing from the copyright owner.

Unless otherwise noted, *ALL* Scripture references are taken from the King James Bible Version; with some rewording for clarity. Within Scripture quotations, words in *italics* and/or *ALL CAPITALS* are this author's emphases. And some of the author's own words are in either *italics* or *ALL CAPITALS* for emphasis regarding certain Bible Truths.

Scripture quotations marked KJV are from the Holy Bible, King James Version (Authorized Version). First published in 1611. Quoted from the KJV Classic Reference Bible, Copyright © 1983 by The Zondervan Corporation.

The views expressed in this work are solely those of the author and do not necessarily reflect the views of the publisher, and the publisher hereby disclaims any responsibility for them.

Any people depicted in stock imagery provided by Getty Images are models, and such images are being used for illustrative purposes only. Certain stock imagery © Getty Images.

Print information available on the last page.

Rev. date: 06/14/2019

**To order additional copies of this book, contact:**
Xlibris
1-888-795-4274
www.Xlibris.com
Orders@Xlibris.com
790587

# Contents

| | | |
|---|---|---|
| Introduction | | ix |
| I | Chief information about our chief adversary | 1 |
| II | Favorite hiding-place—political correctness | 13 |
| III | Political correctness in the Old Testament | 29 |
| IV | Political correctness in the New Testament | 57 |
| V | Religious correctness—The worst kind | 73 |
| VI | The blame-game | 103 |
| VII | Celebrity role models | 109 |
| VIII | Bible Interpretation I | 111 |
| IX | Bible Interpretation II | 131 |
| X | Bible Interpretation III | 155 |
| XI | Money | 161 |
| XII | Sex | 173 |
| XIII | Prayer | 181 |
| XIV | Fear | 185 |
| XV | Death | 205 |
| Conclusion | | 219 |

# Acknowledgments

I acknowledge first of all Jesus Christ, my Lord and Savior, Who has given me all the revelation contained in this book. I also want to thank my wife, Joan, and the other members of **Living Way Fellowship** for their sustained patience and support of me in all my authoring endeavors. May this book and all of my other publications honor each of them.

# Introduction

*The devil never approaches human beings as his real self and yells*: "Boo, I am going to deceive you, and destroy you!" No, *the devil being a big bluff, he cannot afford to divulge his real character to people he seeks to destroy. No SANE person would fall for the devil's lies if he or she knew they were lies.* Proverbs 1:17 expresses that truth: "*Surely in vain is the net spread in the sight of any bird.*" Who would deliberately step into a trap they watched somebody set for them? *Christians certainly ought to know that Bible Truth*: "*Lest Satan should get an advantage of us* [believers]; *for we are not ignorant of his devices* (2 Corinthians 2:11)." But, many believers today are thoroughly ignorant of Satan's devices! One good reason for this *TIMELY* work. *This book has the DIVINE PURPOSE of re-educating believers, who have been thoroughly DECEIVED by both various religious traditions and nonsensical concepts propagated by this fallen-world system. Many in the modern church have become impressed by everything they ought not be impressed by, while they DELIBERATELY IGNORE GOD'S WORD*—the only *DOCUMENT* that may safely be trusted.

During my 40-plus years of ministry, I have learned that many people (even many church members) actually want to be *DECEIVED!* It is crazy, but true. Isaiah 30:9-10: "Israel is a rebellious people, *lying children, who WILL NOT HEAR the law of the LORD.* They say to the Seers: 'See not'; and to the prophets, '*Prophesy not unto us right things.* Speak unto us smooth things. *Prophesy DECEITS.*'" And Jeremiah 5:30-31: "An astonishing and horrible thing is committed in this [My] land: The prophets prophesy *FALSELY*, and the priests bear rule by their own means; and *My people love it that way.*"

Now, let us be honest. If that was prevalent among God's own people back in those ancient days, *be not deceived into thinking the same attitude is not hiding in today's church.* In fact, 2 Corinthians 2:11 is *a warning to Christians regarding that very possibility. Why warn Christians of Satan's devices if they neither exist nor pose any danger?* Think abut this:

*The devil's destructive character and tendencies have not changed over thousands of years since his INITIAL rebellion.* Moreover, *this fallen world we live in is virtually the same as always* (except for *technological advances*). And, *religion has remained the same, except for its modern-day garb; which is basically the world's concepts and practices camouflaged as Christianity, and donned by MODERN WOLVES IN SHEEP'S CLOTHING; which Jesus warned us about in* Matthew 7:15.

Those are the reasons WE MUST UNCOVER THE DEVIL'S HIDING-PLACES. And surprisingly, *many even in the church will likely be SURPRISED at some of the devil's camouflages! Four of his FAVORITE hide-aways are identified on the front cover of this book; and those etceteras scattered on the front cover suggest that there are other hiding-places as well. Yet, all of those hiding-places have a common denominator—The Adversary himself. The devil has to hide behind some sort of diversion, so he can perform his DIRTY DEEDS without being detected. Thus, just as many illegal enterprises make use of legitimate businesses to launder illegal funds, SO does Satan HIDE his EVIL works behind organizations and activities that seem legitimate, but are in many cases contrary to Scripture. (Of course, money-laundering itself is one of the devil's dirty deeds. His laundromat cleans not, but dirties its inventory!)*

Upcoming chapters will *DEAL IN DEPTH with some of the devil's obvious hiding-places; and some places which are not so obvious. The first chapter focuses on the character known as the devil, and Satan, as Holy Scripture identifies him.*

(Although this work uncovers many of the devil's favorite hiding-places, this volume is not intended to be exhaustive. However, *the lessons you learn from this book about Satan's hide-aways will SHARPEN YOUR SKILLS in uncovering other satanic camouflages you may encounter on your own.*)

# Chapter One

## Chief information about our chief adversary

First Peter 5:8 is a warning to us believers: "Be sober, be vigilant [constantly alert]; because *your adversary, the devil*, just as a roaring lion, walks about [on earth], seeking whom he may devour." So *Satan is called our adversary.* Why is he our adversary? Because we believers belong to God, and the devil is God's chief adversary! He cannot get to God Himself, so the best the devil can do is get to us—God's children. *We who are BORN AGAIN are children of God—made in the very image of God!* Satan hating the Head of the family (Hebrews 3:6), he hates every member of His *heavenly household.*

But *how did the devil's adversariness come about?* God's Word provides all the information we need. Isaiah 14:12-15: "How are you *FALLEN* from heaven [his original habitation], *LUCIFER*, you son of the morning! How are you cut down to the ground, who weakened the nations [All of that occurred before Adam was created.]! For you have said in your heart: '*I WILL ASCEND* into heaven, and *EXALT MY THRONE* above the *STARS* of God. [Then,] *I WILL SIT* upon the mount of the congregation [*on God's throne AFTER expelling God Himself*], on the sides of the North. I will ascend above the heights of the *CLOUDS* [*Lucifer had a God-given kingdom on earth.*]. *I will be LIKE the Most High.*' But you will be brought down to hell, to the sides of the pit [*instead of the sides of the North*]." This refers to Lucifer's fall—how he became the devil.

Ezekiel 28:12-19 provides even more *biblical truth about that ancient origin of Satan—HOW he became our Adversary.* "Son of man, take up a lamentation upon the *King of Tyrus*, and say to him: 'You sealed up the sum; full of wisdom, and perfect in beauty. *You have been in EDEN the garden of God* [not Adam's and Eve's Eden, because]; *every precious stone was your covering; the sardius, topaz, diamond, beryl, onyx, jasper, sapphire, emerald, carbuncle, and gold.* [In addition,] the workmanship of your tabrets, and pipes [some musical instruments], was prepared in you on the day that you were created. [Nothing like this was written about Eden or Adam. Nor this:] *You were the anointed cherub* [said only of angelic beings] *that covers*; and I [God] have set you so [His original position was the plan of the Creator.]. You were on *the holy mountain of God* [located up in heaven]; you have walked up and down in the midst of the stones of fire. *You were perfect in all your ways from the day you were created until iniquity was found in you* [could not have been stated of any human being after Adam]. By the multitude of your merchandis[ing (making deals)] they [other rebellious angels] have filled the midst of you with violence, and you have sinned. I therefore will cast you as profane out of the mountain of God. Thus, I will destroy you, Oh covering cherub, from the midst of the stones of fire. Your heart was lifted up [in pride], because of your [angelic] beauty, and you have corrupted your [original God-given] wisdom by reason of your [angelic] brightness. I *will throw you to the ground*. I will lay you before kings, that they may gaze on you [in your fallen state]. You have defiled your sanctuaries by the multitude of your iniquities, by the iniquity of your traffic[ing]. Therefore, will I bring forth a fire from your midst, and it will devour you; and *I will bring you to ashes on the earth in the sight of all who gaze at you.* And those who know you among the people will be astonished at you. You will be a terror, and will never be any more [not be annihilated, but ruined].'" (Lucifer was also given an earthly kingdom; from which he invaded heaven—Isaiah 14:13-15.)

Isaiah 27:1—future destruction of the devil: "In that day, the LORD, with His sore, great and strong sword will punish leviathan, the piercing serpent, even leviathan, that crooked serpent; and *He will slay the dragon that is in the sea.*" That has to be Satan, *the dragon* of Revelation chapter twelve.

But, before we get into the fine details of the devil's final fate, let us look at more biblical details of his real character. Notice that Isaiah 27:1 refers to the devil as a *serpent*. Early on in his shady earth-career, Satan got tagged as a serpent. The obvious reason being: *the devil tempted Eve through one of Eden's most beautiful and shrewd creatures—the serpent; a snake.* Consider Genesis 3:1: "Now, the serpent was more subtle [shrewd] than any [other] *beast of the field*, which the LORD God had made." Moreover, Genesis chapter three and other Scripture passages seem to suggest that, the serpent, before the fall, could both *talk*, and *stand upright*—had legs. *Why else would Moses record that the serpent talked to Eve?* And, why did Eve not act surprised when the serpent spoke to her? Furthermore, why did God curse the serpent so that from that day forward serpents (snakes) had to crawl on the ground (Genesis 3:14; Isaiah 65:25)? If snakes were legless before that curse was pronounced, then God's words made little sense. Let us believe what the Bible plainly teaches!

The *obvious point* I am pointing out here is the same as I pointed out up front in the introduction—*That Satan rarely approaches his intended victims in person.* He did tempt our Lord in person, but that seems to be rare. Satan hid behind the serpent to get to Eve, then used Eve to get to Adam. The devil tried to get to Job through his wife (Job 2:9); and Peter to get to Christ (Mark 8:33). Then, he commissioned a fallen angel (hiding behind the religious leaders) to harass Paul (2 Corinthians 12:7). *Religious people* seem to be *Satan's most useful tools* in causing other people to fall, or get hurt. Read the New Testament with that in mind. But now, read this:

Job 1:6-7: "There was a day when the sons of God [quite obviously, the angels that had not rebelled] came to present themselves before the LORD. Satan came also among them. The LORD said to Satan: 'Where did you come from?' Satan answered the LORD: *'From going to and fro in the earth, and from walking up and down in it.'*" The same thing happened in Job 2:1-2. What was the purpose of Satan's earth-walk? First Peter 5:8 answers that: *"Your adversary the devil, as a roaring lion, walks about seeking WHOM HE MAY DEVOUR."* Our adversary is LOOKING FOR VICTIMS! Peter tells us how to keep from becoming one of his victims—1 Peter 5:9.

What is the planned fate of Satan's victims? John 10:10: "The thief [*obviously referring to Satan, the chief thief*] comes not, but for to *steal* and to *kill* and to *destroy.*" Satan has no other purpose than to VICTIMIZE God's creation. Therefore, it ought to be obvious why the devil has to camouflage his evil deeds. *Just as the terrorists who hide behind civilians, using them as human SHIELDS, in order to protect themselves from exposure and damage, Satan himself HIDES BEHIND people others DO NOT SUSPECT, in order to take down other people*; making them victims as well. In other words, *the devil uses victims to make other victims!* A Scripture revealing that very principle is John 8:44: "You are of your father the devil, and *the lusts of your father you will do.* He was a murderer from the beginning, and *remained not in the truth*; because, *there is no truth in him.* When Satan lies, he does so from his own [resources]. For, he is a liar, and the father of [both lies and liars]." And, Jesus said that to some Jews who had believed on Him (John 8:31)! *Like father, like son*, was the scriptural principle our Savior established here. The devil's SPIRITUAL CHILDREN act just like their SPIRITUAL FATHER—the devil. And the devil does have children—multitudes of them. First John 3:10: "In this the *children of God* are manifest, and *the children of the devil*: Whoever does *NOT* do righteousness is *NOT of God*, neither he who loves *NOT* his brother." If one is *NOT* of God, then he or she *IS* of Satan! There is *NO* middle ground. So says Matthew 6:24; and so teaches 1 John 5:19: "We know that we are of God, and that *the whole world lies in wickedness* [under the *SWAY* of the wicked one—different translations]." Moreover, consider Matthew 7:13-14: "Enter in[to God's Kingdom] at the strait gate. For, wide is the gate, and broad is the way [path] which leads to destruction; and many there be who go in thereat. Because strait is the gate, and narrow is the way, which leads unto life; and few there be who find it." These passages and many others prove that most people go to hell when they die. *Most humans are lost!*

The Bible reveals that the devil is somehow connected to every human problem. Ephesians 6:12: *"For, we wrestle not against flesh and blood*, but rather against the principalities [fallen angels, and evil] powers, and *rulers of the DARKNESS of this world; against SPIRITUAL wickedness in high places."*

Just as many of the Scripture references in this book fit under more than one chapter-subject, so the *NEXT* passage fits *THIS* chapter-subject, as well as others. *It is appropriate here in that it mentions the devil's fall.* In Paul's instructions to Timothy about installing church leaders, Paul specifically laid down this rule: "Not a novice [a new believer], lest being lifted up with pride [as Lucifer was] he [the new believer] fall into the condemnation of the devil [the same condemnation Lucifer fell into—becoming Satan, the Adversary]. Moreover, he must have a good report of those who are outside [people who are lost]; lest he fall into reproach, and the snare of the devil (1 Timothy 3:6-7)." This Scripture passage adds to our knowledge about how the devil became the devil; and a little about how he presently operates. *The world constantly looks for any scrap of supposed evidence that might be used to put the Christian believer in a BAD light; so those worldlings will think they are excused from obeying God.* And, *they are even more than willing to help Christians sin, so they can create a disclaimer, and dismiss the Gospel message as though it did not apply to them.* Satan is obviously behind that deception. By such tricks he can snare both believers and unbelievers!

And now for Satan's prophesied end. Way back in Jesus' days on earth *demons knew they were condemned to eternal punishment.* Matthew 8:29 fills us in on that: "And, behold, they [the demons inhabiting their victims] cried out, saying, 'What have we to do with You, Jesus, Son of God? *Have You come to torment us before the time?'" The demons questioned not the fact of their infernal future, but protested the timing of it.* Was Jesus cutting short their evil careers on earth?

And, although most prophesies of the book of Revelation are yet future, *the devil obviously presently knows that they will come to pass, and that his loose-time on earth is limited. If demons knew about their time-limit long ago, then Satan is aware of it right now!* Revelation 12:12: "Woe to inhabitants of the earth and the sea! For, the devil has come down unto you, having great wrath, *because he knows that he has only a short time* [left to tempt mankind before he is incarcerated in the abyss for a thousand years, then released for a short season, then cast into the eternal Lake of Fire]." Both Satan and demons know more truth than many church members!

But, not only will Satan burn forever in the Lake of Fire, every human being who is *aligned with Satan* will suffer the same eternal fate—only in different degrees. Matthew 25:41: "Then, He [Christ] will say to those on His left hand, *'Depart from Me, you accursed, into the everlasting fire, prepared for the devil and his angels.'" That destiny was not intended for human beings* (or for any angel) *at creation, but was instead PREPARED for Satan and his angelic rebel rabble.* However, Jesus made it clear in the previous passage that the Lake of Fire will be the eternal abode of human rebels, the same as angelic rebels. Yet, human beings can repent in this life and be saved, although angels cannot. *And most people do not!*

Still another Scripture passage proving that *people* go to hell is Revelation 20:11-15: "And I saw a great white throne, and Him Who sat on it, from Whose face both the earth and heaven fled away. But there was found *NO PLACE* for them. Then I saw the dead both small and great stand before God. Then *the books were opened*; and *another book was opened*, which is *the Book of Life*. The dead were judged out of those things which were written in those books, according to their works. Then, *the sea gave up the dead which were in it*; *and DEATH and HELL delivered up the dead which were in them.* Then, everyone was *JUDGED*, according to his or her works. Then *death and hell were cast into the Lake of Fire*; which is the second death. And, whosoever was not found written in the Book of Life was cast into the [same] Lake of Fire."

As for the varying degrees of torment suffered by people in that fire, Luke 12:47-48 explains: "The servant who knew his Lord's will, yet prepared not himself [to obey it], neither did [his Lord's revealed] will, *WILL BE BEATEN WITH MANY STRIPES* [will suffer greatly]. However, he who knew not [his Lord's will], yet, [during this life] committed things *WORTHY OF STRIPES, WILL BE BEATEN* [but] *WITH FEWER STRIPES* [will suffer less intensely]. *To whomsoever much* [knowledge and privilege] *has been granted*; *of him, or her, will much be required.* To whom men have committed much, of him they will ask the more." (And Deity will certainly do the same!)

The devil will occupy the lowest and hottest room of that *FIRE PIT*, and suffer the most. But, ultra-evil human beings will also be confined to those lower and hotter quarters:

Deuteronomy 32:22: *"A FIRE is kindled in My [Jehovah's] anger, and it will burn to the LOWEST HELL."* Moreover, "We know Him, Who has said: *'Vengeance belongs unto Me. I will recompense [repay],'* says the Lord. And yet again, *'The Lord will judge [even] His people.'* It is a fearful thing to *FALL* into the hands of The Living God (Hebrews 10:30-31)." Because: *"Our God is a consuming fire* (Hebrews 12:29)." Therefore,...

Even though this chapter primarily concerns the biblical facts in regard to *the devil's own rise and demise*, I want to expose as well yet another of his favorite hiding-places—*his keeping hidden the Bible Truth that the sinner's eternal fate is closely connected to the devil's eternal fate.* And so,...

A good place to begin is Isaiah 13:9-13: "Behold, the day of the *LORD* comes, cruel, both with wrath and fierce anger, to lay the land desolate. And, *He will destroy the sinners out of it.* The stars of heaven and the constellations will not give any light. And the sun will be darkened [Joel 3:15, Matthew 24:29, Mark 13:24] in his going forth, and the moon will not cause her light to shine. *And, I* [Deity] *will punish the world for their evil and the wicked for their iniquity. I will cause the arrogance of the proud to cease, and lay low the haughtiness of the terrible. I will make a human more precious* [rare] *than fine gold;* [rarer] *than the golden wedge of Ophir. Therefore, I will SHAKE the heavens* [Hebrews 12:26]; *and the earth will REMOVE out of her place* [orbit] *under the wrath of the LORD of hosts in the day of His fierce anger."* Now add to that,...

Nahum 1:2: *"GOD IS JEALOUS [of His reputation and His creation]. Thus, the LORD revenges. The LORD revenges and is furious. The LORD will take vengeance on His adversaries; and reserves wrath for His enemies."* Add this as well,...

Zephaniah 1:14-15: *"That great DAY of the LORD is near.* It is near and hastes greatly; even the voice of the day of the LORD. [On that day,] The mighty man will cry there bitterly. [Because,] *That day is a day of wrath, a day of trouble, and distress, a day of wasting and desolation, a day of darkness and gloominess, a day of clouds and thick darkness."* People on earth on that day who are not right with God will perish.

*MORE* Judgment-Day prophecies in the *NEW* Testament: Matthew 3:7: "When he [John the Baptizer] saw many of the Pharisees and Sadducees come to his baptism, he said unto them: 'Oh generation of vipers [snakes—connecting them to the Serpent—the devil], *who has warned you to flee from the wrath to come?'"* Now that refers to *future wrath*, but,...

John 3:36: "He who believes on the Son *HAS* everlasting life. But he who believes not on the Son will not see life; but *the wrath of God* [presently] *ABIDES on him."* Now-wrath!

Romans 1:18: "The wrath of God is revealed from heaven against *all ungodliness and all unrighteousness of those who hold the truth in unrighteousness."* (Preachers be warned!)

Romans 2:5-6: "But, after your hardness and impenitent heart, you *TREASURE UP* for yourself wrath against the day of wrath, and revelation of the righteous *JUDGMENT* of God; Who will render to *EVERY* man according to his deeds."

Romans 2:8-9: "*To those who are contentious, and do not obey the truth, but obey unrighteousness* [instead, will come] *indignation and wrath. Tribulation and anguish upon EVERY soul who does evil*; of the Jew first, and also of the Gentile." God is no respecter of nationalities! And more Bible Truth:

Ephesians 2:2-3: "*IN TIME PAST you* [Christians] *walked* [lived] *according to the course of this world, according to the prince of the power of the air, the spirit that now works in the children of disobedience* [There is the sinner's connection to the devil.]. *Among whom also we all* [including Paul] *had our conversation* [lifestyle] *in times past...and were by nature the children of wrath, even as others* [who are still lost]." So,...

Ephesians 5:3-6: "*Allow neither fornication, uncleanness, nor covetousness to be once named among you* [saints], *as is proper for believers. Neither filthiness, nor foolish talking, nor jesting, which are not convenient. But rather, giving thanks. Because you know that no whoremonger, or unclean person, or covetous man, who is an idolater, has ANY INHERITANCE in the Kingdom of Christ, and of God. Let no one deceive you* with vain words. For because of such [evil] things comes the wrath of God [both now and in the future] on the *children of disobedience* [they being the devil's children—1 John 3:10]."

Colossians 3:6 agrees with Ephesians 5:3-6, saying: *"For which things' sake the wrath of God comes on the children of disobedience."* Only *repentant sinners* escape God's wrath!

More intense is 2 Thessalonians 1:7-9: "You [Christians] who are troubled, rest with [the rest of] us [believers], *when the Lord Jesus will be revealed from heaven with His mighty angels, in flaming fire, taking vengeance on those who know not God; who OBEY NOT the Gospel of our Lord Jesus Christ: Who will be PUNISHED WITH EVERLASTING DESTRUCTION from the presence of the Lord, and from His glorious power."*

Jude 5-7: *"I bring to your remembrance, even though you once knew this,* that the Lord, having saved [Israel] from the land of Egypt, *afterward destroyed all of those who believed not. And, those angels that kept not their first estate, but left their own habitation, God has reserved in everlasting chains under darkness to the judgment of the great day. And just as Sodom, and Gomorrah, and those cities around them, in like manner* [to the fallen angels], *gave themselves to fornication, going after strange flesh* [sexual perversion], *are set forth as examples, suffering the vengeance of eternal fire."*

Revelation 6:15-17: "[At Jesus' coming,] The kings of the earth, great men, rich men, chief [military] captains, mighty men, and every bondman and freeman will hide themselves in the dens and rocks of the mountains; saying to the rocks and mountains: *'Fall on us, and hide us from the face of Him Who sits on the throne, and from the wrath of the Lamb. The great day of His wrath has come; and who can endure it?'"*

Revelation 14:19-20: *"The angel thrust his sickle into the earth, and gathered of the* [fruit of the] *vine of the earth, and cast that fruit into the great winepress of the WRATH of God. And the winepress was trodden outside the city* [Jerusalem], *and blood came out of the winepress up to the horse bridles, by the space of* [about 180 miles]." *Wrath to the uttermost!*

*And Jesus Christ will be personally involved in meting out that wrath.* Revelation 19:15: "*Out of His* [our Lord's] *mouth goes a sharp sword, that with it He should smite the nations. And, He will rule them with a rod of iron. And, He treads the winepress of the fierceness and wrath of Almighty God.*"

Now, back to exposing the devil's past and future. Isaiah 14:12-15 *both indicted him, and prophesied his final demise*: "How are you *fallen* from heaven, Oh Lucifer, you son of the morning! How are you *cut down* to the ground [happened in the past one time already], who did *weaken* the nations! For you have said in your heart: '*I will ascend* into heaven. *I will exalt* my throne above the stars of God. *I will sit* also on the mount of the congregation, there on the sides of the *NORTH* [location of God's throne]. *I will ascend* above the heights of the clouds. And *I will be like* the Most High.' But you will be brought down to hell, to the sides of the pit [instead]."

Revelation 12:7-9 *prophesies the Adversary's future close encounter with earth's landscape*: "*War broke out in heaven. Michael and his angels fought against the dragon* [the devil]; *and, the dragon fought, along with his angels,* [against those angels under Michael]. *But, they* [the devil's army] *prevailed not; neither was a place found anymore for them in heaven. And, that great red dragon was cast out* [of heaven]; *that old serpent*, called the Devil, and Satan, who deceives the whole world. *He was cast out* [of heaven], *to the earth,* [for the final time], *and his angels were cast out with him.*" (Satan loses!)

And verse ten continues: "I heard a loud voice in heaven, saying…'[Satan] the *ACCUSER* of our brethren is cast down, who accused them before our God day and night.'" Then:

Revelation 20:1-3: "I saw an angel [*Just one angel!*] come down from heaven, *having the key* [to unlock] *the bottomless pit; and a great chain in his hand* [that had the devil's name on it]. *And the angel laid hold of the dragon, that old serpent called the Devil, and Satan, and BOUND HIM for a thousand years.* And cast him down into the bottomless pit, and shut Satan up, and set a seal on him, that he should deceive the nations no more, till that thousand years would be fulfilled. And after that, [Satan] must be loosed for a little season."

Revelation 20:7-10: "Then, when the thousand years are expired, *Satan will be loosed from his prison, and will go out to deceive ALL the nations that are in the four quarters of the earth, Gog, and Magog, to gather them together to battle.* The number of them is as the sand of the sea. And they went up on the breadth of the earth, and compassed the camp of the saints, and the beloved city [Jerusalem]. And [this time] fire came down from God out of heaven, and devoured them all. And Satan who deceived them was cast into the Lake of Fire and brimstone, where the beast [*the Antichrist*] and the false prophet [have been incarcerated for a thousand years], and they will all be tormented day and night for ever and ever."

From Genesis to Revelation, *the Scriptures reveal Satan's diabolical personality, and his ultra-evil designs against God and His creation.* Many passages expose his heinous deeds. Moreover, *there are certain passages that assign titles to the devil.* And of course, *DEVIL* is one of those telling titles.

The list: Adversary, Devil, Dragon, god of this age, Prince of this age, Satan, Thief and Tempter. Certain English Bible versions call him the Evil One. (I could have missed a title.)

So, let us begin with the *ADVERSARY* tag. First Peter 5:8: "Be sober. Be vigilant [on alert]. Because your *ADVERSARY*, the *DEVIL*, as a roaring lion, walks about [on earth], seeking whom he may devour." God's adversary is our adversary!

*DEVIL, DRAGON, SATAN* and *SERPENT*. Revelation 12:9: "That great *DRAGON* was cast out, that old *SERPENT*, called the *DEVIL*, and *SATAN*, who deceives the whole world."

Revelation 20:2: "And he [just one angel] laid hold on the *DRAGON*, that old *SERPENT*, called the *DEVIL*, and *SATAN*, and bound him [in the Abyss] for a thousand years."

One more title: "*The god of this world* [*age—god* not to be capitalized] has blinded the minds of those who believe not, lest the light of the glorious Gospel about Christ, Who is the image of God, should shine unto them (2 Corinthians 4:4)." *Satan was never god of the earth; just god of this evil age!*

Ephesians 2:2: "In time past you walked *according to the age of this kosmos, according to the PRINCE of the power of the air, the spirit* [obviously the devil] *that now works in the children of disobedience."* In John 14:30, Jesus called Satan the *PRINCE* of the *kosmos* (Greek)—the sinful *world system.*

John 8:44: "You are of your [spiritual] father the *DEVIL,* and therefore the lusts of your father you will to do. *He was a murderer from the beginning; neither abode he in the truth, because there is NO truth in him.* Whenever he speaks a lie, he speaks of his own. For *he is a liar,* and the father of it."

John 10:10: "The *THIEF* comes not, but to steal, kill and destroy. I [Jesus] have come that [believers] might have life; and have it more abundantly." Satan is the *CHIEF THIEF!*

In both Matthew 4:3 and 1 Thessalonians 3:5, the devil, who tempted our Lord, and is still in the tempting business, is actually named the *TEMPTER.* (A most appropriate title.)

The good news of both Scripture and this vital volume is that Christ our Savior has: *"...Delivered us from the wrath to come* (1 Thessalonians 1:10)." And, for that reason alone we are assured that: *"God has not appointed us* [who believe] *to wrath* [now or in the future], *but* [rather,] *to obtain salvation by our Lord Jesus Christ* (1 Thessalonians 5:9)." *Hallelujah!*

The Gospel reason: *"He* [the Savior] *Who ascended, what is it but that, He also descended first into the lower parts of the earth* [went to hell—Matthew 12:40, Acts 2:27, 31]? *He Who descended is that One Who also ascended far above the heavens; that He might fill all things* (Ephesians 4:9-10)."

*Jesus bore God's wrath on the cross, so that we would be rescued from wrath.* Romans 5:9-10: "Being justified by His [shed] blood, *we will be saved from wrath through Him.* For, if when we were enemies, we were reconciled to God, by the death of His Son, much more, *being now reconciled, we will be saved* [*from present and future wrath*] *by His life."* One of Satan's favorite hiding-tricks is to hide that scriptural truth from both sinners and saints. And one way he does it is,...

# Chapter Two

## Favorite hiding-place—political correctness

*Of all the books on the Christian market that address the subject-matter of exposing our enemy—Satan—none of them DARE to expose the truth about the devil's hiding-places like this work does.* I believe I can validly claim such; *although I have NOT READ ANY of them. I only know they are out there.* Moreover, I believe the same can be said about this chapter. *How many CHRISTIAN books deal with political correctness? Even discussing political correctness in public is a big no-no; especially in church circles.* Churches and preachers ought to stay out of politics, is the general consensus. However,...

Try your best to stay out of politics, politics will not stay away from you! Like it or not, *political correctness affects all segments of society (ESPECIALLY Christian believers). Those liberal politicians often cry:* "Separation of church and state!" But, their concept is one-sided. True separation would apply to church AND state. However, *liberal politicians demand on one hand that churches stay out of government business, but on the other, continually stick their long political noses in the church's business.* A demonic political-correctness ploy!

My purpose in this chapter is to *prove beyond doubt* that political correctness is one of our Adversary's hiding-places. In other chapters, we will look at *Bible records of incidences of political correctness.* And, *we will investigate the history of some believers who were heavily involved in government.*

Other than that little introduction, how do I start such a chapter? *To grasp what I am endeavoring to get across here, we have to zoom out to the big picture; NOT focus on isolated incidents. Once you perceive that Satan camouflages himself behind one political word, or action, you will see him in every political maneuver.* It is so simple and enlightening! *You will begin to detect that behind every societal perversion, the very inventor of perversion—Satan himself—conveniently hides.*

People question whether or not television is evil, because they *SEE* so much evil onscreen. *Some have even concluded that the devil must have invented the internet because of the gross evils invading people's lives through that medium.*
Some might actually *BLAME* God for those evils, because He prophesied in Daniel 12:4 (many hundreds of years ago), that, *IN THE LAST DAYS knowledge will increase.* The world has always been *inundated* with some kind of knowledge, so what kind of knowledge was that ancient prophecy referring to? *Today's technological advances—modern inventions! But can we blame Deity for how humanity uses those inventions?* (Of course, there is also great increase in Bible knowledge.)
*Time and labor-saving gadgets are handy, but do not and cannot alter sinful human nature.* In fact, *modern inventions make it EASIER TO SIN!* And Satan takes advantage of every such opportunity. And his primary instrument for achieving his evil agenda is *political-correctness—pressure to conform!*

Earlier I provided a list of Satan's titles. *Although the list did not include the word PERVERT, that is one characteristic of the devil.* According to Christ's words in John 8:44, *Satan is THE CHIEF PERVERT—THE LUSTS of your spiritual father you will do.* In other words, *people-perversions are the result of their connection to the devil—THE CHIEF PERVERT.* Christ said Israel was a *perverse generation* in Matthew 17:17. The Greek word *perverse* in that verse means *distort*, or *corrupt*. *The devil was obviously behind all those Jewish perversions.* But Philippians 2:15 says the entire lost world is a *perverse generation*. And Paul, in Galatians 1:7, said some wanted to *pervert the Gospel of Christ.* Although the Greek word there is a different term, it also means to pervert, or corrupt. *Who would want to pervert the Gospel more than the devil?*

That establishes the Bible fact that, *the devil is the Chief Pervert*. Thus, *perversion is the devil's PRIMARY ACTIVITY in this fallen world*. And his primary perversion-tool is political correctness. I will explain that in detail later, but first let us backtrack to *prehistory*, and focus on Satan's appearance in history. *Satan's attempt to replace his Creator would require perverting BOTH his own character, and that of his Creator! His becoming LIKE the Most High* (Isaiah 14:14) *would mean that God would no longer be THE Most High. There could not be TWO Most Highs! Lucifer attempting to raise his status to his Creator's level, he instead lowered it to the devil level.*

After thoroughly failing at that project, the fallen Lucifer, now the devil, *came into the Garden of Eden and applied his perversion-tactic there. The first thing he distorted was what God had said to Adam and Eve about the forbidden tree.* You see, *in the human realm, it all started in the Garden of Eden. Both perversion and political correctness were introduced to paradise.* The devil right then became "the god of this age (2 Corinthians 4:4)," *and began spreading his perversions from Eden throughout the earth; continuing to this day.*

Let us look closely at some *political-correctness practices*, learn how to detect them, and become *EXPERTS* at avoiding their pitfalls. *Political correctness* being very common, it has certain *recognizable earmarks. Once you see THE GENERAL PATTERN, you spot political correctness immediately. And by removing its camouflage, you reveal its TRUE nature. Political correctness being easily spotted, it is easily avoided.* Mature Christians are not readily drawn into political correctness.

Satan is a liar (John 8:44). *Jesus said there is no truth in him. A LIE is a falsehood—which is a distortion or perversion of the truth.* The devil is out to steal, kill, and destroy (John 10:10); all of which are distortions and perversions of God's original purpose for creation. If you are willing to look, with an open heart, and mind, *you will BEGIN to perceive satanic perversions in every department of human life.* And political correctness is *the major tool* by which the devil brings about those perversions—their effects always being *DETRIMENTAL* to the human race; and to God's people in particular.

The *RANGE* of political correctness covers the entirety of life on earth—from federal governments to family structure. At this writing, all sorts of evidence is coming out about the hypocritical, and even criminal, actions of *many government officials in Washington D.C.* Some of that information I want to emphasize concerns the *COVER-UPS* of those *hypocritical and criminal* deeds. *Why do guilty parties want to cover their unlawful activities? To avoid penalty! And how do they cover* their indiscretions? With lies! But, how do many of them get away with their *hypocritical and criminal actions* for so long? They have help—others who cover for them. *But, why would other people COVER for them? Unlawful activity is often more widespread than the one culprit.* So, they lie for one another! And, what is the pressure they use to assure that everybody involved *keeps the lid on information* that might incriminate them? Political correctness! Maintain the status-quo—those politicians who are in power, and will do anything to stay in power. *Political correctness is a highly-developed social and political art that knows how to say just the right things to the right people at the right time to get them to elect you to office, and keep you there.* Anyone who opposes either their words or actions is shamed or ostracized by the status quo—those already in power. *Vultures of a feather do flock together!*

*That politically-INcorrect statement opens the door for me to mention yet another unsavory entity that powerfully helps guilty politicians continue to get away with hypocritical, even criminal, activities—leftist,* so-called *liberal, news networks.*

*News networks are SUPPOSED to report actual news. But most of the current news networks have become propaganda machines for certain politicians and their political party. Just recently, those liberal news networks have hastily broadcast inaccurate news articles about a person in the political party which they* (the so-called reporters and their networks) *hate and despise (WHICH INFORMATION THEY KNEW UP FRONT WAS INCORRECT), then had to retract their statements when the actual truth about it all came out from other news outlets.* The goal of that game: *Those reporters and their propaganda networks hope the first broadcast has done some damage to their enemy; even though they had to retract that news when confronted with the truth.* Gullible viewers take the bait!

And that proves this: *If those BIASED news networks did not back certain deceitful political candidates with their OWN lies and deceptions, none of those untrustworthy candidates would EVER be elected to office.* Just How many law-abiding citizens would knowingly elect liars and crooks to represent them in government? *If they lie to get into office, they will lie after they get into office! Those people obviously care nothing about the people who put them into office; just about getting into, and staying in, a POWERFUL and LUCRATIVE position.* The truth would have a negative effect on their career, their prestige, *AND* their salary. Those politicians have learned to use *political correctness* to get into power and stay in power.

Other news outlets have recently been exposing some of the hypocrisy of some of the liberal news networks; so some of the so-called reporters who put out *fake news broadcasts* have been fired. But, I challenge you to think about this: No one person does all the research, assembling of information and reporting of any news article. Many are involved. Which tells me that *the firing of only one individual in such cases is just another politically-correct maneuver of the network head to divert public attention off him or herself. That fired anchor becomes a scapegoat for the higher-ups in that organization.*

The primary point I want to make from this eye-opening revelation is that: *Political correctness is the deceptive power that protects the guilty from exposure.* And, *it being deceptive proves it to be a work of Satan. Political correctness ALWAYS pressures people to do the WRONG thing. The devil ALWAYS tempts people to do the WRONG thing. Satan NEVER tempts people to do the RIGHT thing. And the right thing is ALWAYS what God says is right!* I have noticed that *IN EVERY CASE, political correctness pressures people to act contrary to God's Word—proving EVERY CASE OF POLITICAL CORRECTNESS to be of Satan!* It is one of his primary destructive tools. So, ought it not be obvious that *believers need to learn to detect political correctness in all its forms, then expose it and defeat it with God's Word?* Instead, the very reverse has happened: *Political correctness has invaded the Lord's church, reducing its effectiveness on earth, and even threatening its existence.* More on that later; but now, continuing the secular side,...

Having focused for a little while upon *crooked politicians, let us now zero in on crooked policies that crooked politicians have made into crooked laws*—crooked when compared with God's Word. (And, in some cases crooked because they were made into laws by *unauthorized* legislative means.) *All kinds of immoral concepts and activities have been forced upon the citizens of this country* (USA) *by means of ungodly laws that make it politically INcorrect for one to refuse to acknowledge, and especially to speak out against, the evils of such laws.*

Case in point: Abortion—Premature termination of some military mission, or the life of an unborn human being. Like it or not, believe it or not, unborn babies are human beings; not just blobs of *TISSUE!* Truth is, *upon the coming together of the human sperm and egg, another human being is in the making!* Thus, *the termination of that unique human being is outright murder!* More and more evidence of that reality has piled up in recent years, so the political perpetrators of that *demonic concept and practice* have softened the terminology; renaming it "women's rights"—the current *politically-correct* term. *Changing the wording SUPPOSEDLY protects the guilty parties.* Challenging abortion would be denying the rights of half the population of the USA—*POLITICALLY INCORRECT!*

That is the *moral* and *scriptural* side of the *SIN* known as abortion. But the *legal* (actually, *illegal*) side of abortion lies in the fact that it was *NOT* legislated by an act of congress, but was decided by the Supreme Court of the United States. *This country was founded upon the premise of separation of powers* (three powers) *in government.* I understand that *the legislative branch of government* (House and Senate) *makes our laws. Then, the executive branch* (President) *executes the laws—puts them in force. If a law is challenged it goes to the judicial branch* (Supreme Court), *which determines whether the law is constitutional.* So the abortion law is *NOT A VALID LAW*, but rather a *BREACH* of our constitutional system.

Recently, congress has been either negligent or impotent regarding its legislative role in our constitutional system, so presidents often bypass congress, *legislating their own laws by executive action*—which is legal to a degree; but has been carried far beyond their constitutionally-allowed authority.

Not only that; recently, in many cases, *local governments and even state authorities have refused to acknowledge and abide by some of the duly-legislated laws*; thereby becoming lawless—*just as the apostle prophesied*. Matthew 24:12 says that toward the end *lawlessness will prevail*. Lawlessness is also evidenced by *widespread violence and rebellion of many lawless individuals and groups in our country and across the globe*. Therefore, *lawlessness* has become politically correct! We are beholding that happening before our very eyes every day in these *LAST* days. *The devil being behind lawlessness, and lawlessness being politically correct in our society today, it is obvious that Satan is the inventor of political correctness.*

If anyone speaks for biblical morality and decency, *many insist that morality cannot be legislated. But lawmakers CAN and DO legislate immorality! Law books are full of manmade laws that diametrically oppose and violate God's moral laws.* Moreover, most of those immoral laws not only make it legal to commit immoral acts, but make it illegal to call them sin.

But, let us look at some *Bible lingo* about such things. In Psalms 94:20, the psalmist rebukes authorities, "*who frame mischief by the law*." Isaiah 10:1 is an even clearer warning: "Woe to all those who *decree unrighteous decrees, and write grievousness* [by unjust laws,] *which they have prescribed.*"

*The modern lawlessness mentality is obviously preparing for the arrival of the Antichrist*; who will: "hurl great swelling words against the Most High, and will wear out the saints of the Most High, and who will think to *change times and laws* [to fit his agenda, and thwart God's agenda] (Daniel 7:25)."

And Proverbs 28:4 plainly states: "*Those who forsake the law* [of God, and any God-approved laws of the land] *praise the wicked. But, those who keep the law contend with them* [the wicked]." *What personality would want the wicked to be praised?* The devil! *The devil being the Wicked One, praising the wicked is praising the devil! And what does he use to get people to praise him?* You guessed it—*Political correctness!*

One more enlightening observation about the *moral flaw* called *political correctness*: Man's law, at least in the United States of America, has established "*statutes of limitation*" in connection with certain crimes, including murder. *In divine law,* (which everyone will eventually be judged by,) *there are NO "statutes of limitation." ALL sinners will stand before God at that Great White Throne Judgment, at the very end of this age,* and will be judged for *EVERY* ungodly intent, thought, word and action; from their very first infraction to the last.

A thousand years earlier, *believers will have stood before the Judgment Seat of Christ to be JUDGED for every ungodly thought, word, and action that has not been repented of, and forgiven, then washed away by the shed blood of our Savior.* Check out Romans 14:10 and 2 Corinthians 5:10 for details on that *future judgment of every born-again believer.*

That *political-correctness camouflage* is also being pulled off *certain celebrities in the ENTERTAINMENT and BUSINESS worlds. Sexual harassment allegations are on the rise on the West Coast, as well as on the East Coast*—Washington D.C. Thus, *they are finding out that political correctness is NOT A SURE-FIRE GUARANTEE that their sins will not be detected.* "Be sure your sins will find you out!" Who said that? Moses, in Numbers 32:23. That is God's law; which supersedes *ALL* other laws. Man's law is temporary. Divine law is eternal!

My intent here is *NOT TO GLORIFY* political correctness, but rather, to *PROVE* that political correctness is a powerful weapon the devil uses to contaminate, and desecrate, every societal entity. *Satan obviously wants to pervert and destroy every human institution, as well as every human.* "The thief comes *NOT BUT* for to steal, kill and destroy (John 10:10)."

Another *human/demonic* practice people today are using political correctness to shield from *exposure* and *elimination* is homosexuality—two or more men committing sexual acts with other men; or two or more women doing the same with other women. *Such degrading practices are forbidden in both Old and New Testaments of God's Word.* Sadly, practicers of those sickening practices do not realize that *the degradation of the human race is the devil's very purpose.* Satan is out to *defile, demean* and *destroy* all of creation (John 10:10). *And in so many cases people perpetrate their very own defilement and destruction. Then brag about it!* Romans 1:32 shows the utter stupidity of such ungodly attitudes and actions.

Leviticus chapter eighteen explicitly describes numerous immoral activities that the heathen nations practiced before Israel took over their land (*exactly the reason God had Israel cleanse that land*). Deity forbade the males from committing sex acts with other males, and both males and females from performing sex acts with animals (*which Canaanite heathen had done in their worship of their false gods*). Those heathen also sacrificed some of their little babies to false gods—which were actually demons (Leviticus 17:7, Deuteronomy 32:17, Psalms 106:37, 1 Corinthians 10:20). *Captivated by one sex sin* (or any other kind of sin), *sinners always SINK to deeper levels. The devil never stops taking his victims to lower levels of degradation and destruction.* Upon ensnaring a person in one kind of sin, Satan will allure him or her into still others; *until that person is completely destroyed, and God's creation is totally debased. That has been the devil's agenda from the very beginning. Sin is a downhill path toward loss, pain, hell and destruction* (John 10:10). In many cases, *the sinner also experiences SOME HELL ON EARTH before being thrown into the eternal flames.* And, neither Satan's plan nor God's plan has ever changed! Satan destroys; God saves repenters!

(*Jehovah warned Israel over and over not to worship Him the same way the heathen had worshipped their idols—false gods—demons. And sexual immorality was always involved. The gods men worshipped were invented by the devil, so you can understand why God forbade His own people to worship idols; or to worship Him the way they worshipped their idols. PERVERTED WORSHIP serving Satan's purposes, why ought he to have any say-so in how people worship the True God? Satan helps people worship God in a demeaning manner!*)

The New Testament Scripture that *condemns all kinds of sexual perversion, including homosexuality,* is 1 Corinthians 6:9-11: "*Do you not know that the UNRIGHTEOUS WILL NOT INHERIT THE KINGDOM OF GOD? Be not deceived therefore: No fornicator, idolater, adulterer, homosexual, thief, covetous one, drunkard, reviler, or extortioner will inherit the Kingdom of God. And such* [sinners] *WERE some of you* [who are now believers]. *But, you are washed, sanctified, and justified, in the name of the Lord Jesus, and by the Spirit of our God.*"

Some of the Corinthian believers had been homosexuals before they got born again; *but were no longer, because they were now Christians, having been delivered from that former ungodly lifestyle. From the biblical standpoint, THERE IS NO SUCH THING AS A PRACTICING CHRISTIAN HOMOSEXUAL, Christian thief, Christian murderer, Christian drunkard, etc.*

How does political correctness fit this pitiful scenario? *In the USA, it is now politically INcorrect for anyone to publicly tell the truth about homosexuality and lesbianism being sins.* Can you not see the devil behind that political maneuver? *If he can shield sinners from biblical truth about such sins, by bluffing Christians so that they are afraid to publicly discuss Bible Truth about such sins, then sinners may never hear the truth of salvation from sin, and have opportunity to be saved from their sins, and the ETERNAL punishment due their sins. Political correctness is designed to DESTROY people.* Sinners must be convinced that their lifestyle is a sin, in order to be persuaded that they need to be *DELIVERED FROM* their sin. *Holy-Spirit-conviction of that truth comes to sinners through somebody preaching Gospel Truth with Holy-Spirit-anointing, and Holy-Spirit-boldness to preach it in the FACE of possible persecution. FEAR of persecution is what motivates cowardly Christians to YIELD to political-correctness pressure, thereby cheating sinners out of hearing the Gospel.* Thus, it ought to be obvious that political correctness is of the devil!

Remember, Satan leads sinners from one sin to another. *The homosexual clan having gotten their way on the political playing-field, they have descended to an even lower level of sexual perversion.* It is not enough for them to demand that same-sex marriage be accepted as the norm in this country: Now they are demanding to have their sex organs surgically altered to turn them into the gender they see themselves as. And not surprisingly, *they are demanding that the American taxpayer foot the medical bills for such ungodly procedures.*

Consider this *Bible Truth*: THERE IS NO SUCH THING AS SAME-SEX MARRIAGE. *Marriage is what the Creator says it is. Any distortion of God's original cannot be called marriage. Neither homosexuals nor lesbians can increase or sustain the human race—God's plan through one man and one woman.*

*Some doctors and hospitals are beginning to provide birth certificates that allow for a third gender: Male, female and X. Parents can CHOOSE the gender they want their child to be. Can you not see Satan behind that distortion of humanity?* It is one more *PERVERSION* of God's purpose for His creation. *Can you imagine the Creator going along with such perverted concepts and practices?* Political correctness is an invention of the devil—his primary hiding-place in this fallen world.

How can any parent claim their baby is male, when it is obviously female; or female when it is obviously male? *Such reasoning is utterly stupid.* And what sex is X? The devil has brought the human race down to that low level—at least the politically-correct portion of it. *And they are pushing to pass laws making it a CRIMINAL offense to publicly speak against such demonic perversion and stupidity.* And that itself is the devil's baby—*punishing the innocent for exposing the guilty!*

Proverbs 17:15: *"He who justifies the wicked and he who condemns the just; both are an abomination to the LORD."* To whom will we be loyal? To God, or to the politically-correct? Acts 5:29: "Then Peter and the other apostles answered and said, 'We ought to obey God, rather than men.'" *Amen!*

Also, whatever the child's sex, it is *politically INcorrect* to discipline him, her, or it, with *old-fashioned Bible discipline*; spanking. *Another example of modern wisdom* (ha, ha). *But, what does Holy Scripture say about such important matters?*

Proverbs 13:24: *"He who withholds the rod* [of discipline] *HATES his son* [or daughter]. *But he who LOVES him* [or her] *disciplines him* [or her] *promptly."* Surely, the Creator knows more about what humans need than modern psychologists; who have decided it is *politically INcorrect* to spank children. *They say it might warp their personality. Psychologists have the warped personalities. Satan has scrambled their brains!*

Proverbs 22:15: "Foolishness is *BOUND* in the heart [and mind] of a child; but the rod of correction [that is, spanking] will *drive it far from* him [or her, or it]." Rather than warping a child's personality, "The rod and reproof give wisdom. But *the child left to himself brings his mother to shame* (Proverbs 29:15)." "Correct your son, and he will give you rest; yes, *he will* [eventually] *give delight to your soul* (Proverbs 29:17)."

Another controversy: Free Speech! *Our constitutional first amendment guaranteeing free speech was meant only for the rebels in society, the protestors insist.* (?) They claim to have the constitutional right, not only to *SAY* whatever they want to say (*including derogatory defamation and filthy language*), but to engage in *DESTRUCTIVE DEMONSTRATIONS* they feel are *VALID* expressions of their anger and frustration against the status-quo—*the status-quo including even Deity Himself.*

On the other hand, people who represent the status-quo ought not be allowed to express their convictions about any subject; for *ANYTHING THEY SAY is considered by rebels to be HATE SPEECH.* You can surely see Satan behind that!

Of course, it is those decent, law-abiding, God-believing, church-attending people who are the status-quo. The rebels see them (us) as *HATE-MONGERS. Calling sin sin is HATE in their eyes.* Satan is obviously behind that *politically-correct* mindset and activity! If the devil can persuade sinners that avoiding God's Word is in their best interest, *they will shield themselves from His saving power.* The devil just smiles!

*Satan is out to steal, kill and destroy all of creation* (John 10:10). Christ prophesied in Matthew 24:22 that unless the *Tribulation* will be shortened *no flesh will be saved!* Through Antichrist, Satan plans to annihilate the entire human race. Revelation 11:18 also says that *Deity will destroy those who destroy the earth.* Those passages expose the devil's *PLAN* to destroy all of creation. *And what he uses most to achieve his goals is political correctness—the most destructive weapon in his arsenal—by the which he controls most human beings.*

There are many more areas in which *political correctness is attempting to destroy traditional institutions; especially the traditional family structure.* That should be evident from the information presented in the previous pages of this chapter. Political correctness *NEGATIVELY AFFECTS* the social fabric of every modern society across the globe. It seeks to destroy democracy and get the world ready to receive the Antichrist. *The Antichrist, fully energized by the devil, will be the devil's greatest attempt to rule the whole world before Christ comes.* Daniel 8:12—*The Antichrist will CAST TRUTH to the ground.* Satan is already doing such with political correctness!

*A key ingredient of political correctness is the alteration of certain word meanings, and opposition to using certain terms that are offensive to the politically-correct crowd.* Such terms offend them because they s*how them up* for what they really are—outright hypocrites—the devil's kids. Yes, the devil has kids (John 8:44, 1 John 3:10). It is now *politically INcorrect* to call illegal aliens illegal aliens, or terrorists terrorists. The correct term for the former is *undocumented immigrant*, and for the latter (??). *What term would better describe a terrorist than terrorist?* And the number of altered words is growing.

But, I want to focus on two politically-correct words that are just as *hypocritical* as those who insist on their political correctness—*LIBERAL* and *PROGRESSIVE*. *The definitions of both words are positive; rendering them a perfect camouflage for satanic lies.* However, *LIBERAL politicians are liberal with OTHER people's cash and freedoms; not their own.* Yet, *they call their political platform PROGRESSIVE;* which supposedly means that every citizen is better off under their leadership. But I challenge you to investigate their poor political record! *It is accessible to the public.* In reality, *they are progressively pulling this nation down into chaos and destruction.*

I want to cap off this chapter with a discussion of one of the most *asinine, ludicrous, absurd* and *stupid* concepts the devil has ever sold to mankind—the theory of evolution. The theory is only that—a theory! *No real proof whatever!* Let me provide you with *some real proof that the theory of evolution is nothing but a big lie.* Of course, *it is politically INcorrect to question that satanic falsehood*; but let us dare be *politically INcorrect* anyway! Let us face the actual truth about this.

Notwithstanding the clear scriptural account of creation, *those evolutionists claim that nature provides NO evidence of intelligent design.* Both the vast universe and life itself came into being by accident; and has ever-so-slowly *become more and more complex* as billions of years have passed. (?????)

Approaching that subject from *a practical standpoint*, let me ask *a practical question.* Has anybody today, or any time in history, *produced one practical product* without intelligent design? *From machinery, cars, houses, tools, to healthy food recipes, intelligent design is imperative.* Nobody in their right

25

mind believes that car parts *evolve from dirt and slowly and ACCIDENTALLY assemble themselves together, to produce a beautiful, practical, comfortable, driving machine. Intelligent design is an absolute necessity in the cooking, building, and manufacturing industries in our universe—Which supposedly came into being without ANY intelligent design. Why is it that human beings, who supposedly developed without intelligent design, can produce NOTHING without intelligently designing it, and intelligently building it? I question the INTELLIGENCE of those who BLINDLY push that EVOLUTION nonsense!*

Moreover, to question the Bible account of creation is to question all the rest of Bible history. *If one part is a lie, how can anybody believe the rest of it?* Yet, I have to present this observation. *Evolutionists are correct in their claim that the universe is much older than 6000 years. But Creationists are correct in their claim that man was created about 6000 years ago.* Both entities are both correct and incorrect. Scientists being minutely accurate in their calculations in space travel proves their *calculation of distance between stars* to be quite accurate. Even the smallest inaccuracy in their calculations would have made travel to the moon impossible. *Spaceships would never have been able to find distant planets and send back pictures.* Although light travels 6 trillion miles per year, 6000 years would allow light to cross only a small portion of our own galaxy, the Milky Way; which is 100,000 light years across (average galaxy size). And, distance between galaxies is far greater than the size of any galaxy. This is all correct.

*HOW* do we resolve the differences between Evolutionists and Creationists? *Believe the biblical account of creation and the indisputable scientific facts of the environment. And then question the unfounded speculations of BOTH.* For instance: *Dinosaurs populated this planet BEFORE man was created, and did not exist alongside man;* as those Creationists claim. But also true: *Man was created around 6000 years ago, and DID NOT EVOLVE from a bug millions of years ago;* as those Evolutionists claim. Deity created Adam, then made Eve from part of Adam's physique. The time-line of human history can be roughly calculated from the Bible account of the line of the Messiah. It has been approximately 6000 years. *So there!*

And, what about this: *God told Noah to take onto the ark animals, birds and bugs, in order to preserve each species of those creatures. So if dinosaurs did exist, and were taken on the ark, where are they now? Why would Deity burden Noah with dinosaurs for over 150 days if He knew that they would become extinct soon after the flood?* Moreover, *there was not enough room on the ark for dinosaurs, plus food necessary to sustain them* (and everyone else) *during the flood*. No matter what the Creationists claim, the dimensions God gave Noah for the ark would prohibit the inclusion of dinosaurs (*which obviously did not exist*). Be honest with the Bible account.

*No matter the controversies surrounding this controversial issue, the Scriptures clearly reveal that there was some earth history before Adam was created.* Lucifer had already fallen, and came into the Garden of Eden as a foe; not an emissary of God (*despite the claim of one popular preacher that Adam caused Lucifer's fall after God had sent that angel to Eden to help Adam.* Help Adam how? Crazy preachers out there!).

Genesis 1:2 is a picture of judgment, not creation. Isaiah 45:18 says God did not create this earth *EMPTY*. That verse has *THE SAME* Hebrew word as Genesis 1:2. Jeremiah 4:23 actually echoes Genesis 1:2: "*I beheld the earth, and it was without form, and empty.*" Both Jeremiah 4:23 and Genesis 1:2 *picture judgment, not creation. Therefore, Genesis 1:3-31 describes the RENOVATION of the earth. It is NOT an account of the original creation.* More scriptural evidence:

Second Peter 3:5-7 speaks of the *heavens* and *earth* that were of old, and the *heavens* and *earth* which now exist. So, Peter agrees that the original universe was tainted and then judged. Peter meant not the waters of Noah's flood, because *neither earth, nor heaven, was destroyed by that inundation: ONLY everything outside the ark that had breath.* Therefore, once again we find Bible evidence of a world before Adam.

Isaiah 14:13 says that *Lucifer wanted to exalt his throne above the STARS*. Then verse 14, *above the CLOUDS*. Where are clouds? In earth's atmosphere. *Lucifer's throne being on this EARTH means he ruled some kind of social system here. That pre-Adamite flood did not do away with the evidence of that former system, but obviously buried it deep in the earth. Deeply-buried fossils are evidence of pre-Adamite creatures.*

Paul said in 1 Corinthians 15:39 that *fish* have one kind of flesh; *birds* another kind of flesh; *animals* another kind of flesh; and *man* another kind of flesh. That destroys any and all arguments of the theory of evolution. God having created each category of living being with its very own distinct flesh, IT WOULD BE IMPOSSIBLE FOR ONE SPECIES TO EVOLVE INTO ANOTHER SPECIES. End of that asinine argument!

In a college biology class, the professor filled us students in on *the complicated functions of each system of the human body*. We have a *skeletal* system. We are not mush. We also have a *muscular* system. That provides movement. But flesh and bones have to be joined together by *ligaments*, so we do not fall apart. All that must have *nourishment*, so we have a *digestive* system. *Hand to mouth, chewing, swallowing, then digesting and distributing nourishment to the rest of the body (and eliminating the waste)*. But how does it get distributed? The *circulatory* system. How does each system know what it is supposed to do? The *nervous* system governs all the other systems. Then there is a *glandular* system, *skin* to cover the other parts, *hair, nails, reproductive organs, etc.*, and so on. My point is: *There is NO WAY a bug could develop into such a complicated organism, no matter the time frame*. Each part of each system MUST FUNCTION PERFECTLY within its own system. Moreover, *each of the many different systems has to work IN COOPERATION WITH each and every other system: Which proves that human beings did NOT start out as bugs*. I refuse to believe that worms could be my ancestors!

*I rarely recommend books other than my own, for though other good books do exist, most have some major flaws. One I do recommend is Dake's annotated Bible. If you really want to know, then Dake's Bible is the place to go. Small print, not cheap, and you will spend months chasing down references proving those things I have presented in this chapter; and a lot more.* Dake provides ABUNDANT BIBLICAL EVIDENCE of the pre-Adamite world; as well as details of end-time events.

*The entire world system operates on political correctness; and many incidents of such were even recorded in Scripture.* The next two chapters provide *abundant proof of that truth*.

# Chapter Three

## Political correctness in the Old Testament

*Preparing for and writing the previous chapter jogged my memory about several Bible accounts of political correctness. And having gotten into it, I have discovered more such cases than I had originally thought existed—from cover to cover!*

The world uses *political correctness* to pressure people to conform to *worldly standards. That worldly pressure is used on everybody, including believers.* God's Word WARNS God's *people to resist that demonic power because of its destructive effects on both those who wield it and those who yield to it.*

Colossians 2:8: "Beware, lest any man *spoil* you through philosophy and vain deceit, after the *traditions of men,* after the *rudiments of the world*, and not after Christ." Know that being *spoiled* means being robbed of your possessions, your dignity, etc. How do believers get spoiled? By capitulating to the rudiments (*basic principles*) this world operates by. That definitely includes *political correctness.* Manmade traditions become established, and people are pressured to perpetuate them. *How can the warning get any plainer?* And Colossians 2:20 continues: "Wherefore, *if you be DEAD with Christ from the rudiments of this world* [political correctness, etc.], WHY, *as though* [you were yet] *living in the world* [system], *are you subject to* [the world's] *ordinances?"* Christians have DIED to the world and its evil principles, and have become citizens of God's Kingdom; which operates on honest principles.

The earliest *BIBLE* case of political correctness I found is nestled in Genesis 10:8-11:9. We learn that Nimrod formed the very first kingdom on this planet; which means he ruled over its citizens. And since *political correctness* has been the *preferred tool of oppression* throughout fallen-man's history, *the same tool was obviously used to keep people in line then as well*. This world has not really changed all that much!

Genesis 11:4 tells us the people began construction on a skyscraper for their protection from *ANOTHER* flood; and as a memorial of their genius. Babel also became a commercial center, as well as the headquarters of rebellion against God. *Deity, being aware of lost-man's propensity toward evil, and even in that fallen state had the ability to do great things, He disrupted their rebellious plans by confusing their language; causing them to scatter in all directions* (Genesis 11:6-9).

One early case I found exemplifying *resistance to political correctness* is Genesis 14:21-23, where: "The King of Sodom said to Abram: 'Give me the persons [Sodomite citizens who had been kidnapped, *but whom Abram had returned safely*], but take the goods for yourself.' But Abram said to the King of Sodom: '*I have lifted my hand to the LORD, the Most High God, the Possessor of heaven and earth, that I will NOT take even a thread or shoelace* [from you], *and that I will not take anything that is yours*; LEST YOU should SAY: "I have made Abram rich."'" Do you see that world-principle? If the King of Sodom made Abram rich, *he would have something hanging over Abram's head. He would have power by which he could control Abram*. He who makes rich can control the rich!

Abraham did yield to political correctness when in Egypt (Genesis 12); then in Gerar (Genesis 20): "Abraham said of Sarah his wife: 'She is my sister.' And so Abimelech, King of Gerar, sent and took Sarah [into his harem] (Genesis 20:2)." "And Abimelech said to Abraham: '*WHY DID YOU DO THIS?*' And Abraham said: '*Because I thought surely the fear of God is not in this place; and they may slay me for my wife's sake* (Genesis 20:10-11).'" *Abraham based HIS protection plan on fear of what a human might do to him*—political correctness. In so doing, Abraham both put his wife's life in danger, and *gave Satan an opportunity to pollute the line of the Messiah!*

*Another Bible example of political correctness, but played out on a much smaller scale—family tradition—is recorded in* Genesis 29:23. Jacob had made a *DEAL* with Laban to work seven years *for the hand in marriage of his younger daughter Rachel*. But, "It came to pass in the evening, that he [Laban] took Leah, his [older] daughter, and brought her to [Jacob]; and Jacob went in to her [marriage *TRADITION* back then]." Laban *DELIBERATELY DECEIVED JACOB* by *NOT* informing him about that exchange. *Political-correctness deception!*

"And it came to pass the next morning, Jacob saw it was Leah. And Jacob said to Laban: 'What is this you have done to me? *Did not I serve with you for Rachel?* So why have you beguiled me?' Laban replied: '*It MUST not be so done in our country to give the younger girl before the firstborn. Fulfill her week, and I will give you Rachel ALSO for the service which you provide for me another seven years* (Genesis 29:25-27).'" Family tradition is *one powerful form of political correctness.* Laban *JUSTIFIED* taking advantage of Jacob by appealing to the family tradition of getting the first-born married first. In Laban's mind, *it mattered not that he had to be dishonest in pulling off that transaction. CLASSIC* political correctness!

Genesis records one more case of political correctness in 37:5-11: This one *starting out as a family matter, but ending on a political note.* Joseph, Jacob's favorite son at that time, had two *God-given dreams*—both picturing Joseph someday having authority over *ALL* the other members of that family. His father Jacob rebuked him, and his older brothers hated and scorned Joseph; finally selling their very own brother to passing-by slave traders. Genesis chapters 39-50 relate the rest of that story—how Joseph's dreams *DID* come true; and how his family members *DID BOW* down to his authority.

There are two *political-correctness elements* found in this account. That *historical period* is often called the *patriarchal dispensation—which means that the father of the family was looked upon as the patriarch, or absolute head, of the family.* Thus, *the thought of Joseph ruling EVEN over his father was repulsive to Jacob; so he rebuked Joseph for those God-given dreams.* Secondly, *the first-born son of a family would be the future family patriarch, and Joseph's dreams put him in that position ahead of the first-born in that family.* A big no-no!

Next case of political correctness in Scripture: In Exodus chapter one, we find that Israel had been enslaved in Egypt. But even in slavery *they prolifically multiplied and became a possible THREAT to the Egyptian status-quo*. Thus, Pharaoh decided to solve the precarious problem by commanding the Hebrew midwives *to kill all the Hebrew boy-babies, but keep the girl-babies alive*, when they attended the Hebrew women in child-birth—*the politically-correct action to take*. However, *the two Hebrew midwives feared the Lord, and refused to do what Pharaoh had commanded them. Yet, although they had been politically INcorrect, the Lord protected those midwives. Pharaoh then turned to the Egyptian populace, commanding them to do away with all the male Hebrew babies*. That was when Moses came along. Exodus chapters 2-14 report that *God first saved Moses, then through Moses saved Israel from their slave-masters, and all of their politically-correct ploys*.

In that ancient world, it was politically-correct to have a *VISIBLE* god. For the Hebrews encamped in the wilderness, who had been influenced by Egyptian idolatry for centuries, Moses was the closest thing they had to a visible god. Thus, "When the people saw that Moses delayed coming down out of that mountain, they gathered together to Aaron, and said to him: *'Up, MAKE us some gods, which will go before us*; for as for Moses, the man who brought us up out of the land of Egypt, *we know not what has become of him.'* So Aaron said to them: *'Break off the golden earrings that are in the ears of your wives your sons and your daughters, and BRING THEM TO ME.'* So the people broke off the golden earrings that were in their ears, and brought them to Aaron. And Aaron received the gold at their hand and FASHIONED it with a graving tool; making it into a molten calf*. Then, all the people said: 'These be your gods, Oh Israel, which brought you from the land of Egypt (Exodus 32:1-4).'" *And what spin did Aaron put on his actions when he got caught?* "Let not your anger be hot. For *you know the people that they are set on mischief.* They said to me: *'Make us gods to go before us.* For, as for Moses, who brought us up from Egypt, we know not what has happened to him.' So I said to them: *'Whoever has gold, bring it to me.'* And they gave their gold to me, and I cast it into the fire, and this [perfectly-sculpted] *calf came out* (Exodus 32:22-24)."

*Note the dishonesty of religious AND political correctness! Aaron yielded to the PRESSURE of the crowd to be religiously and politically correct, fashioning their gold god with his own hands; then twisted the facts about it all to Moses, saying: "I put a bunch of gold into the fire, and this gold calf came out." Did that fire all by itself fashion that blob of gold into a calf? Religious and political correctness invent unbelievable lies to cover their demonic tracks, by putting fantastic spins on their lies in the face of factual evidence to the contrary. Who is the FATHER OF LIES AND LIARS? THE DEVIL! Obviously, then, Satan is behind both religious and political correctness. (The ancient world combined religious and political correctness.)*

*Jehovah WARNED Israel NOT to make any covenant with the Canaanite people, or to learn any of their heathen habits. Their satanic lifestyle was the reason God commanded Israel to destroy the ENTIRE population of those ungodly nations.*

Exodus 34:12: "Take heed unto yourself, lest you make a covenant with the inhabitants of the land where you go, lest [that covenant] become a snare in your midst." Therefore,...

*Israel had BOTH to be cleansed from that IDOLATRY they had been exposed to for centuries down in Egypt, and to RID their NEW habitation of its EVIL practitioners.* Leviticus 18:3: "*After the [EVIL] doings of the land of Egypt where you dwelt you must NOT do. [Moreover,] after the doings of that land of Canaan whereto I bring you, you must NOT do. Neither walk after their ordinances." Their religious rites were ultra-evil!*

Leviticus 18:24-25: "Defile not yourselves in any of these things. *For in all these things the nations are defiled, which I cast out before you.* Even the land itself is defiled! Therefore, I [God] *do visit its iniquity upon it, and the land vomits out its own inhabitants." Sin polluted the very SOIL they walked on!*

Isaiah 24:5-6: "The earth is *defiled* under its inhabitants because they have *transgressed* [divine] laws, have *changed* [God's] ordinance and have *broken* the everlasting covenant. Therefore, has the curse devoured the earth; and those who dwell therein are desolate." To reverse that curse:

"Let the people praise You, Oh God. Let the people praise You. Then, will the earth yield her increase; and God, even our God, will bless US (Psalms 67:5-6)." *Earth's productivity depends more on our honoring God than it does on fertilizer!*

Numbers 33:55-56 posted a further warning to Israel: "If you do not drive out the inhabitants of the land [of Canaan] from before you, *those you permit to remain will be pricks in your eyes, and thorns in your sides, and will vex you in the land* [of Canaan] *wherein you dwell. Moreover, I will even do to you as I thought to do to them.*" God's purpose was *NOT* to rid the land of Canaan of one set of devil-worshippers, then fill it with another people who would commit the same evils.

Deuteronomy 7:5-10: "*But, you* [My people] *must destroy their altars, break down their images, cut down their groves, and burn their graven images with fire. For, you are a HOLY people to the LORD, your God;* [Who] *has chosen you to be a special people to Himself, above all other people who are on the face of the earth. The LORD did NOT set His love on you, nor choose you, because you were more in number than any other people; for, you were the fewest of all the peoples. But, because Jehovah LOVED YOU, and because He would KEEP THE OATH WHICH HE SWORE to your fathers has the LORD brought you out with a mighty hand, and redeemed you from the habitation of bondage, from the hand of Pharaoh, King of Egypt.* Know therefore, that the LORD, your God, He is God, the Faithful God, *Who keeps covenant and mercy with those who love Him, and KEEP His commandments, to a thousand generations. And repays those who hate Him to their face, to destroy them. He will not be slack to him who hates Him. He will repay him* [the rebel] *to his face.*" Therefore,...

Deuteronomy 12:30-32: "*TAKE HEED to yourself, so that you be not snared by following* [their satanic practices even] *after they have been destroyed from before you* [*for that very thing*]; *and be sure you enquire NOT after their gods, saying:* 'How did these nations serve their gods? Even so, we will do likewise.' *You must NOT DO to the LORD YOUR GOD* [as they DID to THEIR gods]. *For, every abomination, which the LORD God hates, have they done to their gods. For, even their sons and their daughters they have BURNT in the fire to their gods* [demons]. *Whatever I command you therefore, observe to do. You must not add to* [My Word]; *nor diminish from it.*"

God knowing the power of political correctness, He knew that if Israel left any *DEMON-WORSHIPERS* in Canaan, they would influence His people to practice those same evils.

In fact, *He knew Israel would someday want to be like all the other nations.* Such is the political-correctness pressure. Israel's theocratic form of government and lifestyle would be looked upon as odd by all the surrounding heathen nations. (*Even today, many believers want NOT to be LOOKED UPON AS ODDITIES by this world, so yield to worldly standards, in order to be accepted by sinners, instead of being examples to sinners of how our Creator wants us all to live. One current divine purpose for Christians is that our lives demonstrate to the world the Creator's original purpose for the human race.*)

Deuteronomy 17:14-15: "When you [Israel] have come to that land which the *LORD* your God gives you, and possess it, and dwell therein, then say: 'I will set a king over me, like all of the nations that are about me'; you must set him king over you, [ONLY] whom the *LORD* your God will choose. *One from among your brethren you must make king over you. You may not set a stranger over you; one not your brother* [kin]."

Meantime, *neither Israel nor Joshua their new leader did a perfect job obeying Gods orders, for they carelessly made a covenant with one of the Canaanite clans.* In Joshua chapter nine, the Gibeonites (a local tribe) acted as though they had travelled from a far country, and *tricked the Israelite leaders into making a covenant with them to protect them from all the other Canaanite nations.* Joshua 9:14: "And the men took of their victuals [as though Israel really needed food, etc.], and *asked not counsel at the mouth of the LORD.*" Divine counsel protects from the deception of political correctness, whereas *neglect to consult God,* regarding important life-decisions, is an *inexcusable error,* which often results in *undesirable and unending consequences. Even after having been commanded to DESTROY all Canaanites, Israel carelessly obligated itself to PROTECT the Gibeonites, a Canaanite tribe* (Joshua 10)!

Now, this example of *political correctness*: Judges 8:4-17: "And Gideon came to Jordan, then passed over, he, and the three hundred men, who were with him; faint, yet pursuing them. Then he said to the men of Succoth: 'Give, I pray you, loaves of bread to the people following me, for they are faint; and I am pursuing after Zebah, and Zalmunna, the kings of Midian.' And, the princes of Succoth said: 'Are the hands of

Zebah and Zalmunna *NOW* in your hand, that we ought to give bread to your army?' Gideon said: 'When the LORD has delivered up Zebah and Zalmunna into my hand, *then I will TEAR your flesh with the wilderness thorns, and with briers.*' Then he went up from there to Penuel, *and spoke unto them likewise.* And, the men of Penuel answered him the same as the men of Succoth. Then, Gideon spoke also unto the men of Penuel, saying: 'When I come again in peace [after I have captured those two kings], I will break down this tower.'"

It seemed politically correct at the time for those cowards in their walled cities to withhold bread from Gideon's hungry soldiers, for they feared that those two kings might overcome Gideon, then come back and harm them. Political correctness ALWAYS yields to fear—based on appearances; *not on faith!*

How did it turn out? Judges 8:15: "[After *defeating* those Midianite monarchs,] Gideon came to those men of Succoth and said: 'Behold Zebah and Zalmunna, with whom you did upbraid me, saying: "Are the hands of Zebah and Zalmunna *NOW* in your hand, that we should give bread to your men, who are weary?"' And Gideon took *the elders of the city,* and took thorns of the wilderness, and briers, and with them he taught the men of Succoth. Then he beat down the tower of Penuel, then slew the men of that city." Political correctness sure got those cowards into big trouble! You see, power can suddenly switch hands. *Better be on God's side!*

Just as God had prophesied long before, Israel desired to have a king. And, *some of Israel's spiritual leaders provided the very occasion for the general population to WANT a king.* Beginning with the high priest Eli, 1 Samuel 2:22-24 states: "Now, Eli was very old, and he heard all that his sons did to all Israel; and how *they lay with the women who assembled at the door of the tabernacle of the congregation.* And he said to them: 'Why do you do such things? For *I hear of your evil dealings by all this people.* No, my sons; it is no good report that I hear. You make the LORD'S people to transgress.'"

First Samuel 2:29-31 is *GOD'S RESPONSE*: "Why do you kick at My sacrifice and My offering, which I commanded in My habitation? And you honor your sons above Me, *to make yourselves fat with the chiefest of all of the offerings of Israel MY people?* Wherefore, the LORD God of Israel says: 'I said indeed that your [Eli's] house, and the house of your father, should walk before Me forever.' But now the LORD says: 'Be it far from Me [to do so]; for *those who honor Me I will honor, and those who despise Me will be lightly esteemed*. Behold, the days will come when I will cut off your arm [power], and the arm of your father's house, so that there will not be any old man in your house.'" Sow evil, reap evil (Galatians 6:7).

*Eli raised Samuel from childhood, and Samuel eventually took Eli's place as high priest. But, some of the problems that had plagued Eli plagued Samuel as well*: "For Samuel's sons walked not in his [godly] ways, but rather *turned aside after lucre* [ill-gotten gain], *taking bribes and perverting judgment*. Then, all the elders of Israel gathered together, and came to Samuel at Ramah and said to Samuel: 'Behold, you are old, and your sons walk not in your ways. So, make us a king to judge us like all the other nations.' But the thing displeased Samuel, when they said: 'Give us a king, to judge us.' Then, Samuel prayed to the LORD. And, the LORD said to Samuel: 'Hearken to the voice of the people, in all that they say unto you. For, they have not rejected you, but they have rejected Me, that I should not reign over them (1 Samuel 8:3-7).'"

"Samuel reported all the words of the LORD to those who had demanded a king, saying: 'The king, who will reign over you, will take of your sons and appoint them for himself, for his chariots, and some for his horsemen; and some will run before his chariots. And that king will appoint captains over thousands, over hundreds, and over fifties; and set them to ear [to till] his ground, to reap his harvest, and to make his instruments of war and instruments of his chariots. And he will take of your daughters to be confectionaries, cooks, and bakers. And your king will take away your fields, vineyards, and olive-yards; even the very *BEST* of them, giving them to his servants. And he will take the tenth of your seed, and of your vineyards, giving them to his officers and his servants. And he will take your menservants, and your maidservants, and your goodliest young men, and your donkeys, and put them to *HIS* work. He will take the tenth of your sheep. And you will be the king's servants. Then you will cry out in that day, because of your king, which you have wanted; and *the LORD will not hear you in that day*.' Nevertheless, the people refused to obey the voice of Samuel; and they said: 'No; but we will have a king over us; that we also may be like all the nations; and that our king may judge us, and go out before us, and *fight our battles.*' Samuel heard all their words, and rehearsed them in the ears of the LORD. And the LORD said to Samuel: *'Hearken to their voice, and make them a king* (1 Samuel 8:10-22).'" *God knew that Israel would be sorry they had desired to be under a king. They would despise political correctness once they were under its politically-correct spell.*

What did their first king do? "King Saul tarried for seven days, according to the *SET* time Samuel had appointed. *But Samuel came not to Gilgal; so the people were scattered from Saul.* So King Saul said to them: 'Bring me a burnt offering, and peace offerings.' And he offered the burnt offering. And, *as soon as King Saul had finished offering the burnt offering, Samuel arrived.* So Saul went to meet Samuel to salute him. *But Samuel asked him:* 'WHAT HAVE YOU DONE?' And Saul answered: *'When I SAW that the people were scattered from me, and that YOU came not within the days YOU appointed, and that the Philistines had gathered* [in array] *at Michmash;* I said: "The Philistines will come down on me to Gilgal, and I have not made any supplication to the LORD." So, I FORCED MYSELF TO OFFER THE BURNT OFFERING.' Samuel said to Saul: *'You have acted foolishly by not keeping the command of the LORD your God, which He commanded you. The LORD* would have established *YOUR KINGSHIP* over Israel forever. *But now your kingship is terminated. And instead of you, the LORD has SOUGHT for Himself a man AFTER His own heart, and the LORD HAS COMMANDED HIM to be captain over His people—because you have NOT kept* [obeyed] *what the LORD commanded you* (1 Samuel 13:8-14).'" *ONLY official priests were allowed to offer sacrifices. Such was off-limits to kings.* King Saul violated that office. Later, King Uzziah committed the same sin, and became a leper (2 Chronicles 26:16-23).

*There is a MAJOR difference between political correctness and biblical correctness. In fact, they are exact opposites. So one cannot walk both directions at the same time.* More than that: *When one falls under the SPELL of political correctness, he or she will CONTINUE going downhill.* King Saul did.

Not only did King Saul intrude into an office barred from kings (*reserved only for the descendants of Levi; particularly the family of Aaron*), he yielded to political correctness again by disobeying God's command to destroy EVERY Amalekite. "GO SMITE AMALEK, AND UTTERLY DESTROY ALL that they have. Spare nothing. Slay man, woman, infant and suckling, ox and sheep, camel and donkey (1 Samuel 15:3)." All of it!

"But, Saul and the people spared King Agag and the best sheep, oxen, fatlings, and lambs, and all which was good [in their sight], and *did not utterly destroy them*. But everything vile and refuse [as *THEY* saw it] they destroyed utterly. *Then came the Word of the LORD unto Samuel*, saying: 'It repents Me that I have set up Saul to be king, for he has turned back from following Me, and HAS NOT PERFORMED [ANY of] My commandments.' And it grieved Samuel. And he cried to the LORD all night...Then, Samuel came to Saul. And *Saul said unto Samuel*: 'Blessed be you, of the LORD: I have performed the commandment of the LORD.' But Samuel said unto Saul: 'What then means this bleating of the sheep in my ears, and the lowing of oxen which I hear?' Then Saul said: 'They have brought them from the Amalekites. For, the people spared the best of the sheep and oxen to sacrifice to the LORD your God; and the REST we have utterly destroyed.' Then, Samuel said to Saul: 'Stay, and I will tell you what the LORD has said to me this night.' Then Saul said to him: 'Say on.' And Samuel said: 'When you were little [humble] in your own sight, were you not made the head of the tribes of Israel; and the LORD anointed you king over Israel? Then *the LORD sent you on a mission*, and said: "Go, and utterly destroy the SINNERS, the Amalekites, and fight against them until they are consumed." Why then did you *not obey the voice of the LORD, but did fly upon the spoil, and did EVIL in the sight of the LORD?'* Then, Saul said unto Samuel: 'I have obeyed the voice of the LORD, and I have gone the way which the LORD sent me, and have brought Agag the king of Amalek, and have utterly destroyed the Amalekites. But, *the people took of the spoils*; sheep and oxen, the chief of the things which should have been utterly destroyed, to sacrifice to the LORD your God in Gilgal.' But, Samuel said to King Saul: 'Has the LORD as great delight in burnt offerings and sacrifices, as in obeying the voice of the

LORD? Behold, *to obey is [FAR] better than sacrifice, and to hearken [BETTER] than [offering] the fat of rams. Rebellion is AS the sin of witchcraft, and stubbornness is [the same] AS iniquity and idolatry.* Because you have rejected the Word of the LORD, the LORD has ALSO rejected you from being king (1 Samuel 15:9-23).'" *Unpleasant harvest of disobedience!*

Can you now see that *veering off the Word of God in any degree is outright disobedience? Inviting divine rejection and wrath?* And what pressure was applied to Saul to move him to disobey Deity's clear command? Political correctness! The people (his political constituents) put pressure on King Saul to alter the expressed will of God. What seemed right to that crowd dictated how their God-appointed ruler acted. Today, politics operates essentially the same way. *Political pressure put on elected officials motivates them to yield to the people's desires.* Whether that is good or bad depends upon whether or not what the people want lines up with God's Word.

First Samuel 17:38-40 recorded another case of political correctness: "And Saul armed David with his armor, and he [Saul] put a helmet of brass on David's head. He also armed David with a coat of mail. And David girded his sword upon his armor, then struggled to move; for he had not proved it. And David said unto Saul: *'I cannot go with these; for I have not proved them!'* So, David put the armor off him, and took his staff in his hand, and chose him five smooth stones out of the brook, and put them in a shepherd's bag which David had, even in a scrip; and his sling was in his hand. Then he drew near to the Philistine." *And surely you know the rest of that story:* David, using the weaponry he was familiar with, GOT THE JOB DONE—defeating Goliath. *Political correctness pressures people it seeks to control to use its preferred tools, but then moves the controllers to envy when their pressure is rejected, and the politically-INcorrect tools work* (like what is going on in Washington D.C. and the media at this writing.)

"And it came to pass, when David had returned from the slaughter of the Philistine, the women came out of the cities of Israel, singing and dancing, to meet King Saul, with their tabrets, with joy, and with instruments of music. And those women answered one another as they played, singing: 'Saul has slain his thousands, and David, his tens of thousands.'

And Saul was wroth. For, their singing displeased him. And he said: 'They have ascribed unto David tens of thousands, and to me they have ascribed but thousands. And what can he have more, but the Kingdom?' And Saul eyed David [*with suspicion; and harbored hatred toward David*] from that day on (1 Samuel 18:6-9)." *Political-correctness displeasure!*

David himself later fell into that *political-correctness PIT, when he committed adultery with Bathsheba,* the wife of one of his soldiers, who was on the battlefield fighting for Israel. King David schemed to cover his sin by having the woman's husband killed. Notice the following politically-correct plot:

"David wrote in a letter, saying: '*Set Uriah in the forefront of the hottest battle, THEN back off from him, that he may be smitten and die.*' *So Joab assigned Uriah to a place where he knew valiant men were...And there fell some of the people of David's servants; and Uriah the Hittite died also.* Then, Joab sent David *information concerning the war*; and charged the messenger with this: 'When you have made an end of telling the matters of the war to the king, if the king's wrath arises, and he says to you: "*WHY* did you approach so near the city in the battle? Knew you not that they would shoot from the wall?"...Then you say: "*Your servant Uriah the Hittite is dead also.*" So the messenger told David all Joab had told him to say...'Surely, the men prevailed against us, and came out to us into the field, then, we were upon them to the entering of the gate. And, the shooters shot from off the wall upon your servants; and some of the king's servants be dead; and your servant Uriah the Hittite is dead also.' Then David said unto the messenger: 'Thus you must say unto Joab: "Let not this thing displease you, because the sword devours one, as well as another. Make your [effort] stronger against the city, and overthrow it. And encourage Joab (2 Samuel 11:15-25).""'

*Do you NOW see the deception political correctness injects into one's life?* Political correctness *BLINDED* God's formerly faithful servant King David, so that he forgot righteousness, and *committed sins just as EVIL as the unsaved*. Nathan the prophet later confronted King David, and he did repent; but David's foolishness set into motion great disaster in his life.

It all boils down to this issue: Are false gods really gods? Or is fallen-man his own god? "Elijah came to all the people and asked: 'How long will you halt between two opinions? If the LORD [Jehovah] is God, follow Him. But, if Baal [is god], then follow him.' And the people answered Elijah not a word (1 Kings 18:21)." *Political correctness can be silenced.* Jesus did it more than once (Matthew 22:34, 46). (Also, *some have used Christ's words* in John 10:34-35, quoting Psalms 82:6, *to teach that MEN ARE GODS.* But, in Genesis 1:26, *God did not say: "Let Us make gods," but: "Let Us make man."* Before making *TOO MUCH* of John 10:34-35 and Psalms 82:6, you might ought to consider Jeremiah 10:11: *"The gods that did not make the heavens, and this earth, will PERISH from this earth, and from under the heavens." That refers to false gods those ancient people worshipped—and many STILL worship.* God called them gods only in the sense they were *leaders* in Israel—*judges* over the people. Some English Bibles contain notes indicating that. It is wise to study before doctrinizing!)

In 1 Kings 18, the Baal-worshippers called on their false god all day long, *and nothing happened.* Then, Elijah prayed to the True God, Jehovah, Israel's God, and *the fire fell from heaven and consumed Elijah's sacrifice*; proving at the same time that Baal was not god, and that Jehovah was. Political correctness had led Israel astray; which led to the slaughter of many of God's faithful people. *So it had become politically INCORRECT to worship Jehovah, and politically CORRECT to worship Baal, a false god.* Obviously, the devil's plan!

Yet, "I [God] have left Me *seven thousand in Israel*, whose knees have not bowed to Baal, and whose mouths have not kissed him (1 Kings 19:18)." *In every generation, Deity has a faithful few, who spurn political correctness, and serve ONLY Him. And EVERY human MUST CHOOSE between the two!*

King Asa, *one of Judah's better kings at first,* made some foolish choices later in his life; after making some important reforms for Israel earlier. "King Asa, in the thirty-ninth year of his reign [after making several of those foolish decisions], became diseased in his feet, until his disease was exceeding great. Yet, in his disease, *Asa sought not to the LORD, but to the physicians.* So Asa died [unhealed] in the forty-first year of his reign (2 Chronicles 16:12-13)." *Man CANNOT heal!*

That is a biggie! Why was that recorded? *Does it make a difference with Jehovah-Rapha whether His people trust the doctors for their healing or The Healer Himself?* The nation of Israel had *NO* physicians for a few hundred years; *until King Solomon imported a few hundred wives from other countries; who brought with them THEIR heathen gods and physicians.* I go into detail about all that in my books on divine healing. *Deity essentially rebuked King Asa for looking to man for his healing instead of Jehovah-Rapha: Who promised His people that He would heal them, and keep them well, if they trusted and obeyed Him* (Exodus 15:26, 23:25, Deuteronomy 7:15).

King Asa had started his *downhill slide* a few years back, when, *in another situation, he put his trust in man instead of God, in a war with Israel. Asa had hired a heathen king and his army to defend Judea, instead of trusting Deity to deliver them.* King Asa was rebuked for that as well, through one of God's prophets. *And King Asa's treatment of the prophet*: He jailed him. *King Asa even oppressed some of his own people.* Read *ALL* of 2 Chronicles chapter sixteen, and *observe how political correctness pulls those deceived by it down to lower and lower levels of disobedience?* No person can trust BOTH GOD AND MAN at the very same time (Psalms 46:1, 60:11, 124:8, 146:3, Isaiah 31:3, Matthew 6:24, John 6:63, etc.).

Another Judean king made a similar mistake. "Amaziah HIRED also a hundred thousand mighty men of valor out of Israel for a hundred talents of silver. But, there came a man of God to King Amaziah, saying: *'Oh King, let not the army of Israel go with you, for the LORD IS NOT WITH ISRAEL* [now]. But, if you do go, be strong for the battle. *For God will make you fall before the enemy. God has power to help, and power to cast down.'* Amaziah said to the man of God: *'What about the hundred talents, which I have already payed the army of Israel?'* And, the man of God answered: *'THE LORD IS ABLE TO GIVE YOU MUCH MORE THAN* [what you squandered by trusting man and not God] (2 Chronicles 25:6-9)." Amaziah heeded PART *of that command. But partial obedience gleans PARTIAL BLESSINGS. The man's less-than-total commitment to Deity spawned further disobedience; which eventually led to his demise.* Only total obedience will secure total victory!

I mentioned this earlier, but these are the sordid details: "When [King Uzziah] was strong [well-established upon his throne], his heart was lifted up, to his own destruction. For, *he transgressed against the LORD his God by going into the temple of the LORD to burn incense upon the altar of incense.* Azariah the priest went in after Uzziah; and with him eighty priests of the LORD, who were valiant men [against political correctness]. And they withstood Uzziah, the King, saying to him: *'It appertains NOT TO YOU King Uzziah, to burn incense to the LORD, but only to the actual priests, the sons of Aaron, who are DULY consecrated to burn incense.* So, go out of the temple sanctuary. *For, you have already trespassed. Neither will the LORD God count your action honorable to you.'* Then, Uzziah was wroth, and he had a censer in his hand to burn incense. But, while he was wroth with those priests, leprosy appeared on his forehead, before the priests, in the house of the LORD, right beside that incense altar. Azariah, the chief priest, and all the priests, looked upon him, and, behold, he was leprous on his forehead. Then they thrust him out from thence. Yes, even himself hasted also to go out, because the LORD had smitten him. King Uzziah was a leper to the very day of his death, and dwelt in a separate house, he being a leper; for he was *CUT OFF* from the house of the LORD. And Uzziah's son Jotham was over the King's house, judging the people (2 Chronicles 26:16-21)." Political correctness varies, according to who is in power. But the devil always uses it to lead people astray, so that they violate God's commands.

One of the few kings who made some right decisions was Hezekiah. During one Assyrian invasion of Judah, Hezekiah said, "'With Sennacherib King of Assyria is the arm of flesh. But, with us [God's people] is the LORD our God, to help us, and *to fight our battles.' And so the people rested themselves upon the words of King Hezekiah* (2 Chronicles 32:8)." *Faith words always encourage people, and bring God to the scene*:
"*The LORD sent one angel, who cut off all the mighty men of valor, and leaders and captains in the Assyrian camp.* So, the King of Assyria returned with shame of face to his land. And when he had come into the house of his god, those who had come from his own bowels [his sons] slew him with the sword (2 Chronicles 32:21)." *No safety in the world system!*

*The BRAND of political correctness that is the trend at any given time depends on the political regime that is currently in power. So, in different locations, and different times, political correctness takes on different forms, and different degrees of seriousness, and danger, for God's people. The devil himself, however, is the real culprit behind ALL political correctness.*

Ecclesiastes 5:8 in some English Bible versions seems to be speaking to this political-correctness issue. That passage clearly infers that, in countries characterized by oppression, the more powerful government officials dominate those who occupy lower positions; while all are kept in line by the *TOP* official. A perfect picture of how political correctness works. *That explains why some freshman electees become corrupted even in the good old USA after they go to Washington D.C.*

The book of *EZRA* tells of some of the problems the Jews faced upon their return to their homeland after the 70 years of captivity in Babylon. Note the following recorded history:

"When the *ADVERSARIES* of Judah and Benjamin found out that those [returned Jews were rebuilding] the temple of the *LORD* God of Israel, they approached Zerubbabel [their governor] and the chief of the fathers, and [deceptively] said unto them: '*Let us build with you, for we seek your God, just as you do.* And we do sacrifice to Him ever since the days of Esarhaddon, King of Assur, who brought us here.' However, Zerubbabel and Jeshua, and all of the chief of the fathers of Israel, answered [those adversaries]: '*You have nothing to do with us to build a house to OUR God.* We ourselves will build to the *LORD* God of Israel; as King Cyrus, *the King of Persia,* commanded us.' Then, the people of the land weakened the hands of the citizens of Judah by *TROUBLING THEM in their building efforts; and even HIRED counsellors against them to frustrate their purpose ALL the days of Cyrus, King of Persia, until the reign of Darius, King of Persia* (Ezra 4:1-5)." At first, the Jews' enemies *tried to join them* in their building project, in order to trouble them from within. When that plan failed, *they used the law and politics to stop the Jews from obeying the command to rebuild the temple and resume their worship of God. Our obedience to God annoys the devil's bunch!*

Israel's enemies appealed to some *government document*, which had been signed and filed by a previous Persian king: One informing the current king of Israel's *rebellious history. Their purpose was to convince that king that Israel intended to rebel again*; their rebuilding project being evidence of such treason. Satan always *accuses* believers (Revelation 12:10).

Over the years, letter after letter was sent from the Jews' enemies to one Persian king after another; UNTIL one finally responded: "'I commanded, and search has been made, and it is certainly true that this city of old [Jerusalem] has made insurrection against kings; and that rebellion, and sedition, have been made therein. Also, there have been mighty kings over Jerusalem, who have *RULED OVER* all of the countries beyond the river; *and toll, tribute, and custom WAS PAID TO THEM!* So, give commandment to cause those [Jewish] men to cease [building]; that their city be not built, until another commandment may be given from me. Take heed now, that you fail not to do this. Why should damage grow to the hurt of the kings?' Now, *when that copy of King Artaxerxes' letter was read before Rehum, Shimshai the scribe, and all of their companions, they went in haste to Jerusalem, to those Jews, and MADE them cease by force and power.* Then ceased the work of [building] the house of God, which is at Jerusalem. Thus, it ceased until the second year of the reign of Darius, King of Persia (Ezra 4:19-24)." *Using law to stop God's work!*

*While the devil was using the SWORN ENEMIES of God's people to put a stop to their city and temple construction, God was moving His prophets to move that project forward.* "The prophets Haggai and Zechariah prophesied to the Jews that were in Judah, and in Jerusalem, in the name of the God of Israel. Then arose Zerubbabel, and Jeshua, and [the people] started [once again] to build the house of God at Jerusalem. And even God's prophets were helping them (Ezra 5:1-2)!"

God's enemies used man's laws to put a stop to the work of building Jerusalem, which was the official, God-approved place the Jews were commanded to worship God. Check out Deuteronomy 12:11, 16:2, 31:11 and 1 Kings 8:29, 48. God chose Jerusalem as the permanent location of His temple.

Then, *Satan launched another politically-correct attack on the returned Jewish captives—attempting to stop the worship of Jehovah.* (Human beings are caught right in the middle of the ongoing battle between the devil and the Creator.)

After the Jews renewed their temple-building project, "At the same time, came Tatnai, the governor on this side of the river, and Shetharboznai, along with their companions, and they said to those Jews: 'Who commanded you to build this house, and to make up this wall?'...But, the eye of God was upon those Jewish elders, and *their enemies could not cause them to cease building; until the matter came to King Darius.* [The Jews' enemies sent a letter to King Darius, saying:] 'Be it known to the King, that we went to the province of Judea, to *the house of the great God*, which is being built with great stones, and timber being laid in the walls; and the WORK is going FAST on, and prospers in their hands. Then asked we the elders: "*Who commanded you to build this house, and to make up these walls?*" We demanded their names too,...And they answered us: "*We are the servants of the God of heaven and earth*, and we rebuild this house which was built many years ago, which a great king of Israel [King Solomon] built. But, after our fathers had provoked the God of heaven unto wrath, He gave them into the hand of *Nebuchadnezzar, King of Babylon, who destroyed this house and carried the people away into Babylon.* But in the first year of Cyrus the King of Babylon, *that same King Cyrus made a decree to build this house of God.* And also, the vessels of gold and silver of the house of God, which Nebuchadnezzar took from the temple in Jerusalem, and brought them into the temple of Babylon, those did Cyrus the King take out of the temple of Babylon, and delivered them to a man whose name was Sheshbazzar, whom he had made governor. Then said to him: 'Take these vessels, go, carry them into the temple that is in Jerusalem, and LET THE HOUSE OF GOD BE BUILT in its place.' *So the same Sheshbazzar laid the foundation of the house of God in Jerusalem. And since that time even until now has it been in building, but it is still not finished.* Now, therefore, if it seems good to the King [petitioned the Jews], *let search be made in the King's treasure house*, which is at Babylon, *whether it is so that King Cyrus made a decree to build this house of God at Jerusalem* (Ezra 5:3-17).'"" (*The prevailing document!*)

"Then King Darius made a decree, and search was made in the house of the rolls where the treasures were laid up in Babylon. *And there WAS FOUND at Achmetha, in the palace that is in the province of the Medes, a roll, and therein was a record thus written:* 'In the first year of Cyrus, the King, *that same King Cyrus made a decree concerning the house of God at Jerusalem:* "*LET* the house be built, the place where they offered sacrifices. *LET* the foundations of it be strongly laid. [Then Cyrus gave the dimensions.]...*and let the expenses* [of building that temple] *be given out of the King's* [own] *house.* And also, let the gold and silver vessels of the house of God, which Nebuchadnezzar took out of the temple at Jerusalem, and brought to Babylon, *NOW* be restored to the Jerusalem temple; every vessel put in its [proper] place in the house of God.'" Now therefore, Tatnai, governor beyond the river, and Shetharboznai and all your companions, the Apharsachites; let the *WORK* of this house of God alone! Let the governor of the Jews and the elders of the Jews build this house of God in his place. Moreover, I make a decree of what you must do for the elders of these Jews for the building of this house of God: Out of the King's goods, even out of the tribute beyond the river, forthwith expenses must be given unto these men, *so that they be not hindered.* And that which they have need of, young bullocks, rams and lambs, for the burnt offerings of the God of heaven: wheat, salt, wine and oil, according to the appointment of the priests which are at Jerusalem, let it be given them, day by day, without fail. That they may offer sacrifices of sweet savors unto the God of heaven, and pray too for the life of the King, and his sons. Also, I have made a decree, that whosoever alters this word, let timber be pulled down from his house, then being set up, let him be hanged thereon; and let his house be made a dunghill for this. *And the God Who has caused His name to dwell there destroy all kings and people, who put their hand to alter and to destroy this house of God at Jerusalem.* I, King Darius, have made a decree: 'Let it be done with speed.' Then Tatnai, governor on this side of the river, Shetharboznai, and their companions, according to what King Darius had sent, they *DID* speedily. And, the elders of the Jews built and prospered through the prophesying of Haggai the prophet and Zechariah. And they built, and finished it, according to the commandment of the

God of Israel, and according to the commandment of Cyrus, and Darius, and Artaxerxes, Kings of Persia. And this house was finished on the third day of the month Adar, which was in the sixth year of the reign of King Darius (Ezra 6:1-15)."

*I have included this lengthy portion of material on Israel's later history, in order to establish the indisputable FACT that political correctness is one of the devil's primary weapons in his onslaught against God's people and God's Kingdom. But, just as true is the FACT that God is able to turn the tables on the devil and his human crew*; and has often done just that. In fact, *God had long before this event planned His strategy.* Isaiah was written a few hundred years before the activities of the book of Ezra took place; and there you can see God's pre-established plan for Israel's returnees from Babylon:

"God said of King Cyrus: 'He is My shepherd, and he will perform all of My pleasure—Even saying to Jerusalem: "*You will be built*"; and saying to My temple: "*Your foundation will be laid* (Isaiah 44:28).""" More information on God's plan:

"Thus says THE LORD to His anointed [one], King Cyrus, *whose right hand I have held, to subdue nations before him* (Isaiah 45:1)..." And why did God do such for King Cyrus?

"'I have raised him up in righteousness. And, I will direct all of his ways. He will build My city; and he will let go [free] My captive people; not for price, or reward,' says THE LORD (Isaiah 45:13)." More biblical proof of God's preplanning:

"In the *FIRST* year of King Cyrus of Persia, that the word of the *LORD* spoken through the prophet Jeremiah might be accomplished, the *LORD* stirred up the spirit of Cyrus, King of Persia, *so that he made a proclamation throughout all his kingdom*; also putting it in writing: 'Thus says Cyrus King of Persia: "All the kingdoms of this earth has the *LORD* God of heaven given me. And, He has commanded me to build Him a house in Jerusalem, in Judah. Who is there among you of all his people? The *LORD* his God be with him, and let him go up [back to his homeland] (2 Chronicles 36:22-23).""

Ezra 1:1-4 contains basically the same words, but adds: "Whoever [of Israel] *remains in any place* where he sojourns, let the men of that place help him with silver, and gold, and goods, and beasts, beside the freewill offering for the house of God that is in Jerusalem." *Tables turned on the enemy!*

One more passage: "I, even I, Artaxerxes the King, make this decree to all of the treasurers who are beyond the river; that *WHATEVER* Ezra the priest, the scribe of the law of the God of heaven, will require of you, it be done speedily. *Up to an hundred talents of silver, and up to an hundred measures of wheat, and up to an hundred baths of wine, and up to an hundred baths of oil, and salt without measure.* Whatever is commanded by the God of heaven, *LET* it be diligently *DONE* for the house of the God of heaven. For why should there be wrath against the realm of the King, and his sons? Also, we certify you that touching any of the priests, Levites, singers, porters, Nethinims, or ministers of the house of God, it will not be lawful to impose toll, tribute, or custom, upon them. And you, Ezra, after the wisdom of your God, that is in your hand, set magistrates, and judges, who may judge all of the people who are beyond the river; all such as know the laws of your God; and teach all of them who know them not. And whoever will not do the law of your God, and the law of the King, *let judgment be executed speedily upon him; whether it be death, banishment, confiscation of goods or imprisonment* (Ezra 7:21-26)." Wow! Talk about turning the tables!

Other intervening events concerning the *rebuilding of the temple and the walls of Jerusalem* are written in Nehemiah; which you can read about in your own Bible. However, I will present a little snippet of that most enlightening material:

"The [Jerusalem] wall was finished in fifty-two days. And it came to pass that; *when all of our enemies heard about it, and all of the heathen that were about us saw these things, they were much cast down in their own eyes. They perceived that this work was wrought of our God* (Nehemiah 6:15-16)." It requires *supernatural power* to defeat *political correctness*; because evil spirits—the devil and demons—are behind it.

The book of Esther records events that took place *during the Jews' captivity in Persia, not after their captivity,* as both Ezra and Nehemiah report. *But the book of Esther shows the same kind of confrontation between political correctness and God's people and God's plan. And, both Esther and Mordecai exercised the same sort of HOLY boldness to conquer political correctness as did Ezra, Nehemiah and the other returnees.*

"Then Haman said to King Ahasuerus: *'There is a certain people scattered abroad, and dispersed among the people, in all of the provinces of your kingdom, whose laws are diverse from all people; neither keep they the King's laws. Therefore, it is not for the King's profit that they be tolerated.* If it please the King, let it be written that they may be destroyed. And, I will pay ten thousand talents of silver to the hands of those who have the charge of the [killing] business, to bring it into the King's treasuries [*And the King fell for his flattery.*].' And the King took his ring from his hand, and gave it to Haman, the Jews' enemy. And the King said to Haman: *'The silver is granted you and the people also, to do with them as it seems good to you* (Esther 3:8-11).'" Mordecai would not bow down to Haman, so VAIN Haman hated Mordecai and his people.

"*Letters were sent by posts into ALL the King's provinces; to destroy, kill and cause to perish, all the Jews—young and old, little children and women; all in one day*—the thirteenth day of the twelfth month, Adar. And [of course,] *to TAKE the spoil of them for a prey* (Esther 3:13)." Political correctness!

Esther had become queen, but the King knew not about her pedigree. She was a Jew, Mordecai's cousin. He told her to keep quiet about her nationality for the present time. Yet, after that edict, *she would be killed like the rest of the Jews.* Therefore, *Mordecai asked her to appeal to the King in behalf of her people. That was risky even for the queen in that land, because, if she had not been summoned by the King, even as the Queen she might be condemned; unless the King held out his golden scepter.* Esther could be killed right on the spot!

"Mordecai commanded to answer Esther: '*Think not with yourself that you will escape* [because you are in] *the King's house, more than the other Jews.* For, if you altogether hold your peace [*cowardly yield to that political correctness*] now, there WILL arise deliverance to the Jews from another place. And you and your father's house will ALL be destroyed. Who knows whether you have come into this kingdom for such a time as this (Esther 4:13-14)?'" (Verse fourteen has inspired many sermons.) Esther took that *RISKY STEP*, and the King held out to her the scepter; *extending to the queen his favor.*

51

Meantime, Mordecai discovered a plot to assassinate the King, and reported it to Esther, who informed the King; and the would-be assassins were hanged. Mordecai was credited with foiling their plot, and it was filed in the official records. That too came in handy later on; for Haman hated Mordecai more all the time, and sought how to do away with him. But Deity had a different plan. First however; Haman happened upon a most-pleasing plan, and quickly put it into action.

"Then said Zeresh his wife and all his friends to Haman: *'Let a gallows be made fifty cubits high, and tomorrow speak to the King, that Mordecai may be hanged thereon. Then, go merrily with the King to the banquet* [Esther had prepared].' And the thing pleased Haman; and he caused the gallows to be made (Esther 5:14)." But, as it turned out,...

"Haman came in, and the King said to him: *'What should be done to that man whom the King delights to honor?'* Now, Haman thought in his heart: *'Whom would the King want to honor more than myself?'* And so Haman answered the King: 'For that man whom the King delights to honor, let the royal apparel be brought in which the King used to wear, and the horse the King rides upon, and the royal crown which is set on his head. And let the apparel and horse be delivered into the hand of one of the King's most noble princes, so that he may array the man withal whom the King delights to honor, and bring him on horseback through the streets of the city, and proclaim before him: "Thus be it done to the man whom the King delights to honor."' And, the King said unto Haman: 'Make haste and bring that apparel, and that horse, as you said, and do so to Mordecai, the Jew, who sits at the King's gate. Let nothing fail of all that you have spoken.' Then took Haman that apparel, and that horse, and arrayed Mordecai, *then brought him on horseback through the city streets, and proclaimed before him: 'Thus be it done to the man whom the King delights to honor* (Esther 6:6-11).'" Devastated, Haman hung his head in shame and went home (Esther 6:12).

Now, *at that banquet Esther revealed her nationality, and informed the King of Haman's plot against the Jews*. Haman pleaded for his life at Esther's feet, but the King took it that the man was attacking the Queen! "So, *they hanged Haman on the gallows that he had prepared for Mordecai. The King's wrath was then pacified* (Esther 7:10)." *Tables turned again!*

"And the King took off his ring, which he had taken from Haman, and gave it unto Mordecai. *And Esther set Mordecai over the house of Haman* (Esther 8:2)." Remember, however, the King had signed an *irreversible edict* that upon a certain day the Jews were to be slaughtered. Not able to rescind the first edict, the King made a second one; giving the Jews the freedom and weaponry to protect themselves on that day.

"The Jews gathered together in the cities, throughout all of the provinces of King Ahasuerus; *to lay their hands upon all who sought their harm. And no one could withstand them; for the fear of them fell upon the people.* And, even the rulers of the provinces, with the lieutenants, deputies, and officers of the King, HELPED the Jews—*because the fear of Mordecai fell on them—for Mordecai was great in the King's house. His fame went throughout all of the provinces. Mordecai became greater and greater. The Jews smote all of their enemies with the sword, slaughter and destruction; and did whatever they wanted to ALL who hated them* (Esther 9:2-5)." Haman's ten sons were also hanged (Esther 9:13-14). *What a turnabout!*

"Mordecai the Jew was [second-in-command] under King Ahasuerus, and great among the Jews, and accepted by the multitude of his brethren; seeking the wealth of his people, and speaking peace to all of his seed (Esther 10:3)."

Psalms 1:1-3 *perfectly illustrates the scriptural message I am endeavoring to get across in this chapter*: "Blessed is the man, who *walks NOT in the COUNSEL of the ungodly* [yields not to political-correctness pressure], nor stands in the way [path] of sinners, nor sits in the seat of the scornful. But his delight is in the law of the LORD. And, in God's law does he meditate day and night. That man will be like a tree planted by rivers of water, which brings forth its fruit in its season. [Thus,] its leaf will not wither; and whatever that man does will prosper." *Blessed by overcoming political correctness!*

Psalms 12:8: "The wicked [those who are concerned only about their own concerns] walk on every side [they infiltrate every facet of society], when the vilest men are exalted." The pressure to be politically correct (go along with the in-crowd for your own safety) negatively affects everyone when crooks control local, state and federal governments. (And church!)

However, when believers trust and obey God, "The LORD brings the counsel of the heathen to nothing. He makes the [devious] devices of the people of *NO* effect (Psalms 33:10)!"

Now let us look at some *Proverbs truths*: Proverbs 14:12: "There is a way that *seems right* to a man, but at the end of [that way] are the ways of death." *No one can outsmart God. Political correctness is that way which seems right to a man, but which ends in death—the devil being behind it.* Proverbs 16:25 is a repeat of 14:12. Its message must be important.

Proverbs 16:2: "All of the ways of a man [estranged from God] are clean in *HIS* own eyes [estimation]. But, the LORD weighs the spirits." God sees lost man as he really is—lost.

Now, this *ancient observation* that describes our modern world—Proverbs 20:6: "*Most men will proclaim each his own goodness. But a faithful man who can find?*" Therefore,...
Proverbs 30:12: "There *IS* [an entire] generation that are pure in their own eyes, and yet they are *NOT WASHED* from their filthiness." (Modern political-correctness filthiness.)

And Deity has this to say about believers who capitulate to that political correctness: Proverbs 24:10: "If you faint in the day of adversity, your strength is small." Our God is not small, so *if my strength is small, that means I am trusting in something much smaller than God.* And then this warning:
Proverbs 25:26: "*A righteous man falling down before the wicked is as a troubled fountain and a corrupt spring.*" *Deity does not approve of believers bowing to political correctness.*
Rather, "When a man's ways please the LORD, He makes even his enemies [*who put pressure on him through political correctness*] to be at peace with him (Proverbs 16:7)." He did not say they would like it; but that they will be powerless to do us harm. Psalms 91 lays out the fine details about that.
Proverbs 26:27: "He who digs a pit [to harm another] will fall in it: And, he who rolls a stone [to crush someone else], it will return upon him." We can serve God without fear!
Proverbs 29:25: "The fear of man brings a snare. But, he who puts his trust in the LORD will be safe." So, *the people of God do not have to compromise with political correctness!*

*The very gist of political correctness is that it reverses the roles of right and wrong, good and evil.* Political correctness always protects both lies and liars—*making bad people look good and good people look bad. God condemns both evils*:

"WOE to those who call evil good, and good evil; who put darkness for light, and light for darkness; who put bitter for sweet, and sweet for bitter (Isaiah 5:20)!" Almighty God will bring the politically-correct bunch to their knees; if not here on earth during their lifetime, certainly in the Lake of Fire.

One way that evil bunch establishes political correctness is by *deceptively gaining powerful political positions* in local, state and federal governments, then either passing laws, or, pressuring lawmakers to pass laws, that push their political agenda. Once again, what does God's Word say about that?

"*WOE to those who decree unrighteous decrees and write grievousness which they have prescribed* (Isaiah 10:1-2)." In this fallen world system, multitudes of laws *favor the guilty, and condemn the innocent*. In some states today, *a thief can break into someone's home to steal their goods, and while in the house fall, and get hurt, and then sue the homeowner for damages.* And politically-correct judges will favor that thief! (Isaiah actually described modern political correctness.)

That politically-correct crowd trusts in the powers of this fallen world system for their success. God had something to say about that too! "*Egyptians are men, and NOT GOD. And their horses are FLESH, and NOT spirit. Therefore, when the LORD stretches out His hand, both he who helps and he who is helped will fall; they will all fail together* (Isaiah 31:3)."

Additional divine comment regarding *people who trust in anything less than the Lord*: "Behold, all of you who kindle a fire, who compass [surround] yourselves about with sparks. Walk in the light of your fire, and in [the light of] the sparks you have kindled. *THIS* is what you will have from My hand: You will lie down in sorrow [torment in hell] (Isaiah 50:11)."

One more case of *political correctness* found in Daniel: "It pleased Darius to place over his kingdom a hundred-twenty princes, who would rule over that whole kingdom. And, over those were three presidents; of whom, Daniel was first: That the princes might give account to them, and the King would have no damage. *Daniel was preferred above the presidents and princes because an excellent spirit was in Daniel.* Thus, the King thought to set him over the whole realm. Then, *the presidents and princes sought to find some occasion against Daniel concerning his official duties. But, they could find NO occasion, or fault, forasmuch as he was faithful.* Neither was there any error or fault found in him. Then, said those men: 'We will not find any occasion against Daniel, *except we find it against him concerning the law of his God.*' So then, those presidents and princes assembled together to the King, and [flattered] him: 'King Darius, live for ever. All the presidents of the kingdom, the governors, and princes, the counsellors, and captains, have consulted together to establish a *ROYAL STATUTE* and to make a *FIRM* decree [political correctness]; that whoever makes a petition to any god, or man, for thirty days, except you Oh King, *he will be cast into a den of lions.* Now Oh King, *establish the decree and sign the writing*, that it cannot be changed; according to the law of the Medes and Persians, which alters not.' King Darius signed the writing, and the decree. And when Daniel knew that the writing was signed, he went into his house; and his windows being open in his chamber, toward Jerusalem, he kneeled down on his knees three times each day, and prayed, and gave thanks to his God [as was his daily custom] (Daniel 6:1-10)."

Once again, *political correctness condemned the innocent and endeavored to promote the guilty.* But as often happens, *Deity reversed the fortunes of both. The lions NOT being able to hurt Daniel impacted King Darius.* And he knowing Daniel was not guilty of wrong, but those other officials were,...

"The King commanded that they bring the men who had accused Daniel, and they cast them into *THE SAME DEN* of lions; *they, their children, and their wives.* And the lions got mastery of them, and broke all their bones in pieces, or ever they came at the bottom of the den (Daniel 6:24)." Just as it had happened to Haman, *who was HANGED on the gallows he had built for Mordecai, those men and their families were thrown into the same DEN of lions they had hoped would be Daniel's demise.* Political correctness *BACKFIRED* on them!

# Chapter Four

## Political correctness in the New Testament

The *Old Testament* covers a lot of human history; history which reveals *MANY* cases of political correctness. So in the previous chapter, because of limited time and space, *I could not adequately deal with them all, but restricted the coverage to the cases that best demonstrate Bible Truth on that issue.*

Therefore, on the very first page of this chapter, *I need to mention one more Old Testament passage which tells us how to deal with those people who push political correctness.*

The last portion of Jeremiah 15:19: "If you take forth the precious from the *VILE* you will be as My [God's] mouth. Let them [Jeremiah's enemies] return unto you; but return *NOT* unto them." *The purpose of politically-correct personalities is to pressure everyone else to conform to their deceptive ideas:* Why Christians are commanded to reject pressure from the politically-correct! *If anybody does any changing, it must be the politically-correct bunch!* That Scripture also reveals that *political correctness is VILE, which explains why Deity hates it, and commands us believers to both reject it and expose it.*

*LEFTIST groups CONTEND that we ought to all get along: Meaning that those who have different ideas ought to accept leftist ideas.* But: "No man can serve two masters. For, either he will hate one and love the other; or else he will hold to one and despise the other. You cannot serve God *AND* mammon [money gained by political correctness] (Matthew 6:24)."

Politically-correct fools serve money. *True believers serve God alone!* Therefore, *Christians who compromise with those politically-correct satanic slaves, to GAIN money or any other advantage, are switching their loyalty from the Savior, Jesus Christ, to the devil, the god of that politically-correct crowd.*

Mammon consists of *wrong attitudes* concerning money, AND the *misuse* of it (*MONEY IS NOT EVIL IN ITSELF. LOVE OF MONEY is what Paul rebuked* in 1 Timothy 6:10.). Satan is behind wrong attitudes about, and the misuse of, money. Many are *unenlightened* about that reality, so they ought to ponder what Christ said in Luke 11:35: *"Take heed that the LIGHT that is in you be not DARKNESS!" Dark-light perfectly describes political correctness. ONLY light coming from God's Word will expose political correctness!* But one problem with sinners; and saints: *"This is the condemnation, that light has come into the world* [that light being Christ and His Gospel], *and men loved* [to stay in the] *darkness, rather than* [coming to the] *light, because their deeds were evil* (John 3:19)." This is a clear *denunciation* of religious and political correctness.

Politically-correct patrons are also blind to another Bible reality: *"Now is the judgment of this world. Now the prince of this world* [the devil] *will be cast out* (John 12:31)." That was over 1900 years ago! This world system was divinely judged, and its evil leader, Satan, was cast out. *That was connected to Christ's cross-event, because in the very next verse, Jesus spoke of being lifted up* (crucified). *Both Satan and all of His stuff were condemned—including political correctness.* Christ confirmed that reality in John 16:11: *"The ruler of this world* [Satan] *HAS BEEN JUDGED." That means everything aligned with Satan was judged and condemned with Satan—sinners and political correctness—*Which is why in Revelation 20:10, Satan is thrown DIRECTLY into the Lake of Fire with no trial. His trial took place on the cross! (The White Throne Judgment of sinners will only determine their LEVEL of punishment.)

Now, some New Testament cases of political correctness: "Then King Herod, when he had privily called the wise men, enquired of them diligently when the star appeared. And he sent them to Bethlehem, and said: 'Go and search diligently for the *young child; and when you have found Him, bring me word again, so that I may come and worship Him also'*...But, being warned of God in a dream that they should not return to Herod, they departed to their own country *ANOTHER* way (Matthew 2:7-8, 12)." Both history and Scripture reveal that King Herod did not want to worship Jesus, but rather to kill Him. It would have been politically correct to do as the King had requested, but God warned those wise men against it.

"Then Herod, when he realized that he had been mocked by the wise men, became exceedingly wroth, and sent forth, and slew all the children, who were in Bethlehem, and in all the coasts thereof, *from two years old and under*; according to the time he had diligently enquired of the wise men. Then was fulfilled what had been spoken by Jeremy the prophet: 'In Rama, a voice was heard; lamentation, and weeping, and great mourning; Rachel weeping for her children, and would not be comforted, because they are not (Matthew 2:16-18).'" *The REAL NATURE of political correctness—cruelty—surfaces when POLITICALLY-INCORRECT people refuse to bow to it.*

"Behold, *I send you forth as sheep in the midst of wolves.* Be, therefore, wise as serpents, but harmless as doves. But, beware of men. For, they will deliver you up to the councils, and they will *scourge you* in their synagogues. And, you will be brought before governors and kings for My [Jesus'] sake, for a testimony *AGAINST* them, and the Gentiles. But, when they deliver you up, take no thought about how or what you will speak. For, it will be *GIVEN* you in that same hour what you are to speak. For it is not you who speak, but the Spirit of your Father, Who speaks in you. Then brother will deliver up brother to death, and the father, the child. And, children will rise up against their parents, and cause them to be put to death. And, you will be *HATED* by all men for My name's sake. But he who endures to the end will be saved (Matthew 10:16-22)." Why will the world hate believers? Because they not only refuse to fall into the same demonic trap which the politically-correct crowd is trapped in, but have boldness to expose both the trap and those who have fallen into it.

"Think not that I [Jesus] have come to send peace on the earth. I came not to send peace, but a sword [instead]. For I have come to *SET* a man at variance against his father, and daughter against her mother, and daughter-in-law against her mother-in-law. A man's foes will be members of his very *OWN* family. He who loves father or mother more than Me is *NOT* worthy of Me. And, he who loves son or daughter more than Me is *NOT* worthy of Me (Matthew 10:34-37)." *The Lord here condemned family loyalty over loyalty to Him.* If that be the case (and obviously it is, for Christ said so), then *loyalty to business partners or government officials, by YIELDING to political-correctness pressure, will surely incur God's wrath.*

*The underlying SPIRITUAL principle which makes political correctness so utterly evil was taught by the Lord* in Matthew 12:25-30: *"Every kingdom divided against itself is brought to desolation.* And every city or house divided against itself will *NOT* stand. Thus, if Satan casts out Satan, he too is divided against himself. How, then, can his kingdom stand? And if I by Beelzebub cast out demons, by whom do your sons cast them out? Therefore, [your sons] will be your judges. But, *if by the Spirit of God I cast out demons, THEN the Kingdom of God has come unto you. How may a man enter into a strong man's house* [Satan's domain] *and spoil his goods unless he first binds that strong man* [the devil]? Then he can spoil his house [deliver people]. *He who is not with Me is against Me. And, whoever gathers not with Me, scatters abroad."* Political correctness produces THE WRONG KINDS *of division—people against people; against God's people; and even against God!*

Jesus Christ taught that the devil seeks to conquer God's Kingdom by dividing it. Hence, church-divisions. *Christ said division would happen to Satan's own kingdom if he cast out demons. And that religious bunch accused Jesus of using the devil's power to deliver the demon-possessed. But the Savior said such an accusation amounted to blasphemy against the Holy Spirit—blasphemy WHICH WOULD NOT BE FORGIVEN; either in this age or the next!* My purpose for harping on this subject is to make it clear that: *The SAME Bible Truth is true today concerning people who teach that healing-miracles are the devil's work. It would make NO SENSE for the devil to go around healing those he had made sick.* Therefore, teachers who teach such garbage had better repent, and get their act together. *Blasphemy against the Holy Spirit is not the kind of baggage you want with you when you stand before God.*

Although *much less voluminous* than the Old Testament, *the New Testament records an impressive number of cases of political correctness. Most believers today, however, seem to be unaware that political correctness is splashed all over the pages of the New Testament books.* It begins in the Gospels; Jesus Christ Himself exposing political correctness:

Explaining to His disciples the *significance* of the parable of the wheat and tares, "Jesus said: 'He Who sows the good seed is the Son of man; the field is this world; the good seed are the children of the Kingdom; *the tares are the children of the Wicked One; the enemy that sowed them is the devil*; the harvest is the *END* of this [evil] age; and, the reapers are the angels. As the tares are gathered and burned in the fire; so will it be *AT THE END* of this age. The Son of man will send forth His angels, and they will gather out of His Kingdom all things that offend [badmouth God and His people], and that practice iniquity; then the angels will cast the offenders into a furnace of fire. There will be wailing and gnashing of teeth (Matthew 13:37-42).'" Satan sows his seed (sinners) into the world, *in order to take over the world; or at least to make the good seed unproductive.* And what does the devil use to pull off that dastardly deed? *Political-correctness pressure!*

"Herod laid hold on John [the Baptizer], and imprisoned him because of Herodias his brother Philip's wife. John had said to Herod: *'It is not lawful for you to have her.'* So Herod desired death for prophet John; *but he feared the multitude*, because they revered John as a prophet. But, when Herod's birthday came around, the daughter of Herodias danced for the crowd; pleasing Herod: *Whereupon, he promised with an oath to give her whatever she would ask.* She, *being already instructed by her mother*, said: 'Give me John Baptist's head in a charger.' Then king Herod was very sorry. Nevertheless, for his oath's sake, and for those who sat with him at meat, he commanded it to be given her. So he sent and beheaded John in the prison. And his head was brought in a charger, and given to the damsel. She then brought it to her mother. John's disciples came and took his body, and buried it, and went and told the Lord (Matthew 14:3-12)." *Perfect picture of political pressure to conform to the will of the ungodly!*

*That same political pressure pressured Pontius Pilate, the Roman governor of Judea, to do the political thing.* Perceiving that a riot was brewing, "When Pilate *SAW* that he prevailed nothing, but rather that a tumult was made, he took water, then washed his hands before that multitude, stating: *'I am innocent of the blood of this just person. You see to it!'* Then, answered the people, saying: *'HIS BLOOD BE ON US* and *ON OUR CHILDREN* (Matthew 27:24-25).'" Then Pilate yielded to the *political pressure* of that mob; although he had power to disperse them and make a decision based on law, *instead of MOB-rule. The common people yielded to the pressure of the religious leaders to demand Christ's crucifixion.* Then, Pilate yielded to that *mob-pressure*; thereby granting the religious leaders their religious wish. *Political correctness all around!*

*Political correctness seems to have no end*: "Behold, some of the watch [those soldiers watching Jesus' gravesite] came into the city, and told the chief priests all those things that were done [*grave was open and Jesus was gone*]. And when they had assembled, along with their elders, and had taken counsel, they gave large sums of money unto those soldiers; and commanded them: *'Say that His disciples came by night and stole Him away while we slept.'* And if this comes to the governor's ears, we will persuade Pilate, and secure you. So they took the money, and did as they were taught. And this saying is commonly reported among the Jews until this day (Matthew 28:11-15)." *Questionable compensation, and lying, always accompany political-correctness projects! ALWAYS!*

Why that conflict between political correctness and plain honest correctness? Investigate the personality behind each kind. Remember, mammon (filthy money) and lying go hand in hand—both being products of Satan. *Dirty money* (getting money by the wrong means, and for the wrong reasons) and *deliberate deception* are both obviously demonic operations.

Dirty money pollutes those who go after it; revealing that *the devil, who tempts people to go after dirty money, is out to pollute everything, and every person.* Moreover, the fact that lies always accompany the pursuit of illicit gain reveals that Satan is definitely involved. *If such projects were honest and aboveboard, lying would not be necessary for their success!*

John 15:18-21 reveals *the reason for the conflict between political correctness and just being honest*: "If the world hate you [Christ's disciples], *know that it hated Me before it hated you. If you were of this world, this world would love its own. But because you are not of this world, but I have chosen you out of this world,* [for that very reason,] *this world hates you.* Remember, I said to you: *'The servant is not greater than his Lord. If they have persecuted Me they will persecute you too!* If they have kept My sayings they will keep yours also. But, *all of these* [hateful] *things will they do to you for My name's sake; because THEY KNOW NOT HIM WHO SENT ME.'"* John 8:44: "You are of your father the devil, and the lusts of your [spiritual] father you *WILL TO DO.*" Satan hating God with a passion, *he hates anyone connected to God; so motivates his slaves to harbor that SAME hate he has for God AND family.* Jesus repeated that principle in John 17:14 in His prayer to the Father: *"I have given them Your Word; and the world has hated them, because they are not OF the world, even as I am not OF the world."* WE CHRISTIANS ARE CITIZENS OF TWO DIFFERENT WORLDS—earth and heaven (Philippians 3:20, Colossians 3:1-3). *Make proper use of both citizenships!*

More political correctness in Acts: "About that time, King Herod stretched forth his hands *TO VEX* certain ones of the church. Herod killed James, brother of John [one of the 12], with the sword. And *WHEN HE SAW THAT IT PLEASED THE JEWS* [religious and political correctness], he then proceeded to take Peter (Acts 12:1-3)." People's lives MEAN NOTHING to the politically-correct. *It is ALL about money and power, and doing whatever it takes to GET and KEEP money and power.*

You can read about the church getting down to praying, and Peter getting delivered by an angelic jailbreak. However, I want to cover the details of the demise of the one who saw that it *pleased the Jews* to kill one of God's precious saints:

"On a set day, Herod, arrayed in royal apparel, sat on his throne, and made an oration. And those [hypocritical] *people shouted about him: 'It is the voice of a god and not of a man.' And immediately the angel of the Lord smote Herod, because he gave not God the glory. And he was eaten by worms, and gave up the ghost.* But the Word of God grew and multiplied (Acts 12:21-24)." *Big price tag on that political correctness!*

"[Paul's team] *found a certain sorcerer, a false prophet, a Jew, named Barjesus: Who was with Sergius Paulus, deputy of that country; a prudent man, who called for Barnabas and Saul, and desired to hear the Word of God.* But, Elymas the sorcerer (the man's name by interpretation) *withstood them, seeking to turn away the deputy from the faith.* Then, Saul, (who also is called Paul,) filled with the Holy Ghost, set his eyes on him, and said: '*O full of all subtlety and all mischief, you* [very] *child of the devil, you enemy of all righteousness, will you not cease to pervert the right ways of the Lord?* And now, behold, *the hand of the Lord is upon you, and you will be blind, not seeing the sun for a season.*' Then immediately, there fell on him a mist, and a darkness; and he went about seeking someone to lead him by the hand. Then the deputy, when he SAW what was done, believed, being ASTONISHED at the doctrine of the Lord (Acts 13:6-12)." Well, *I guess so!*

*To that sorcerer, the Gospel was not politically correct; not something the deputy needed. So he tried to steer the deputy away from the Gospel.* God certainly foiled that satanic plot!

"When we went to prayer, *a certain damsel possessed by A SPIRIT OF DIVINATION met us, who brought to her masters much gain by soothsaying.* The same followed Paul, and us, and loudly shouted: '*These men are the servants of the Most High God, who show unto us the way of salvation.*' And that she did for many days. But, Paul, being grieved, turned and said to that evil spirit: 'I command you in the name of Jesus Christ to come out of her.' And, he came out the same hour. And when her masters saw that the hope of their gains was gone, they caught Paul and Silas and dragged them into the marketplace unto the rulers; and then, brought them to the magistrates, saying: 'These men, being Jews, do exceedingly trouble our city, and teach customs which are NOT LAWFUL for us to receive, neither to observe, we being Romans.' *And the multitude rose up against them. And the magistrates rent off their clothes, commanding that they be beaten.* Then after they had laid *many stripes* upon them, *they threw them into prison,* charging the jailor to keep them safely: Who, having received such a charge, put them into the inner prison, and made their feet fast in the stocks (Acts 16:16-24)." But Paul started a church there. *Political correctness defeated again!*

Political correctness keeps on keeping on in Acts: "There arose no small stir about that [Christian] way. For a certain man, named Demetrius, who was a silversmith, *made silver shrines for* [the goddess] *Diana, and brought no small gain to the craftsmen: Whom he called together with the workmen of like occupation,* saying: 'Sirs, *you know that by this craft we have our wealth* [what it is all about]. Moreover, you see and hear that, not only here at Ephesus, but almost throughout all of Asia this Paul has persuaded, and turned away, many people, saying that there are *NO* gods made with hands. So, not only is this, our craft, in danger to be set at nought; but also, the temple of the great goddess Diana will be despised, and her magnificence will be destroyed, whom *ALL* Asia and the world worship.' And when they heard that they were full of wrath, crying out: 'Great is Diana of the Ephesians.' *Thus the whole city was filled with confusion.* Then having caught Gaius, and Aristarchus, Paul's traveling companions, *THEY RUSHED* with one accord into the theatre. When Paul would have entered in to the people, the disciples allowed him not. Also, certain of the chiefs of Asia, who were his friends, sent unto him, desiring him that he would not adventure himself into the theatre. Some, therefore, cried one thing, and some another, for the assembly was confused. And, the more part knew not why they had gathered. Then they drew Alexander out of the multitude; the Jews putting him forward. And so, Alexander beckoned with his hand, and wanted to make his defense to the people. But when they knew Alexander was a Jew, all with one voice, about the space of two hours, cried: 'Great is Diana of the Ephesians.' But, when the town-clerk had calmed the people down, he said: 'You men of Ephesus, what person is there who does not know that this city of the Ephesians is a worshipper of that great goddess Diana, and of that image that fell down from Jupiter? *Seeing that these things cannot be spoken against, you ought to be quiet, and to do nothing rashly.* But, you have brought these men here, who are neither robbers of temples nor blasphemers of your goddess. So if Demetrius, and the craftsmen with him, have any matter against any man, the law is open, and there are deputies. Let them implead one another. But, if you enquire anything, concerning other matters, it has to be determined in a lawful assembly. For we are in danger of being called in question for today's UPROAR; there being no cause whereby we might give account for this concourse.' And when he had thus spoken, he dismissed the assembly (Acts 19:23-41)." It should be evident that the devil was behind that tumult, for *confusion, pushing idolatry, persecution of Gospel ministers, deception, and hatred of Jews, all Satan's kind of stuff, were prominent features of that politically-correct uproar.* Now that happened in Asia, on one of Paul's missionary journeys; but sometime later in Jerusalem, Paul again being the target,...

"All that city [Jerusalem] was moved [disturbed], and the people ran together: *And they took Paul and drew him out of the temple.* And forthwith the doors were shut. And, *as they went about to KILL Paul,* tidings came to the chief captain of the Roman band that *ALL of Jerusalem was IN AN UPROAR.* Then, he immediately took soldiers and centurions, and ran down to them. *And when they saw the chief captain and the soldiers, they left off beating of Paul.* Then, the chief captain came near, and took him, and commanded him to be bound with two chains; demanding who Paul was and what he had done. *And some shouted one thing and some another among the multitude. And, when he could not know the certainty for the tumult, he commanded Paul to be carried into the castle.* And when Paul came to the stairs, *he was borne by soldiers because of the violence of the people. For the multitude of the people followed after, crying: 'Away with him!'* Then, as Paul was being led into the castle, he said unto the chief captain: 'May I speak with you?' He said: 'Can you speak Greek? Are you not that Egyptian, *who prior to these days made uproar, and led into the wilderness four thousand men—murderers?'* But then Paul said: 'I am a Jew of Tarsus, a city in Cilicia, a citizen of no mean city. Thus, I beseech you to permit me to speak to these people.' And when he had given Paul license, Paul stood on the stairs, and beckoned with his hand to the people. And, when there was made a great silence, *he spoke to them in the Hebrew language* (Acts 21:30-40)." *The people listened quietly to Paul's presentation, until he told them God had already instructed him to leave town, because, the Jews in Jerusalem would not receive his testimony; and BECAUSE God was sending him far away TO THE GENTILES to preach the Gospel to them.* The uproar began again, and got worse.

*The foregoing may not seem to fit the political-correctness subject, it being a MIXTURE of religious and political activity, but that previous information sets us up to better understand the political-correctness maneuvers of that Roman captain in the following events. Like all politically-correct slaves, he lied and played the hypocrite before his political superiors.*

"The chief captain commanded that Paul be brought into the castle, and bade that he be examined by *scourging*; that he might know wherefore they cried so against him. And, *as they bound Paul with thongs*, Paul asked the centurion, who stood by: 'Is it lawful for you to scourge [beat] a man, who is a Roman citizen [and who has not been condemned by due process of law]?' When the centurion heard that, he went to the chief captain, and said: 'Take heed what you do, for this man is a Roman [citizen].' Then the chief captain came, and asked Paul: 'Are you a Roman?' Paul affirmed. And the chief captain said: 'I obtained such freedom with a lot of money.' Then, Paul said: 'But I was freeborn.' *Then straightway they departed from him who were about to examine him. And the chief captain also was afraid, AFTER he knew that Paul was a Roman, and because he had bound him* (Acts 22:24-29)."

The politically-correct hypocrisy of the captain shows up in the next Acts passage. "The same Roman captain wrote a letter after this manner: 'Claudius Lysias [the captain], unto the most excellent governor Felix, I send greeting. This man [Paul] was taken of the Jews, and would have been killed by them. Then, I came with my army, and rescued him, *having understood that he was a Roman* (Acts 23:25-28).'" Now, *the captain had no idea Paul was a Roman citizen at the time he pulled Paul from the Jews. He knew NOT until AFTER he had commanded that Paul be flogged, and AFTER Paul had TOLD his would-be-floggers that he was an un-condemned Roman. That captain obviously knew that if he told the TRUTH about HOW he found out that Paul was a Roman, he himself might possibly be in big trouble with Rome* (Acts 22:29).

(*Aaron exhibited the same type of hypocrisy when he told Moses that he just threw a blob of gold into the fire, and that gold came OUT of the fire in the form of a calf—the same sort they had worshipped in Egypt for hundreds of years!* Every politically-correct patron will lie and connive to protect their reputation, their money, and their physical well-being.)

*The politically-correct of this world think everyone else is just like they are—selfish and dishonest.* Felix the Governor "*hoped that MONEY would be given him by Paul,* so that he might loose him. Therefore, he sent for him the oftener, and communed with Paul. *BUT,* after two years, Porcius Festus took Felix' place. And Felix, [more than] *willing to show the Jews a* [political] *pleasure, left Paul bound (Acts 24:26-27).*" Paul being a prisoner, *where would he get the kind of money that would interest Felix? And since Jews could be either the enemies, or allies, of Rome, Felix was more interested in the Jews' interests than in Paul's interests. Political correctness!*

Moreover, the politically-correct bunch thinks Christians are *MENTALLY UNSTABLE*—that we are crazy (1 Peter 4:4). "While Paul spoke for himself [in his defense before Agrippa and Festus regarding the Gospel], Festus cried aloud: 'Paul, YOU ARE BESIDE YOURSELF! MUCH LEARNING HAS MADE YOU MAD [insane] (Acts 26:24)!'" Similarly, *one of the elders of my own denomination—many years ago—felt compelled to warn me against TOO MUCH Bible study.* It just might make me lose my mind! Moreover, Jesus' own family members felt the same about Him. *When they learned that one of their kin had strayed from their religious traditions by healing the sick* (something strange to them), *they set out to lay hold of Him,* saying: "*He is out of His mind (Mark 3:21)!*" Therefore, *I have to believe that I am in good company*—Paul, Jesus, etc., etc.

*Cases of political correctness abound in the Book of Acts, the church's only inspired history book.* But the principles of that satanic deception are dealt with in other New Covenant writings as well. Of course, *God expressed His evaluation of POLITICAL CORRECTNESS; and all other satanic and human principles:* "*WHATEVER IS HIGHLY ESTEEMED AMONG MEN IS AN ABOMINATION UNTO GOD (Luke 16:15).*" *And political correctness is chief among such abominations.* What is God's response to Satan's stuff? "*THE WRATH OF GOD is revealed from heaven against all ungodliness and unrighteousness of men, who hold the truth in unrighteousness (Romans 1:18).*" *Truth is held in unrighteousness by BOTH religiously-correct people and politically-correct people; BOTH of whom LIE and CHEAT to achieve their objectives* (with numbed conscience).

"For they who are after the *FLESH* [the politically-correct bunch] *MIND* the things of the flesh; but, they who are after the Spirit, the things of the Spirit. *For to be carnally-minded is death* [See where the *politically-correct crowd* is headed?]; but, to be spiritually-minded is life, and peace. Because, *the carnal* [politically-correct] *mind is enmity against God. For, it is NOT subject to the law of God; neither indeed can it be.* So then, those who are in the flesh cannot please God. But you are not in the flesh, but in the Spirit, if so be that the Spirit of God dwells in you. If any man has not the Spirit of Christ Jesus, he is none of His (Romans 8:5-9)." *Real Christians do not engage in political correctness. That is a worldly pursuit!*

"The natural [worldly, or merely religious,] man does not receive the things of the Spirit of God. For, [spiritual things] are foolishness to him. Neither can he know them. Because, *they are spiritually discerned.* But he who is spiritual judges all things, yet he himself is judged by no man. For, who has known the mind of the Lord, that he may instruct Him? But we have the [very] mind of Christ (1 Corinthians 2:14-16)."

Instructions regarding political correctness: "Let no man deceive himself. If anyone among you [Christians] seems to be wise in this world [Political correctness *IS* the wisdom of this world!], let him become a fool, that he may be wise. For *the wisdom of this world is foolishness unto God.* For as it is written: 'He takes the wise in their very own craftiness.' And again: 'The Lord knows the thoughts of the wise, that *THEY ARE VAIN* (1 Corinthians 3:18-20).'" It is *politically correct* in this world to lie, cheat, steal, step on others on your way up in the world system, and to use any other devious device; *in order to avoid facing the truth about yourself, and especially to avoid having others find out the truth about you.* It is all a demonic farce. Political correctness takes people to hell!

The gist of political correctness may be seen in Galatians 1:10: "Do I [Paul now] persuade men, or God? Or, do I seek to please men? For, *if I still pleased men, then I would not be the servant of Christ."* Political-correctness patrons attempt to *convince their naive comrades that lying, cheating, deceiving, and pursuing selfish goals is the only way to succeed in life.*

"[Christian] servants, be obedient to people who are your masters, according to the flesh, with fear, and trembling, in *HONESTY* of heart, as unto Christ. *NOT* with eye-service, as men-pleasers; *but as servants of Jesus Christ, doing the will of God from the heart*; with good will doing service, as to the Lord, and not to men (Ephesians 6:5-7)." Paul revealed here that *men-pleasers are not out to please other people, or to do them service, but instead to impress others for the advantage of the man-pleaser. So, political correctness is not a Christian virtue, but an evil WEAPON in the devil's arsenal.* Colossians 3:22-25 echoes Ephesians 6:5-7. Galatians 6:7 also warns: "Be not deceived; God is not mocked. *Whatever a man sows he will also reap* (Galatians 6:7)." Thus, *political-correctness practitioners politically correct themselves right into hell.*

"Beware, lest any man spoil [rob] *you through philosophy and VAIN DECEIT* [political correctness], *after the tradition of men, after the rudiments* [the basic success principles] *of the* [rotten-to-the-very-core] *world* [system], *and not after Christ* (Colossians 2:8)." *Political correctness is VAIN DECIET!*

*The height of political correctness comes out in the book of Revelation.* Rarely in world history has one *politically-correct* group been in power over the entire world. Most of the time, different groups (businesses, political parties, nations, etc.) *COMPETE* with each other for the top slot in society. Within each of the competing politically-correct groups, the person who has the loudest voice, the most money, the most clout with his or her constituents, or, in some cases, the greatest military power, will end up *dominating that particular group. The group having the most of everything will then attempt to dominate all the other groups, and become dominant over the entire world.* The last attempt of the devil to do such will be through the Antichrist—as prophesied in Revelation:

"And, he causes all, both small and great, rich and poor, free and bond, to receive a mark [of the beast] in their right hand, or, in their forehead (Revelation 13:16)." The purpose of forcing the taking of that mark is *to control the population by withholding life's necessities from those who will not take the mark. But, even Antichrist will fail to finalize that goal.*

*Human beings will be caught in the middle of the conflict. Satan, through Antichrist, will threaten with DEATH all those who will not yield to his demands, while Deity warns all who bow to the Antichrist that they will BURN in the Lake of Fire forever. The entire human race will have to make some tough decisions during that final segment of the present evil age.*

"A third angel followed them, saying with a loud voice: *'If any man worships the beast and his image, and receives his mark in his forehead, or in his hand, that man WILL drink of the wine of the WRATH OF GOD, which is poured out without mixture* [full strength] *into the cup of His indignation.* And he will be tormented with fire and brimstone in the presence of the holy angels, and in the *PRESENCE* of the Lamb. *And the smoke of their torment will ascend up forever and ever. They will have NO REST, DAY OR NIGHT, who worship the beast, and his image, and whosoever receives the mark of his name* (Revelation 14:9-11)." And there will be *NO* exceptions!

Since all the politically-correct fall into one or more slots in the following, *many will need to read and repent*: "He who overcomes [sin, the world, Satan and Antichrist] will inherit ALL [the good stuff]...But the *fearful* [cowardly], *unbelieving, abominable, murderers, whoremongers, sorcerers, idolaters, and ALL liars, will have their part in the lake that burns with fire and brimstone*—The second death (Revelation 21:7-8)."

"There will in no wise enter into [the New Jerusalem] any thing that defiles; neither whatever works any abomination, or makes a lie. But, they only who are written in the Lamb's Book of Life (Revelation 21:27)." (*Political correctness lies!!!*)

"Outside [the New Jerusalem] are dogs [the very worst of society], sorcerers, whoremongers, murderers, idolaters and *whoever loves and makes a lie* (Revelation 22:15)." Despised by God are both lies and liars—both being of the devil (John 8:44). *And the very core of political correctness is deception.*

A final warning in Revelation: "I testify to every man who hears the words of the prophecy of *THIS* book: 'If *ANY MAN* adds to these things [God has said], God will add to him the plagues that are written in this book. And, if any man takes away from the words of the book of this prophecy, God will take away his part from the Book of Life, and from the holy city [New Jerusalem], and from [all the good] things that are written in this book (Revelation 22:18-19)." What a warning! *How can anyone misunderstand that communication?*

*The party in power determines the parameters of political correctness that party patronizes.* But, *no matter the party or parameters, Satan himself is the ultimate personality behind all political correctness.* That should be obvious by now.

Remember, *the purpose of this book is to uncover Satan's favorite hiding-places.* And we have learned by this research in both Old and New Testaments that *political correctness is one of the devil's MOST COMMON CAMOUFLAGES.* However, we have yet to expose the devil's most devious hiding-place. *Religious correctness* is coming up in the next chapter. *Keep an open mind as we dare explore what Scripture says about that.* God's Word fills us in on what we need to know.

(Let me use this little space to make this point. *The devil hides behind everything, except THE ACTUAL BIBLE TRUTH.* He cannot hide behind God's Genuine Word, for God's Word is the very brightest of *LIGHTS!* And, *the light of God's Word, which cannot be extinguished, EXPOSES the darkness of the devil's lies.* Satan cannot turn off that light, nor overcome it (Read John 1:5 in different versions.), so all he can do is *lie about God's Word,* and/or *substitute his lies for God's Word! The devil hides behind lies! But how can he hide behind lies? By convincing gullible people that his lies are really the truth. Holy Scripture records incident after incident of that tragedy.* How can we make sure we are *NOT* one of the gullible ones? By filling our hearts, our minds, and our mouths with Bible Truth—which exposes the devil's lies! *That is what this book is all about—biblically uncovering the devil's hiding-places.*)

# Chapter Five

## Religious correctness—The worst kind

*This chapter heading might at first be A LITTLE MUCH for some to believe; they questioning its validity.* However, as we investigate *many Scripture passages from both Old and New Testaments*, the indisputable ugly truth about the nastiness of religious correctness will begin to sink in. *It is worse than the world's political-correctness ideas and practices, because religion is MORE dishonest, and MORE cruel, than the world! While many in this old world question if God even exists, the religiously-correct, while claiming to believe that Deity exists, both lie to and about Him.* It sounds absurd, but it is true.

*Flattery is giving praise without sincerity. In other words, flatterers are outright liars.* So check this out: "Nevertheless, they FLATTERED Him [God] *with their mouth, and they LIED TO Him with their tongue* (Psalms 78:36)." The Creator, Who sees and knows all, *sees right through flattery*; so to attempt to flatter Deity is the height of insanity. It is stupidity in the extreme! The flatterer might fool others, and definitely does fool him or herself, but he or she *CANNOT* fool God! Such is the religiously-correct bunch for you. *Not all that smart!*

"This people [Jews] *draw near Me with their mouths, and, with their lips they do honor Me, but they have removed their hearts far from Me; and their fear toward Me is taught by the precept of men* (Isaiah 29:13)." Not from the heart! But,...

"The hour is coming, and now is, when *true worshippers will worship the Father in spirit and in truth; FOR, the Father SEEKS such people to worship Him.* God is Spirit. Therefore, people who worship Him *MUST* worship Him in *SPIRIT* [from their heart] and in truth [reality] (John 4:23-24)." With God, flattery will get you nowhere! (Nowhere positive, that is.)

*Jesus proved that the same religious hypocrisy as existed in Isaiah's day was still rampant among the Jews during His time on this earth:* "You hypocrites, well did Isaiah prophesy about you, stating: 'These people draw near to Me with their mouth, and they honor Me with their lips; but, *their heart is far from Me. They worship Me IN VAIN; teaching for doctrines the commandments of men* (Matthew 15:7-9).'" *VAIN* worship means *empty, useless, worthless* worship—*even offensive to God*. Vain-worshippers, instead of advancing themselves, or anyone else, in the Kingdom of God, actually *DECEIVE* both themselves and everyone else who is influenced by them.

The vain practice of lying to God was not confined to *Old Testament personalities*. Acts 5:4 recorded one such case by *New Covenant church members*. It having become *popular* to give one's extra cash to a special church fund, *Ananias and his wife Sapphira pretended to give ALL their extra cash, but actually withheld a certain amount of it*. While that does not sound like it should be counted a serious crime, *lying about it to men was the very same as lying to the Almighty*. "While that land remained [your property], was it not your own [to do with as you saw fit]? And, after it was sold, was it not in your own power [to do with the money as you desired]? Why have you conceived this thing in your heart? You have *NOT* lied to men but to God." Serious infraction! *Peter was God's representative, so lying to Peter was lying to God!* Is that not just as true today as it was in those days? Why would it not be? When did that biblical principle change? *Honesty seems to be more important to God than money!* But, in the modern church, honesty has taken a back seat to money. *Lying has become religiously correct in many churches today; like lying is politically correct out in the corrupt world system. To many churches the most important thing is to keep their money and their prestige intact. HONESTY IS RELATIVE.* Threaten either their money or their prestige, and watch them squirm.

But let us now go back to the Old Testament and look at several Scripture passages that establish the *biblical truths every believer needs to know and understand about religious correctness. It is scattered throughout biblical history!*

I have not enough time or space in either this chapter or book to go into detail on *Israel's long history of disobedience to God, and joining every group that was hostile to their God, and thus yielding to the pressures of those entities to become politically and religiously correct—thereby following man and Satan, rather than the True and Living God—their Redeemer.* After Joshua passed on, *God-appointed judges ruled Israel a few hundred years; and after that, many kings. During most of that time, BOTH the people and rulers of Israel repeatedly rebelled against God, by aligning themselves with practically every politically-correct and religiously-correct practice which was in vogue.* Eventually, *Israel became so far removed from God and the truth that they treated God and his prophets as enemies.* They wanted nothing to do with their HOLY God!

"[My people] *say to the Seers [those who could SEE INTO the spirit realm]: 'SEE NOT'; and to the prophets: 'PROPHESY NOT TO US WHAT IS RIGHT, PROPHESY SMOOTH THINGS; PROPHESY DECEIT. Depart from the way* [of righteousness]; *turn aside out of the path* [of truth]; *and cause the Holy One of Israel to cease from before us* (Isaiah 30:10-11).'" Can you see how foolish and dangerous *BOTH* political and religious correctness are? And Israel fell into those very deceptions!

Also, Jeremiah said: "*An astonishing and horrible thing is committed in the land. The prophets prophesy FALSELY; and the priests bear rule by their own means; and My people love it like that. However, what will you do in the end* (Jeremiah 5:30-31)?" It does not pay to disobey the Almighty!

Jeremiah's kin hated him: But, "'I [Deity] have made you [Jeremiah] this very day a defensed city, an iron pillar, and brazen walls against the whole land; against all the kings of Judah, against the princes, against the priests, and against the people of the land. *They [even your kin] will fight against you; but they will not prevail against you; for I am with you,*' says the LORD, '*to deliver you* (Jeremiah 1:18-19).'" AMEN!

Remember, Jeremiah was a priest of Anathoth. *So it was his own kin who wanted him dead.* "Thus says the LORD, of all the men of Anathoth, who are *SEEKING* your life, saying: 'Prophesy not in the name of the LORD, that you die not by our hand.' Therefore, thus says the LORD of hosts: 'Behold, *I will PUNISH* them. Their young men will die by the sword; their sons and their daughters will die by famine. There will be none left. For, I will bring evil upon the men of Anathoth in the year of their visitation (Jeremiah 1:1, 11:21-23).'"

Jeremiah chapter twenty-three paints a negative portrait of the Jewish leaders in Jeremiah's day. In fact, it is hard to believe they were actually that bad. But knowing that Satan always continues pulling compromisers farther downhill on that road to destruction, it is really not all that surprising.

"'Woe to the pastors [shepherds] who destroy and scatter the sheep [the Jewish people] of My pasture!' says the LORD (Jeremiah 23:1)." *Shepherds DESTROYING God's people! Are not shepherds supposed to FEED and PROTECT their flocks?*
"I have seen also in the prophets of Jerusalem a horrible thing: They [actually] *commit adultery and walk in lies. They also strengthen the hands of evildoers, so that none of them returns from his wickedness. All of them are to Me* [Deity] *as Sodom, and the inhabitants thereof, as Gomorrah.* Therefore, thus says the LORD of hosts, concerning all those prophets: 'Behold, I will feed them with wormwood, and make them to drink the water of gall. For, from the prophets of Jerusalem *profaneness* has gone forth into all the land.' Thus says the LORD of hosts: 'Hearken not unto the words of the prophets who prophesy to you. For *they make you vain.* They speak a vision out of their own heart, and not from the mouth of the LORD. They say still unto those who despise Me: "The LORD has said, 'You will have peace'; and they say unto every one who walks after the imagination of his own heart, *'NO EVIL WILL COME UPON YOU* (Jeremiah 23:14-17).'"" However,...

"If [the false prophets] had stood in My counsel, and had caused My people to hear My words, then they should have turned them from their evil ways, and from the evil of their doings (Jeremiah 23:22)." *But religion always embraces lies!*

"'Behold, I am against those who prophesy false dreams,' says the *LORD*, 'and *cause My people to err by their lies*, and by their frivolity; yet I sent them not, nor commanded them. Therefore, THEY [the *religiously-correct* false prophets] WILL NOT [indeed cannot] PROFIT THIS PEOPLE AT ALL,' says the LORD (Jeremiah 23:32)." *Religiously-correct religious leaders always force their religious correctness on their congregation, so that, instead of God's will being done, Satan's will is done in God's own church—MAKING IT RELIGIOUSLY INCORRECT to think, speak, or act contrary to their ideas and practices. It sometimes even becomes life-threatening to anyone opposing their religiously-correct religious systems!* In Ezekiel's time it happened. *Hear what God Himself had to say about that*:

"Will you pollute Me [God] among My people for handfuls of barley and for pieces of bread, *to slay the souls that ought not die, and save the souls alive that ought not live*, by your lying to My people, who hear your lies (Ezekiel 13:19)?" *God Himself said that some people ought to die!* Most theologians today (*including those in the church college I attended*) deny that Deity has such characteristics. He is a God of love, and so, *could not have said such mean things*. That is part of the *religiously-correct GARBAGE TAUGHT IN MANY CHURCHES*. But, *God is a God of WRATH, just as He is a God of LOVE!*

*Religiously-correct religious lies* obviously occasioned the following most enlightening statement by the Almighty: "*My* [own] *people are DESTROYED for a lack of knowledge*. [Then to the priests:] Because you have rejected knowledge [which My people needed to keep from being destroyed], I will reject you also, *so that you will be no priest to Me*. Seeing that you have forgotten the *LAW* [source of saving knowledge] of your God, *I will also forget your children* (Hosea 4:6)." Here again, God pronounced judgment on the religious leaders of Israel; because one of His divine attributes is that *He is JUDGE*.

"*According to the word* [of blessing] *I covenanted with you when you left Egypt, My Spirit remains among you* [to fulfill that Word]: *Fear not* (Haggai 2:5)!" Yet, while HIS PROMISES OF BLESSING are steadfast, HIS PROMISES OF JUDGMENT AGAINST UNBELIEF AND REBELLION also remain intact.

*Israel's politically and religiously-correct shenanigans got so REPULSIVE that God finally said unto them in frustration:* "'Who is there among you, who would shut the doors [of the temple], *so as not to kindle a fire on My altar IN VAIN. I have NO PLEASURE in you,*' says the LORD of hosts. *'Neither will I* [any longer] *accept an offering at your hand* (Malachi 1:10).'"

Actually, religious correctness is designed by the devil to negatively affect everything about God's Kingdom; including diminishing its financial support. Therefore, Jewish leaders cursed themselves by pushing their religious lies; *which led the general Jewish population to despise that entire religious system, and eventually abandon it in outright disgust. Thus, religious-correctness-pushers destroy themselves in the long run.* (Only God's plans will succeed. All ungodly plans fail.)
"'Will a man rob God? Yet, you have robbed Me. But you say: "Wherein have we robbed You?" In tithes and offerings! You are cursed with a curse. For, you have robbed Me, even this whole nation. Bring *ALL* the tithes into the storehouse, that there may be *FOOD* in My house; and *PROVE ME* now, herewith,' says the LORD of hosts, 'if I will not open you the windows of heaven, and pour you out a blessing, that there will not be room enough to receive it (Malachi 3:8-10).'" *The religious leaders' false ministry failed God, failed the Jewish population, and even failed those leaders themselves; for the tithe was designed by Deity to SUPPORT the leaders of God's worship system.* Therefore, those leaders shot themselves in their own foot, as that old proverb goes, *by pushing religious lies on God's people, who finally came to see the hypocrisy of that religious system, and turned against their leaders—and even against God Himself.* Galatians 6:7 came into play.

But in every generation, God always finds *faithful saints.* "They who feared the LORD spoke often one to another. And the LORD heard it; *and a book of remembrance was written before Him for those who feared the LORD, and who thought upon His name. 'They will be Mine,'* says the LORD of hosts, 'in that day I make up My jewels. And I will spare them as a man spares his son, who serves him. Then, *you will discern between the righteous and the wicked; between the one who serves God and him who serves Him not* (Malachi 3:16-18).'"

Although, as far as I know, the term *religious correctness* does not actually appear in any Bible book, *that principle is abundantly present in almost every Bible book.* And God has made some serious statements about both His view of such evil stuff, and about what He plans to do about that stuff:

"And now also, *the* [divine] *axe is laid unto the root of the trees. Therefore, every tree that brings not forth good fruit is hewed down, then cast into the fire* [of hell] (Matthew 3:10)." That must be referring to everything the devil talks religious leaders into *shoving down the throats of Christian believers*; and *religious correctness* seems to be their personal favorite. *Religious correctness has never brought forth good fruit.* How could it? It is of the devil? *Good fruit is God-honoring fruit!*

Moreover, *why would Jesus make the following comment, unless religious leaders had been teaching the very opposite of God's Holy Word?* "Whoever breaks one of the least of the commandments *and TEACHES men so will be called least in the Kingdom of heaven. But whoever does them and teaches them will be called GREAT in the Kingdom of heaven.* I say to you: *'Except your righteousness exceeds the righteousness of the Scribes and the Pharisees, you will BY NO MEANS enter the Kingdom of heaven* (Matthew 5:19-20).'" Stern warning!

The Scribes and Pharisees were *the cream of the religious crop* in Israel in those days. So, *how could Christ's listeners be MORE righteous than they?* Our Lord BROUGHT TO US A HIGHER KIND OF RIGHTEOUSNESS—*Righteousness from on high*: "For, they being ignorant of *GOD'S* righteousness, and going about to establish their *OWN* righteousness, have not submitted themselves to the God-kind of righteousness. For Christ is *THE END* of the law for righteousness, to everyone who believes (Romans 10:3-4)." Thus, *it was not quantity of righteousness Jesus said the people lacked, but quality.* The BEST of man's righteousness is like filthy rags (Isaiah 64:6). *God's righteousness MAKES believers TO BE righteous!*

The *same principle* is brought out in Jeremiah 2:13: "For *My people have committed two evils*: They have forsaken Me, the Fountain of living waters, and hewed them out cisterns, broken cisterns that can HOLD NO WATER [at all]." *Religious correctness holds NO living water. It is full of religious holes!*

"*NOT* everyone who says unto Me: 'Lord, Lord,' will enter into the Kingdom of heaven; but, he who does the will of My Father, Who is in heaven (Matthew 7:21)." Truth concerning political correctness: *It has NEVER done God's will—NEVER! Political correctness pushes legislation to legalize the murder of innocent unborn babies; and also demands that taxpayers fund those brutal murders. Political correctness sees people's money as belonging to the government; and believes that the government ought to have power to keep whatever amount it wants to keep, and let the people who work for and earn that money keep whatever the government thinks is appropriate. Moreover, political correctness wastes the taxpayer's money with worthless projects, caring not that such waste increases our national debt. Political correctness just raises taxes, then finds more ways to waste that extra revenue, so that there is no reduction in the debt. Political correctness desires to bring this Great Nation of the United States down to the level of the third-world countries. Political correctness legislates the most immoral acts, then makes it a crime to say such acts are sin. Political correctness has the guilty innocent, and the innocent guilty. Political correctness insists that LIBERAL government officials know best how we politically-INcorrect folks ought to live our lives; especially Christians. And, political-correctness practitioners think that they are going to get away with their demonic ideas and practices.* Can you see God, or godliness, in any such politically-correct trash? That politically-correct crowd destroys both themselves and others; thereby serving the devil, not country, God, or the church of Jesus Christ!

What about religious correctness? Is it really any better? Religious correctness teaches that *believers are still sinners, even after having been born again, and having become new creatures in Christ, and old things having passed away, and all things having become new, and those new things being of God* (2 Corinthians 5:17-18). John Calvin's contribution to the church! My book, "Are Christians Just Saved Sinners?", exposes that Calvinist lie. *Religious correctness also teaches that JEHOVAH-RAPHA, THE VERY HEALER HIMSELF, QUIT PERFORMING MIRACLES AFTER THE FIRST CENTURY. That would mean we ought not expect miracle-healings today.* My two HEALING BOOKS BLAST AWAY that satanic lie.

That as well was John Calvin's *DEMONIC* contribution to the church. In James 5:14-16, James commanded believers who are sick to call for the elders of the church; *who should pray for the recovery of those who are sick.* John Calvin said that those instructions were valid ONLY back in James' day. Therefore, *they did NOT apply to the church in modern times (1500s). Calvin provided NOT ONE Scripture passage to back that demonic doctrine.* Still, millions of church members and thousands of cowardly preachers *AGREE* with John Calvin's demonic theology over the plain Word of God. Such tragedy! *How can anyone read God's clear Word on the healing issue, then conclude the opposite of that CLEAR DIVINE WORD?*

(*I have published two more books that expose the satanic nature of Calvin's theology:* "The Calvinist Conspiracy," and "The Calvinist Delusion." *Multitudes today are influenced by various tenets of Calvinism—ALL of which are satanic. There is not one ounce of honesty in any of Calvinism. It pushes the devil's destructive agenda, not God's redemption plan.*)

"Whoever hears these sayings of Mine [Jesus' words] and *DOES* [obeys] them, I will liken him to a wise man who built his house on a rock. And the rain descended, and the floods came, and the winds blew, and *BEAT* upon that house. But, it fell not, for it was founded upon a rock. But everyone who hears My words, and does them not, I will liken to a foolish man, who built his house on sand. And the rain descended, and the floods came, and the winds blew, and *BEAT* on that house; and it fell. And great was its fall (Matthew 7:24-27)."

That is a simple, but graphic, illustration of *the stupidity of those who either hear or read God's Word, then carelessly dismiss it to their own destruction. And religious-correctness is a big factor in persuading people to ignore godly warnings.* Many Jews were *highly developed* in religious correctness:

"Jesus marveled, and said to those who followed: 'Truly I say to you, I have not found so great faith, no, not in Israel.' And I also say unto you: 'Many will come from the East and West, and sit down with Abraham, and Isaac, and Jacob, in the Kingdom of heaven. *But, the children of the Kingdom will be CAST OUT into outer darkness. There will be weeping and gnashing of teeth* (Matthew 8:10-12).'" *Jesus here referred to the Jewish nation, which rejected His message and ministry.*

"Then began He to *upbraid* [fuss on] those cities wherein most of His mighty works were done, because they repented not: 'Woe unto you, Chorazin! Woe unto you, Bethsaida! For if the mighty works [of miracle-healing] which were done in you had been done in Tyre and Sidon [long ago], they would have repented long ago in sackcloth and ashes.' But I say to you: *'It will be more tolerable for Tyre, and Sidon, on the Day of Judgment, than it will for you.'* And you, Capernaum, who are exalted unto heaven, will be brought down to hell. For if those mighty [healing-]works, which have been done in you, had been done in Sodom, it would have remained until this day. But I say to you: *'It will be more tolerable for the land of Sodom on Judgment Day than for you* (Matthew 11:20-24).'"

*The purpose of healing-miracles is not only to HELP those who are physically hurting, but also to bring miracle-viewers to repentance.* If such was the case when Christ walked this earth, it is the case today. *What does that say about modern preachers who MOCK those who believe that miracles are for today, as much as they were for 2000 years ago? How could the words of our Savior,* Who is "the same, yesterday, today, and forever," *have lost their power or authority today?* Thus, our Savior would UPBRAID MANY CHURCHES TODAY as He did those CITIES back in THOSE days! *Religious correctness provokes God in these modern times just as it did back in the first century. It is time to abandon all religious correctness.*

*When religious correctness becomes the norm in churches or denominations, the leaders thereof are compelled to attack whatever APPEARS to threaten it; or them. That is why every new move of God is OPPOSED by established churches;* even churches God moved in before. *Why the Jews hated Jesus!*

"No one puts a piece of new cloth on an old garment [*the old Jewish religious mentality*], for that which is put in to fill it up takes away from the old garment, and the tear is made worse. Neither do men put new [unfermented] wine into old wineskins. Else, [when the *NEW* wine begins to ferment] the *OLD* [brittle] wineskins fracture, and the wine runs out, and the *OLD* wineskins *PERISH* [so both the wine and wineskins are lost]. But they [wisely] put new wine into new bottles, so *BOTH ARE PRESERVED* (Matthew 9:16-17)." What our Lord brought to earth was *both new wine and a new wineskin.*

The Jews had a synagogue on about every corner, as the saying goes today about churches in some cities. And, every synagogue had its leader. But our Savior, seeing beyond the religious establishment, made this disturbing observation:

"When the Lord saw the vast multitudes, He was moved with compassion upon them, because they fainted and were scattered abroad; *JUST AS SHEEP HAVING NO SHEPHERD* (Matthew 9:36)." They had leaders who did not lead, just as many modern churches have. Oh sure, *pastors obviously do lead, but in what direction?* I have said it over and over: "*If it was happening back then, it is happening today.*" Satan has not changed; religion has not changed (because, the devil is behind religion today just as he has always been); the world has not changed (except for modern inventions). How many modern pastors are *REALLY SHEPHERDING* God's sheep?

Consider how the religious leaders responded to Christ's message and ministry: *When their own synagogue members got delivered from demon oppression or possession, religious leaders put their religious spins on those miraculous events.*

"The Pharisees said, 'This fellow does not cast out devils, but by Beelzebub, the prince of the devils (Matthew 12:24).'" I know of such demonic nonsense coming out of Christians' mouths today! So, has anything really changed in *OUR* day? Moreover, *how does religious correctness differ from political correctness? In both circles, the leaders put their own spin on everything that might expose their demonic connection! Those spins, of course, are always lies; and Satan fathers all lies!*

So the Savior asked: "If I by Beelzebub cast out demons, then by whom [by what power] do your sons cast them out? Therefore, they will be your judges. But if I cast out demons by the Spirit of God, *then the Kingdom of God HAS COME to you* (Matthew 12:27-28)." *God's Kingdom produces miracles!*

Because of religious correctness, which religious leaders would not abandon, "The Savior did not many mighty works there, *because of their unbelief* (Matthew 13:58)." Therefore, our Lord finally declared: "*THE KINGDOM OF GOD WILL BE TAKEN FROM YOU; THEN GIVEN TO A NATION PRODUCING THE FRUIT* [it is meant to produce]." Because: "*MY FATHER IS GLORIFIED BY MUCH* [miraculous] *FRUIT* (John 15:8)."

Note this prime example of religious correctness: "Woe to you, scribes and Pharisees; hypocrites! For you *TITHE* mint, anise and cummin [garden herbs], *but you have omitted the WEIGHTIER matters of the law—judgment, mercy, and faith.* These [weightier deeds] you should have done; but not leave that other [tithing] undone. You blind guides, *who strain out a gnat* [small unclean insect], *then swallow a camel* [large unclean animal] (Matthew 23:23-24)." Jesus established the undeniable truth that RELIGIOUS CORRECTNESS ALWAYS CONCENTRATES ON DOING THOSE LESSER THINGS THAT COST THOSE RELIGIOUS PEOPLE LESS; AND SUPPOSEDLY EXCUSES THEM FOR NOT PAYING THAT HIGHER COST OF INVESTING THIER TIME, MONEY AND EFFORT INTO THOSE THINGS IN LIFE THAT REALLY MATTER: SUCH AS OBEYING GOD AND HELPING OTHERS! *And the following reveals their heartless antipathy toward the very Savior of the world; and then their hypocritical patronage of lesser religious rules:*

"Now the chief priests, and elders, and all of the council, *sought FALSE WITNESS against Christ, to put Him to DEATH* (Matthew 26:59)." That is a biggie! Yet, they had *NO* qualms in their conscience when breaking that legal and moral law!

"Then, Judas, who had betrayed Him, when he saw that He [Christ] was condemned, repented himself, then brought again those *thirty pieces of silver* [blood-money] to the chief priests, and elders, and said: 'I have sinned; I have betrayed innocent blood.' And they said: 'What is that to us? See to it yourself [That is your problem, not ours!]!' Then, Judas cast down those pieces of silver in the temple, and departed, and went and hanged himself. Then, the chief priests took those silver pieces, and said: *'It is NOT LAWFUL for us to put them into the temple treasury, for, it is the price of blood* (Matthew 27:3-6).'" *Religious leaders were COMPELLED to comply with LESSER rules* (about money), *but felt NO remorse for illegally incriminating, and then murdering their very own Messiah!*

That is why our Lord said: "*You* [Jews] *outwardly appear righteous unto men, but within, you are full of hypocrisy and iniquity* (Matthew 23:28)." Some of their hypocrisy is evident in Matthew 27:25 and Acts 5:28: "Then said the people: '*His blood be on us, and on our children.*'" But later, their leaders said: "Did not we straitly command you that you should not teach in *THIS* [Jesus'] name? But, *you have filled Jerusalem with your doctrine, and intend to bring this Man's blood upon us.*" The religiously-correct crowd will say anything that lets them off the hook up front; *then will later seek to escape the consequences of their prior self-incriminating words.*

*Even close friends and comrades sometimes fall into that demonic, religious-correctness pit.* Peter did! "*Christ began to teach them that the Son of man must SUFFER many things, then be rejected by the elders, and chief priests, and scribes; then be killed, and after three days rise again.* And He spoke that openly. And Peter took Him, and began to rebuke Him. But when He had turned about and looked on His disciples, Jesus rebuked Peter, saying: 'Get behind Me Satan. For you savor [or value] not the things of God, but the things of men (Mark 8:31-33).'" *Religiously-correct people might not always start out being deliberately opposed to the things of God, but they ALWAYS come against His divine plans in the long run; proving that the devil is behind ALL religious correctness.*

Christ even warned His disciples of *political correctness*: "Jesus called the disciples unto Him, and said to them, 'You know that they who are accounted to rule over the Gentiles exercise lordship over them; and their great leaders exercise authority over them. *But, it must NOT be so among you. For, whoever will be great among you will be your minister. And, whoever of you will be the chiefest will be servant of all. For, even the Son of man came not to be ministered unto, but to minister, and to GIVE His life as a ransom for many* (Mark 10:42-45).'" *He wants no political correctness in the church!*

However, *in some churches and denominations today, the same force that rules this world dominates church members. If any church member gets out of line with that force, various forms of religious and/or political PRESSURE are used to get them back in line.* Contrary to that Mark 10:42-45-demand, *many preachers DEMAND of church members strict loyalty to certain doctrines, a big salary, a good retirement plan, good health insurance, etc. Instead of preachers dominating Satan in behalf of the church members, Satan actually uses them to dominate the church members!* (Just reporting the truth.)

Christ was very smart! "Jesus did not commit Himself to them, because He *KNEW* all men, and needed not that any should testify of man. For, He knew what was in man (John 2:24-25)." *Human beings are fickle.* Jesus knew that, so did not trust His well-being to any man; but to His Father only. *"I have come in My Father's name, but you do not receive Me. If another comes in his own name, him you will receive. How can you believe, who receive honor of one another, and seek not the honor that comes from God only (John 5:43-44)?" The dishonorable have no real honor they can lavish on others!*

When Christ began teaching that to be saved those Jews would need to eat His flesh and drink His blood: "From that time, *MANY* of His disciples went back, and walked no more with Him. Then said Jesus unto the twelve: 'Will you also go away (John 6:66-67)?'" Religious correctness was *SO BLIND* that its patrons refused to hang around long enough to ask for an explanation of what they initially did not understand. Even in the face of that, Christ did not compromise truth to get followers; *but even questioned His inner circle about their loyalty. Before yielding to religious correctness, Christ would start all over and look for disciples who would not bend with religious winds, or hold to manmade traditions* (Mark 7:13).

The bottom line of political correctness: "And *THIS* is the condemnation, that light [Jesus Christ and God's Word] *has come into the world* [bringing light and life], *but people loved darkness rather than light because their deeds were evil. For everyone who does evil HATES the light, neither comes to the light, lest his deeds be* [exposed and] *reproved. But, he who DOES the truth comes to the light, so that his deeds might be made manifest* [made evident], *that they are wrought in God (John 3:19-21)."* More proof of that truth: "The world cannot hate you [that religious bunch]; but Me it hates, *BECAUSE I TESTIFY THAT ITS WORKS ARE EVIL* (John 7:7)." YEP!

"Did not Moses give you the *LAW? But none of you keeps that law* (John 7:19)." Yet, religious leaders *SAW* themselves better than everyone else; saying to that man who had been born blind: "'You were altogether *BORN* in sins, and will you [think to] teach us?' And they cast him out (John 9:34)."

One of the major pitfalls of religious correctness is pride. After the religious bunch had thrown out of their synagogue that grown man, who had been born blind, but whom Jesus had supernaturally healed, "Jesus said to them: 'If you were [actually, physically] blind, you would have no sin. But now you say: "We see"; therefore, your sin remains (John 9:41).'" Both the *politically* and *religiously-correct* always claim they are right, and do not need to do any changing. However, the Lord said that all of them are in deep trouble, if they are not willing to repent and change their ways. *So, neither religious correctness, nor its counterpart political correctness, cleanses anyone from sin or makes any right before God.* They may be temporarily enjoying their hour, and the power of darkness, as Jesus called it, *but unless they repent before it is too late, and accept Jesus Christ as Savior, and Lord, eventually they will find themselves in outer darkness; where they will weep and gnash their teeth in eternal pain.* (Numerous passages!)

Another *troubling fact* about religious correctness is that: The religiously-correct *care little or nothing about the sheep, but only or mostly about themselves. Jesus said exactly that!* "He who is a HIRELING, and not the actual Shepherd, whose OWN the sheep are not, sees the wolf coming, and leaves the sheep. And the wolf [Satan] catches the sheep, and scatters them. The hireling flees, because he is ONLY a hireling, and CARES NOT FOR THE SHEEP (John 10:12-13)." Remember, Jesus said it first! *God-called and faithful ministers consider the sheep as part of their own family, so have the same care for the sheep as Jesus has, for Jesus lives inside us. We are not hirelings!* One way or another, Satan controls hirelings!

When some GENUINE SHEPHERDS [apostles] "spoke [the Gospel] to the people [*in the temple*], the priests, the captain of the temple, and the Sadducees, *CAME UPON* them; *being GRIEVED that they taught the people, and preached through Jesus the resurrection from the dead.* Then they laid [hostile] hands on them and put them in jail unto the next day, for it was already evening. Howbeit, many of those who heard the Gospel believed. And the number of the *MEN* was about five thousand (Acts 4:1-4)." *Religious correctness GRIEVES when people hear the Gospel, believe on Jesus, and get saved!!!!!*

Furthermore, *religious correctness ALWAYS DOWNPLAYS THE MIRACULOUS!* "What will we do to these men? Because indeed, *a NOTABLE MIRACLE has been done by them, which is obvious to ALL dwelling in Jerusalem; and we cannot deny it.* But, that it [the Gospel, with its miracle-healings,] spread no further among the people, *let us threaten them, that they speak from now on TO NO MAN in that name.* So, they called them before the council again, and commanded them NOT to speak at all, nor teach, in the name of Jesus (Acts 4:16-18)." The name of Jesus, to which every knee will eventually bow, and every tongue confess, that He is LORD, obviously scared the daylights out of those religious leaders. So they plotted to lie, and connive, against those faithful servants of God. That HEALING-MIRACLE of the man born lame demonstrated that the Lord's disciples were perpetuating the miracle-ministry of the Savior—Proving that the Jews did not get rid of Christ by crucifying Him after all—and that those religious leaders had been WRONG ALL ALONG. Moreover, those leaders now had opportunity to admit they had been wrong in rejecting Christ as Savior and Lord, and to make things right with God. They opted instead to hold onto their religious-correctness, and to deliberately maintain their lies and hypocrisy. Moreover, *the religious leaders tried to pressure Peter and John to join their hypocrisy, and pass it on to that multitude of unsaved Jews; thus disobeying God, in order to pacify the religiously-correct leaders.* Satan was surely behind that religious shenanigan! NOTHING is godly about religious correctness!

But, praise God, there are some honest and courageous Christians! *Even under such intense pressure to capitulate to religious correctness*, "Peter and John answered the leaders: 'Whether it is right in the sight of God to hearken unto you, more than to God, you judge. *For we CANNOT but speak the things we have seen and heard.*' So, when they had further threatened them, they let them go, *finding nothing how they could punish them, because the people glorified God for what had been done. For, that man was above forty years old, on whom that miracle had been performed* (Acts 4:19-22)."

The apostles *KNEW* that incident would open the door to even more harassment, so when Peter and John reported to those waiting believers their experience with the Sanhedrin, they *ALL* prayed: *"'And now Lord, behold their threatenings; and grant to Your servants, that with ALL boldness they may speak Your Word, by You STRETCHING FORTH YOUR HAND TO HEAL; and that signs and wonders be done by the name of Your Holy Child, Jesus.' And, when they had prayed that, the place where they had assembled together was SHAKEN, and they were ALL filled with the Holy Ghost, and spoke the Word of God with boldness* [the very miracle they had asked God for] (Acts 4:29-31)." Just as it took supernatural power to resist political and/or religious correctness in those days, so it does today! *Healing-miracles will settle that issue in the eyes of common folks; even if they impress not that religious bunch.* But, that is the problem of the religious bunch.

*God honored His faithful ministers, who would NOT BOW DOWN TO religious correctness, by continuing to enable them to perform miracles*—Which revealed that the crucified Savior had *NOT* remained in the grave, but now actually lived in His followers. Jesus had duplicated Himself and His ministry:
"By the hands of the apostles [*Later, others who were not apostles would perform miracles as well.*], *MANY SIGNS AND WONDERS* were wrought among the people; (who were with one accord in Solomon's porch. *But, of the rest of the people, no man dared join himself to them.* But the people magnified [honored] them. [*The modern church has LITTLE honor.*] And believers were the more added to the Lord—multitudes both of men, and women.), insomuch that they brought forth the sick into the streets, and laid them upon beds and couches, so that, at least, *THE SHADOW OF PETER passing by would overshadow some of them*. There came also a multitude out of those surrounding cities to Jerusalem, bringing their sick folks, and those who were *VEXED WITH UNCLEAN SPIRITS*. And they were healed *EVERY ONE* (Acts 5:12-16)." AMEN!

But of course, just as those believers had suspected, the persecution continued. And possibly all of the apostles were brought before the Jewish council this time. The high priest said: *"Did not we sternly command you that you should NOT TEACH in this* [Jesus'] *name? But you have filled Jerusalem with your doctrine, and intend to bring that man's blood on us* (Acts 5:28)." But they had said: *"Let His blood be on us!"*

To that "Peter and the other apostles answered and said: *'We ought to obey God rather than men* (Acts 5:29).'" But did that deter religious correctness? No! For even after Gamaliel warned them against trying to stop those men from obeying God, *they continued in their religious unbelief, and stupidity; BEATING UP those apostles anyway.* (The devil's pawns!)

"And to Gamaliel they agreed [Oh really?]. *But when they had called the apostles and BEATEN them*, they commanded again that they should not speak in the name of Jesus, and [reluctantly] let them go. And [those apostles] departed from the presence of that [angry] council, *rejoicing that they were counted worthy to suffer shame for Jesus' name.* And, in the temple daily, and also in every house [*house-churches*], *they ceased not to teach and preach Jesus Christ* (Acts 5:40-42)."

Remember, *other ministers also* (such as deacons) *began to work miracles among the people.* "Stephen [a deacon], *full of faith and power* [by the anointing of the Holy Spirit], *DID GREAT WONDERS AND MIRACLES* among the people. Then, there arose some of the synagogue known as the *Libertines*, and others the *Cyrenians*, and others the *Alexandrians*, and those also of Cilicia, and Asia, disputing with Stephen. But, they were unable to resist the wisdom, and Spirit, by which he spoke [See Luke 21:15.]. Then, they suborned [stealthily introduced by collusion] men who said: 'We have heard him speak blasphemous words against Moses, and against God.' Thus they stirred up the people, the elders, and the scribes; and they came upon Stephen, and caught him, and brought him to the council, and *set up FALSE WITNESSES* who said: 'This man ceases not to speak blasphemous words against this holy place, and against the law. For we have heard him say that this Jesus of Nazareth will destroy this holy place, and change the customs which Moses delivered us.' And all who sat in that council, looking steadfastly on him, saw his face as it had been the face of an angel (Acts 6:8-15)." Jesus was showing His approval of Stephen by that manifestation.

Those men did listen to Stephen's defense, up to a point: *The point where he rebuked their proud religious correctness by saying:* "'*You stiff-necked and uncircumcised in heart and ears, you always resist the Holy Ghost. Just as your fathers did, so do you! Which of the prophets have NOT your fathers persecuted?* And, they have slain those who revealed before of the coming of the Just One: *Of Whom you have now been the betrayers, and murderers*: Who have received the law by the ministry of angels; AND HAVE NOT KEPT IT.' When they heard those things, they were cut to the heart, and gnashed on him with their teeth. *But, Stephen, full of the Holy Ghost, looked up steadfastly into heaven, and saw the glory of God, and Jesus STANDING on the right hand of God.* Then said: 'I see the heavens opened, and the Son of man *STANDING* on the right hand of God.' *Then they cried out with a loud voice, then stopped their ears, then ran upon him with one accord, then cast him out of their city, and then stoned him.* And the witnesses *LAID* their [outer] garments at the feet of a young man named Saul. And they stoned Stephen, calling on God, saying: 'Lord Jesus, receive my spirit.' Then, *he knelt down, and cried out with a loud voice*: 'Lord, lay not this sin to their charge.' And, when Stephen had said that, he fell asleep [he died] (Acts 7:51-60)." *From that incident, a great persecution broke out against the church, spearheaded by young Saul of Tarsus. The Lord remedied that problem by confronting Saul on the Damascus Road.* Yet, the Jewish *religious-correctness madness* would not go away. The Book of Acts continues:

"Peter said to [Cornelius, family, and friends]: 'You know how that it is an *UNLAWFUL* [*religiously-INcorrect*] action for a Jew to keep company with, or even contact one of another nation [a Gentile]. *But God has shown me that I should NOT call any man common or unclean* (Acts 10:28).'" However,...

Whereas Peter seemed to have learned that lesson, some of his *Jewish Christian brothers* were still in darkness about the fact that God is not a respecter of persons (Acts 10:34).

"When Peter arrived in Jerusalem, those who were of the *circumcision party* contended with him, saying: 'You went in to [went under the roof of] men uncircumcised, and ate with them.' But, Peter rehearsed the whole matter (Acts 11:2-4)." *And some of them reluctantly adjusted their religious beliefs.*

Later, the converted Saul (now Paul) confronted religious correctness in Antioch. *After a successful ministry campaign on one Sabbath day,* "The next Sabbath day came almost the WHOLE city together to hear the Word of God. But, *when the* [unconverted] *Jews saw the multitudes, they were filled with envy, and spoke AGAINST those things that were spoken by Paul; contradicting, and* [even] *blaspheming.* Then, Paul and Barnabas became bold, and said: 'It was necessary that this Word of God first be spoken to you [Jews]. But, *because you have put God's Word* [away] *from you, and judge yourselves unworthy of everlasting life* [by rejecting the Gospel], *we will turn to the Gentiles* (Acts 13:44-46).'" (To reject the Gospel is to judge oneself unworthy of eternal life!) *Those unconverted Jews were envious of Paul and Barnabas because of the big crowds attracted by their Gospel Ministry. LIFELESS religion had never appealed to the multitudes.* Nevertheless,...

"*The Jews stirred up the devout and honorable* [?] *women and the chief men of the city, and raised persecution against Paul and Barnabas, and expelled them from their region.* But Paul and Barnabas shook the dust [of unbelief] off their feet against those Antioch Jews, came to Iconium [and preached there] (Acts 13:50-51)." A major lesson in this passage:

*The religiously correct crowd being fragile, they are easily provoked to ENVY. And envy ALWAYS lashes out at anything unveiling its hypocrisy—proving—THERE IS NO HONESTY IN RELIGIOUS CORRECTNESS! It is a mere demonic deception.*

"[In Iconium Paul and Barnabas] were speaking boldly in the Lord, Who gave testimony to the Word of His Grace, and granted signs and wonders to be done by *THEIR* hands. *But the multitude of the city was divided. Part of them sided with the Jews and part with the apostles.* And when there was an assault made by both the Gentiles, and the Jews, with their rulers [Thus, *political correctness* was involved in this case.], to use [Paul and Barnabas] despitefully, and to stone them, they became aware of it and [left in a hurry] (Acts 14:3-5)."

*Paul and Barnabas FLED to the city of Lystra, where they first preached the Gospel to some heathen idol-worshippers.* One of them even got healed as a result of Paul's preaching. The Gentiles were about to worship Paul as a god, but Paul said: "Sirs, why do you do these things? We are human just like you, *and preach to you that you should turn from these vanities to the Living God*; Who made heaven, earth and sea, and all things therein (Acts 14:15)." So no sacrifice. *Whew!*

As long as the devil runs loose, religious correctness will continue to be a problem. *"And certain men who came down from Judaea taught those* [Gentile believers]: *'Except you be circumcised after the manner of Moses you cannot be saved.'* Paul and Barnabas had *no small dissension and disputation with them,* so they determined that Paul and Barnabas, and certain others, should go up to Jerusalem unto the apostles and elders about the dispute (Acts 15:1-2)." *Even if the devil is unsuccessful in dismantling a church congregation, he will use religious correctness to DISTRACT THE CHURCH from its God-given commission—consuming its time and resources.*

Those *religiously-correct Jews* in the city of Thessalonica made this unsavory comment regarding Paul and company: "These who have *turned the world upside down* have arrived here also (Acts 17:6)." *That reveals how religious correctness thinks!* Paul was ministering the Gospel to a world that was already upside down. Gospel Truth turns the world of those who receive it right side up! *Gospel-rejectors* continue to live in their little upside-down-world (and then gripe about it).

But not everyone in this upside-down-world is as foolish as those in Thessalonica, who had been blinded by religious tradition. Paul next preached to the Jews living in Berea:

*"These Jews were more noble than those in Thessalonica, in that they RECEIVED the Word of God with all readiness of mind, and searched the Scriptures daily, to find out whether those things* [Paul had preached] *were true. Therefore, many of them believed; also of honorable women who were Greeks, and of men, not a few* (Acts 17:11-12)." A MOST enlightening Scripture passage! Respectfully listening to and receiving the Gospel message is both a NOBLE attitude and a NOBLE act. Therefore, a snobbish attitude toward the Gospel is *ignoble.*

Paul preached to the Jews in Ephesus, and encountered this response: *"When some were hardened and believed not, but spoke evil of THAT* [Christian] *WAY before the multitude,* Paul departed from them, and *separated the disciples* [Jews who believed], *disputing* [teaching] *daily in the school of one Tyrannus. And that continued by the space of two years; so that all who dwelt in Asia heard the Word of the Lord Jesus; both Jews and Greeks* (Acts 19:9-10)." (Stealing sheep?)

Some modern preachers would accuse Paul of doing just that; *for many today fear that some slick preacher will come in and STEAL some members of their congregation.* Paul was separating the believing Jews (Christians) from unbelief; not stealing sheep. He was making them Christ's sheep! Before, they were just religious people. *BIG difference!*

The Ephesian elders met Paul at Miletus, where he gave a prophecy *warning the Ephesian elders*: "I know that after I leave here, GRIEVOUS WOLVES will enter in among you, not sparing the flock. AND, EVEN OF YOUR OWN SELVES WILL MEN ARISE, *speaking perverse things to draw disciples after them* (Acts 20:29-30)." Now, that is sheep-stealing! Stealing sheep *FROM JESUS*. And that is still going on today!

Paul himself (*the former Saul of Tarsus*) admitted that *he had ONCE been AN EXTREME EXAMPLE of the CRUELTY of religious correctness*; confessing: "*I truly thought with myself that I OUGHT TO DO many things CONTRARY to the name of Jesus of Nazareth—Which I did in Jerusalem. FOR MANY OF THOSE SAINTS* [New Testament believers] *DID I IMPRISON*; having received authority from the Jewish chief priests. *And when they were put to death, MY VOICE was against them. I punished them often, in every synagogue; compelling them to blaspheme.* Therefore, *being exceedingly ENRAGED against them, I also persecuted them in foreign cities* (Acts 26:9-11)." Jesus had said in John 16:2 that: "*The time will come when those who kill you will think that they do God service.*" Jesus must have had Saul of Tarsus in mind when He said that.

In Galatians 1:13-14, Paul added: "*You have heard of my conversation* [lifestyle] *in time past in the Jews' religion, how that BEYOND MEASURE I persecuted the church of God, and WASTED IT. And I profited in the Jewish religion above many of my equals in my nation, being more exceedingly zealous of the TRADITIONS of my fathers.*" Saul thought he was serving God! Oh, the spiritual blindness of the religiously-correct!

While under house arrest in Rome, Paul preached Christ and God's Kingdom from the law and prophets to those who visited him. *Some believed, and some did not. The Jews who did not believe departed in a huff, after Paul SCOLDED them with a prophecy from Isaiah* (Isaiah 6:9-10—Acts 28:23-25).

Early on, the devil planted seeds of *denominationalism* in the Corinthian church. *That congregation was dividing itself into competing groups: Paulites, Cephasites, Apollosites, and Christites. Denominationalism is a deceptive and dangerous form of religious correctness!* Paul had to put a *STOP* to that: "I beseech you, my brethren, by the name of our Lord Jesus Christ, that you all speak the same thing, and that there be *NO DIVISIONS* among you; *BUT*, that you be perfectly joined together in the same mind and in the same judgment. For it has been declared to me of you, my brethren, by those who are of the house of Chloe, that there are contentions among you. Now this I say, that each one of you says: 'I am of Paul; and I of Apollos; and I of Cephas; and I of Christ.' *Is Christ divided? Was Paul crucified for you? Or were you baptized in the name of Paul* (1 Corinthians 1:10-13)?" Paul taught that *denominationalism appears to divide Christ in the eyes of the world*. Although Jesus Christ Himself, Who is seated at the right hand of God, cannot actually be damaged in any way, His Body on earth, the church, by strife and division, surely can and will be damaged. Paul warned in Galatians 5:15: "If you bite and devour one another, take heed that you be not consumed one of another." *Self-inflicted damage from within the church invites DISDAIN FOR THE CHURCH by outsiders.* It also reveals that those church members need to grow up.

"I, brethren, could not speak unto you as unto spiritual, but as unto carnal, even as unto babes in Christ. I have fed you with milk, and not with meat. For hitherto you were not able to bear [meat]. Neither yet now are you able [to eat the meat of God's Word]. For you are yet carnal [immature]. For whereas there is among you [Christians] envying, and strife, and divisions, are you not carnal, and walk as [mere] men? For while one says: 'I am of Paul'; and another says: 'I am of Apollos'; are you not being carnal (1 Corinthians 3:1-4)?"

Immature believers have the greater tendency to live like the world—very loosely. *And so it happened at Corinth*: "*It is reported commonly that there is fornication among you, and such fornication as is not so much as named among Gentiles*; that one has his father's wife. And, you are *PUFFED UP*, and have not mourned; *that he who has done this deed might be taken away from among you* (1 Corinthians 5:1-2)." So,...

Paul instructed them: *"Deliver such a one unto Satan, for the destruction of the flesh* [If he desires to play around with the devil, then let him have a belly full of the devil.], *that his spirit may be saved in the day of the Lord Jesus.* [If you will severely discipline him, maybe he will repent and be saved.] Your glorying is not good. [They were actually glorying over that gross violation of God's law, rather than mourning over it—verse 2.] *Do you not know that a little leaven leavens the entire lump* (1 Corinthians 5:5-6)?" (So, the church is called A *LUMP!* My little bit of humor.) Quite obviously, the church possesses some kind of protection *for even its members who are committing sin.* Otherwise, why would they need to *turn that man over to Satan* for the destruction of his flesh? Was he not already under Satan's influence? (Unity protects!)

Paul continued: "*I wrote unto you in an epistle* [before his 1 Corinthians letter?] *NOT to keep company with fornicators. Yet I did not mean fornicators of this world, or the covetous, or extortioners, or idolaters. For then, you would need to go out of this world. But now, I have written to you not to keep company, if any man who is called a brother be a fornicator, or covetous, or an idolater, or an abuser, or an extortioner, or a drunkard; with such not even to eat. For, what have I to do to judge those who are outside the church? Do you not judge those who are in the church? But, those who are outside the church God judges. So put away from among yourselves that wicked person* (1 Corinthians 5:9-13)." (Church today heed!)

More on *the subtlety of religious correctness*: "*I Paul fear, lest by any means, just as the serpent beguiled Eve through his subtlety, so your* [pure] *minds should be corrupted from the simplicity that is in Christ. For, if someone comes to you preaching another Jesus, whom we have not preached, or, if you receive another spirit, which you have not received, or, if you accept another gospel, which you had not accepted, you tend to bear with such error* (2 Corinthians 11:3-4)." But,...

"*Such are false apostles, deceitful workers, transforming themselves into the very apostles of Christ. And, no marvel; for Satan transforms himself into an angel of light. Therefore, it is no great thing if his ministers also be TRANSFORMED as ministers of righteousness; whose final fate will be according to their* [evil] *works* (2 Corinthians 11:13-15)." *Hell bound!*

False ministers will come in and persuade believers that their doctrines are *the correct interpretation of Scripture*, and then use *religious-correctness pressure* to keep them in line. Paul was scolding those believers in Corinth for being prone to fall for just such *demonic deception*. Indeed, *it seems that such weakness in today's church in general is common. And no big surprise, for not only was that going on in Corinth, but in those Galatian churches as well*: "I marvel that you are so soon removed from Him [God] Who called you into the grace of Jesus Christ unto *another gospel—Which IS NOT another. But there are some who trouble you and would PERVERT the Gospel of Christ. But, if we, or EVEN an angel from heaven, preach ANY OTHER gospel to you than that Gospel we have preached to you, let him be accursed*. As I said already, so I now say again: '*If any man preach any OTHER gospel to you than what you have received, let him be accursed.*' For, do I now persuade men, or God? *Or do I seek to please men?* For *if I yet pleased men, I would not be a servant of Jesus Christ* (Galatians 1:6-10)." While we must respect other God-called ministers, *we bow only to Jesus Christ; not other preachers*. Let us follow Paul's example in Galatians 2:6: "But, of those who *SEEMED TO BE* somewhat [Peter and John], (*whatever they were, that made no matter to me: God accepts no man's person:*) *Those who SEEMED TO BE somewhat in conference added nothing to me*." Christ, *no one else*, assures us of our calling. WE GET OUR AUTHORITY AND MARCHING ORDERS FROM HIM; *not from denominations or financial donors*.

"When Peter had come to Antioch, I [Paul] withstood him to his face, because he was to be blamed. For, *before certain* [staunch Jewish believers] *came from James* [in Jerusalem], *Peter did eat with the Gentiles*. But when they had come, he withdrew, and separated himself, *fearing those who were of the circumcision* [party]. And, *all the other Jews* [in Antioch] *dissembled likewise with him*; insomuch that Barnabas also was carried away with their dissimulation. But, when I saw that *they walked NOT uprightly, according to the Truth of the Gospel, I* [Paul] *said unto Peter before them all* [in public]: '*If you, being a Jew, lived after the manner of the Gentiles, and not as the Jews, why do you now compel the Gentiles to live as Jews* (Galatians 2:11-14)?'" Religious hypocrisy exposed!

*How does religious correctness get the upper hand in any church?* "Are you so foolish? Having begun [as believers] in the Spirit [by Holy Spirit power], are you *NOW* made perfect by the flesh (Galatians 3:3)?" *It required Holy Spirit power to get you into Christ, but now you think you can maintain your Christianity by your decaying, fleshly energy?* Some English versions render the word for *foolish* as STUPID. About right!

*The fact that Paul had to do so much fussing on believers proves the widespread existence of religious correctness, and its tendency to destroy all who become enslaved by it.* And if such was happening in Paul's day, *it is happening today!!!*
"Stand fast in the liberty, wherewith Christ has made us free, and *be not entangled AGAIN with the YOKE of bondage.* Behold, I Paul say unto you that if you become circumcised, *Christ will profit you nothing* [meaning they would lose their salvation]. *I say again to every man who is circumcised, that he is debtor to do the whole law. Christ has BECOME OF NO EFFECT TO YOU, whoever of you is justified by the law. You have fallen from grace.* For we, through the Holy Spirit, wait for the hope of righteousness by faith. For in Christ, neither circumcision avails any thing, nor uncircumcision, but faith that works by love. *You did run well! Who hindered you, that you should NOT obey the truth?* Such persuasion comes not of Him [God] Who calls you. *A little leaven leavens the whole lump.* I have confidence in you, through our Lord, that you will be none otherwise minded. *But he who troubles you will bear his judgment, whoever he be* (Galatians 5:1-10)." Since Grace by faith is HOW we receive salvation, then falling from grace must mean losing our salvation. How can one fall from a place that one has never been? FALLING from grace, then, has to mean falling from salvation! Think it cannot happen?
"Beware, lest any man spoil [rob] you *through philosophy and vain deceit; after* [either worldly or religious] *tradition of men, after the RUDIMENTS of this world, and not after Christ* (Colossians 2:8)." *Religious correctness is a salvation robber!*

"The Spirit speaks expressly, that in the latter times some will depart from the faith, giving heed to seducing spirits and doctrines of demons; speaking lies in hypocrisy; having their conscience seared with a hot iron (1 Timothy 4:1-2)." *LOST!*

That is a *scorching rebuke* of religious correctness. For it shows this great danger of it: *Having their conscience seared with a hot iron—serious repercussion of religious correctness!* Why would any Christian risk falling into that religious pit? *Departing FROM the faith has to mean losing one's salvation!*

That is why Paul urged Timothy (and all other preachers to): "Preach God's Word. Be ready, in season, out of season; reprove, rebuke, exhort with all long-suffering and doctrine. *For the time is coming when* [believers] *will no longer endure* [tolerate] *sound doctrine; but after their own LUSTS will they HEAP to themselves teachers, having itching ears. Thus they will turn away their ears from the truth, and will be turned to fables* (2 Timothy 4:2-4)." Turn from truth—Lose salvation!

Forming *cliques* in church congregations is still another deceptive guise of religious correctness. I was informed that in some congregations, *new church members are considered INFERIOR to members whose families are either the founders of that church, or at least have been members for a long time.* Many church members have no heavenly or earthly concept of what Christianity is all about! James dealt with a similar problem in James 2:2-9: "If there come unto your assembly [church meeting] a man with a gold ring, in goodly apparel; and there come in also a poor man, in vile raiment; and you have respect to him who wears the nice clothing, and say to him: 'Sit here in a good place.' But you say to the poor man: 'Stand over there, or sit down here under my footstool.' *Are you not*, then, *partial in yourselves, and have become judges with evil thoughts?* Harken to me, beloved brethren: Has not God chosen the poor of this world [to be] rich [by] faith, and heirs of the Kingdom, which He has promised to people who love Him? But you have despised the poor. Do not rich men oppress you, and take you to court? Do not they blaspheme that *Worthy Name*; by the which you are called? *If you fulfill the royal law, according to the Scripture*: 'Love your neighbor as yourself,' you do well. *But, if you have respect to persons, you commit sin; and by the law are proven transgressors.*"

James continued exposing *the satanic nature of religious correctness* by warning: "*If you have bitter envying and strife in your hearts, glory not, and LIE NOT against the truth. This* wisdom descends *NOT* from above; *BUT,* is *earthly, sensual, devilish. Wherever envying and strife are* [invited in], *there is CONFUSION AND EVERY EVIL WORK* (James 3:14-16)." the devil is obviously heavily involved in religious correctness!

*Peter further reveals the depths of depravity believers will be pulled down to when they begin to follow that evil path of religious correctness. This passage refers to people who used to be genuine Christians, but have since fallen from the faith.* "When they speak great swelling words of vanity, *they allure through the lusts of the flesh* [having become the devil's tools to entrap Christians], *through much wantonness, those who are CLEAN ESCAPED from those who live in error. Promising them liberty,* [those allurers themselves] *are virtual servants of corruption. For of whom a man is overcome, of the same is he brought into bondage.* [Sinners are already in bondage to Satan.] For, *IF AFTER THEY HAVE ESCAPED the pollution of this* [unsaved] *world through the knowledge of our Lord and Savior, Jesus Christ, they are AGAIN ENTANGLED THEREIN, and overcome, the LATTER END is worse with them than the beginning. It had been better for them not to have known the way of righteousness* [known it, not merely known about it], *than, after they have known* [experienced] *it, to turn from the holy commandment delivered to them* (2 Peter 2:18-21)."

*Religious correctness is actually an EVIL spirit*: "Beloved, believe *NOT* every spirit, but try the spirits whether they are of God. Because many false prophets have gone out into the world. Hereby you *KNOW* the Spirit of God: *Every spirit that confesses Jesus Christ has come in the flesh is of God. But, every spirit that confesses not that Jesus Christ has come in the flesh is not of God. This is the spirit of the Antichrist, who you have heard should come; and even now is already in the world.* [People under Satan's influence will not confess that Jesus came in the flesh.] You are of God, little children, and have overcome [Satan's bunch]; because greater is He Who is in you than he who is in the world. They are of the world. Therefore, speak they of the world. And so, the world hears them. We are of God. He who knows God, hears us. He who is not of God, hears not us. *BY THIS WE KNOW* the Spirit of Truth, and the spirit of error (1 John 4:1-6)." *SIMPLE!*

Jude contributed some vital information on that subject: "*These* [feasters with the believers at their feasts—Jude 12] *are murmurers, and complainers,* [people] *walking after their own lusts. Their mouth speaks great swelling words, having men's persons in admiration for* [their own] *advantage. But, beloved, remember the words that were spoken before by the apostles of our Lord Jesus Christ.* They told you there would be mockers in the last time, who would walk after their own ungodly lusts. These are people who *SEPARATE* themselves, sensual, *NOT HAVING* the Spirit (Jude 16-19)." Verse twelve says they are twice dead—in the original Greek, *having died twice*; pulled up by the roots. If they had not been in Christ, then *how could they have been pulled up by the roots? What roots? They were still physically alive, so their DYING TWICE had to refer to their spirits.* Sinners are already dead in sins and trespasses, so *dying twice* must mean they had become Christians, then fell away—*becoming lost and dying again.*

*Churches GUILTY of religious correctness*: "I [Jesus] have a few things against you, *because you have there those who hold the doctrine of Balaam, who taught King Balac to cast a stumblingblock before the children of Israel, by eating things sacrificed unto idols, and to commit fornication.* And you also have those who hold that Nicolaitan doctrine; which thing I hate. Repent; or else, I [Jesus] will come to you quickly, and *FIGHT against them with the sword of My mouth* (Revelation 2:14-16)." Once any doctrine (*even a false doctrine*) becomes established in a church, *it becomes a powerful force to force the entire congregation to conform to that doctrine.* And what do the leaders use to enforce such conformity? You guessed it—Religious pressure! *Religious correctness is a dominator!*

*Another sad church example*: "I [Jesus] have a few things against you [Christians in Thyatira], because you allow that woman Jezebel, *who calls herself a prophetess*, to teach and seduce my servants to commit fornication, and to eat things sacrificed unto idols. And I [Jesus] gave her space to repent of her fornication; and she repented not. Behold, *I will cast her into a bed, and those who commit adultery with her into great tribulation; except they repent of their deeds. And I will kill her children with death*; and *ALL* the churches will know that I am He, Who searches the reins, and hearts: And I will give to every one of you *according to your works*. But, to you I say, and to the rest in Thyatira, as many as have *NOT* this doctrine, and who have *NOT* known the depths of Satan, as they say: 'I will put on you *NO* other burden. But that which you have already, hold fast till I come (Revelation 2:20-25).'"

*Worst church condition in the book of Revelation*: "I know your works, that you are neither cold, nor hot. I would that you were cold, or hot. So, then, because you are lukewarm, and neither cold, nor hot, I will vomit you out of My mouth: Because you say, 'I am rich, and increased with goods, and have need of nothing'; and know not that you are wretched, and miserable, and poor, and blind, and naked. Therefore, I counsel you to buy of Me gold tried in the fire, that you may be rich; and white raiment that you may be clothed, so that the shame of your [*spiritual*] nakedness will not appear; and anoint your eyes with [*spiritual*] eye-salve that you may see. As many as I [Jesus] love, I rebuke and chasten. Be zealous therefore, and repent (Revelation 3:15-19)." *A Jesus-rebuke!*

The *mindset* of the leaders in that church having become unscriptural, it also became established in the congregation as the *religiously-correct position* of that church. *But, Jesus rejected their religiously-correct nonsense, and rebuked them sharply.* He would do the same to many churches today!

*Being religiously correct simply means being conformed to the accepted, and established, standards of doctrine and/or practices of a local church or denomination.* Non-conformists may be shamed, shunned, ousted or even persecuted by the church, or denominational, leaders; in order to pressure the non-conformists to conform to the accepted standards. But, *before conforming*, compare their doctrines and/or practices with the Bible standard. Religious correctness has *NO* life in it, for it is the product of man, and man is not the source of life. *God is the Source of life—Who ministers that life through His Word. CONFORM TO GOD'S WORD. Go for divine LIFE!*

(I know Satan does not look like the cover drawings. But, presenting him in that format does get the message across. Everybody ought to know those figures represent the devil.)

# Chapter Six

## The blame-game

The previous chapter was a long one—big subject—while this one is somewhat shorter—but just as enlightening. *One badge of the modern age is the blame game. Another is lying. Both are definitely satanically connected. To blame someone else for something you yourself are guilty of is self-deception. The world is greatly guilty of that stupid sin—and so is God's church—At least many who CLAIM TO BE God's church.* This issue, just as all others, is best understood by honest study of God's Word. *The Bible addresses every societal problem.*

*The blame game is part of BOTH political correctness and religious correctness. The devil spawned all three.* But let me start with the *political-correctness blame-game problem.* As I begin this very chapter, *the blame game is going full blast in Washington D.C. Although it has been heating up for several years now, it seems to be reaching a dangerous temperature. One political party blames the other party for everything that is going wrong, while the same party claims credit for all that seems to be going right.* And although both parties are guilty of some lying, *just a casual observance of actual facts shows which party is lying the most. Many politicians will LIE about something that YOU KNOW IS THE OPPOSITE of documented facts on the issue; that politician knowing that you know, yet he or she holds to those lies anyway. To the one who WANTS their lies to be so, they ARE so in their MIND. Self-deception!*

Thus, *deception, and especially self-deception, is another badge of modern society. And most people seem to think they are going to get away with their dishonest lifestyle!* Scripture actually prophesies: *"Evil men will become worse and worse, deceiving, and BEING deceived* (2 Timothy 3:13)." Therefore, as sickening as that situation is, *it does not come as a shock to those who are familiar with prophecies of end-time events.* I have repeatedly stated: *"As bad as it is now, we have seen nothing yet!"* Read the book of Revelation. Christ prophesied that: *The painful problems that will begin to occur in the near future will be only "the beginning of sorrows* (Mark 13:8)."

And looking back to the past, we find that *the Bible itself provides a lot of essential information about the blame game.* In fact, the book of Genesis tells us how the blame game got started. Genesis 3:12 *tells about the very first instance of the practice of laying the blame for one's own evil actions at the feet of another.* When Deity visited the Garden of Eden, after Adam and Eve sinned, by their eating of the forbidden fruit, and questioned Adam about why he was naked, Adam said: "The *WOMAN* You gave me gave me some of the fruit of that tree, and I ate it." Thus, it was the woman's fault! But more than that, Adam implied that at least indirectly it was God's fault; for He had given Adam the woman who had given him the fruit. Thus, in *MAN'S* eyes, sin is complicated. However, *the Almighty sees things as they really are—Simple. And He is the Judge!* He judges our actions as He sees them, not as we may see them. And the blame-game continuing,...

When the Creator came to Eve and questioned her about her actions, she claimed in effect: *"The devil made me do it."* And when God accosted the serpent, he had nobody to turn to, in order to blame. I relate that to a Three Stooges skit, in which the three stood side by side and saluted a high officer in front of them. When Moe saluted that man, his elbow hit Larry right on his chin. Larry then saluted the man, and his elbow hit Curley on his chin. But, when Curley saluted that officer, there was nobody beside him to take the blow to the chin. Of course, Curley kept saluting, but there was nobody he could *HIT* on the chin. He was very disturbed about that. I remember that episode when I read Genesis chapter three. Who can Satan blame? *No one beside him with a chin to hit!*

God is not mocked (Galatians 6:7), so He began with the serpent in *doling out judgments*; in the which He prophesied of the Christ-event, *through which the devil's enslavement of mankind would be broken; although Jesus had to be bruised in the process.* (See Genesis 3:15, Isaiah 52:14-53:12, John 3:14, 16:11, Hebrews 2:14, Revelation 1:5, etc., etc., etc.)

Then God turned to Eve and pronounced upon her what history has proven to have happened just like God said that it would—*Pain in childbirth and a subservient position below the male in most societies.* Just about every nation has been guilty of oppressing women throughout history. Some more than others. *Eve did not have such in mind when she ate the fruit of that forbidden tree! She had envisioned improvement* (Genesis 3:6), but what she got was Genesis 3:16.

I need right here to point out a prime principle of biblical truth. *The Creator had okayed the partaking of every tree in the Garden except one.* That was actually a pretty good deal. *Yet, the serpent insinuated that God was cheating Adam and Eve out of some good stuff by putting that ONE tree off-limit.* In other words, if they would heed the serpent's words, they would be better off, *for they could then partake of every tree.* As it turned out, *Adam and Eve were not only NOT improved by eating that forbidden fruit; they lost access to all the other trees as well.* The devil is out to steal, kill and destroy (John 10:10), *so heeding his words is the sure path to destruction. The devil being a liar* (John 8:44), *his advice never leads to a better lifestyle.* Only God's Truth blesses (John 8:31-32).

Then God turned to Adam. Another important scriptural principle: *The devil being behind what many people say, our listening to them is the same as listening to Satan.* Preachers included! God said: "*Because you heeded your WIFE'S voice, and ate that FORBIDDEN FRUIT, the very ground is CURSED for your sake!*" Thus, *one does not have to be approached by the devil personally, in order to be guilty of heeding his voice.* Peter was one more *Bible example* of that *Bible Truth.* When the Lord prophesied that He was about to be betrayed, and crucified, Peter rebuked Him for saying such negative things. But, Christ then rebuked Peter, revealing that the devil had instigated Peter's rebuke of Jesus (Mark 8:33).

*Many people in this country (USA) are either very naive or deliberately politically biased. They seem to think that if you hear it on a national news network it has to be on the up and up—accurate and honest* (ha, ha, ha, ha). However, *a casual observation of the different news networks reveals that there are MANY MAJOR DISCREPANCIES between reports that are reported by different networks.* They cannot all be telling the truth. Thus, someone is lying. Moreover, if it is published in a book it must be true (ha, ha once again). *When will people open their eyes to what is really going on in the world today?* Remember, THIS *book is about Satan's hiding-places. One of his favorites is the news media.* He uses what people trust!

Church members seem to be infected with the very same *muddled-mindset* about published materials. If a theologian of a particular denominational persuasion publishes a book on *ANY* Bible subject, *the members of that denomination will accept it as absolute truth, and will push its dogmas; even in the face of INDISPUTABLE BIBLE EVIDENCE to the contrary. A theologian of a competing denomination might not gain the same level of loyalty from those same people to his published works;* yet, some will believe over the Bible certain erroneous theories contained in his books! But, consider Jeremiah 8:8: "The pen of the scribes is vain." The message of this passage is: *Even written material is not necessarily true.* Lies inhabit written words as well as spoken words. *Lies fill newspapers, TV, and the internet—Flooding us with falsehoods!* (The devil hides in the media.) Jeremiah 9:6 says: "They are living in a world of deception." *Sounds just like our world today!*

"Be not soon shaken in mind; or be troubled; neither by spirit, or word, or *LETTER*, as from us, as though the day of Christ had come (2 Thessalonians 2:2)." *They had obviously received a letter, claiming to be from Paul, teaching them the very opposite of what he had taught them when he was with them*—A New Testament example of *written falsehoods.*

*The blame-game-syndrome becoming part of fallen-man's nature, that flaw has been passed on from one generation to the next throughout history. And the curse getting worse, it is more prominent today than ever before.* (Be not deceived!)

One more deceptive slant of the blame game is the claim that "everybody is doing it." So if I am wrong, everybody else is to blame. *No personal responsibility or accountability.* But, *God's Word teaches that every moral creature is responsible; and that God will hold all accountable* (Romans 1:20, 2:5)!

*Another slant on that blame game is the double standard.* That simply means that most human beings have one set of rules they judge themselves by, and different (stricter) rules for everyone else. The guilty party will say something like: *"I meant no harm by doing that. I was just kidding."* However, *if someone else is guilty of the same unkind action*; well, that is different. It matters not whether they meant harm or not. *They are guilty, so they deserve to be punished. Judgment to them, but mercy to me.* (Today's standard double-standard!)

Still one more lopsided practice of the blame game is the so-called apology. *We get that word from the Greek apologia. The early church fathers wrote Gospel apologies; which were DEFENSES of the Gospel. The Greek word apologia originally signified to argue in the support of, or justification of, words or actions. IT DID NOT MEAN TO REPENT OF ANY WORD OR ACT.* In modern English, an apology is yet a defense of one's words and/or actions, *but is presented in such a way that it almost sounds like the apologizer is repenting.* The next time you hear a person apologize to someone else, notice the way they say it. *Most modern apologies are yet defenses of words or actions.* Typical modern apology: *"IF I HAVE offended you in any way, I apologize."* Their words admit *NO* wrongdoing. *The offender might actually APPEAR to have made amends, but did NO actual repenting of any words or actions.* There is a major difference between an apology and true repentance! *In most cases apologies do not rectify any detrimental results brought about by offensive words or actions.* The apologizer might seem to come clean about some offense, but in reality is actually defending his or her words or actions. *It is their way of escaping responsibility. There is no admission of guilt in "IF I have..."* Therefore, it is obvious that Satan is behind most *MODERN APOLOGIES.* Furthermore, *most apologizers apologize ONLY AFTER they are publicly caught and publicly forced to face their error!* (True repentance is voluntary.)

The bottom line of the blame game is: This fallen world "walks by sight [the senses], not by faith." (*And much of the modern church does exactly the same.*) The deliberate design of that blame game is to distract people's attention from the facts of a situation *by the guilty party using carefully chosen words that paint a totally different picture of that situation.* Politicians use *politically-charged* terminology to deceptively achieve their political ambitions. *So do many preachers!!!!!*

*It began in the Garden of Eden, when the serpent painted in Eve's mind a picture of the forbidden tree that the Creator had not painted. God certainly did not portray the tree as the serpent did.* How did the devil get Eve to envision *imaginary blessings* resident in that forbidden fruit? *By lying to her!*

Man's five physical senses may easily be manipulated to cause people to *see what does not exist,* and to *not see what does exist*—the reason God's Word commands Christians to walk by faith, and *NOT* by sight (sight representing all of the five physical senses)! The devil having infiltrated every level of society, he controls most politicians, the dishonest news media, nearly all entertainment, and even *MANY* churches. That has been typical throughout history since the fall; and was prophesied to become worse toward the end-times.

I have mentioned some of what I call *BADGES* of modern society. *And the one BADGE that encompasses all the rest of them is SELFISHNESS.* Selfishness is at the very root of the blame-game, deception, apologies, the double standard, etc. And, of course, the primary purpose of blaming others is to plead that *IT IS NOT MY FAULT!* You cannot blame me! And be not deceived into thinking that the devil's strategies have not infiltrated the church *AS MUCH AS* they have the world. Actually, *selfishness in the church wears the most deceptive garb.* Our Savior warned about "wolves in sheep's clothing." One of Satan's most unnoticed hiding places—the church!

A final thought on that subject: *When everybody blames everybody else for everything, refusing to take any blame for anything, then there will never be any solution for anything, for no one will be willing to take responsibility for anything!*

# Chapter Seven

## Celebrity role models

*Not any and all celebrities; just the politically-liberal kind.* And not all are in Hollywood, California: Sports stars, movie stars, music stars, those ultra-liberal college and university professors, and the ultra-liberal-news-media propagandists. Those *supposed heroic role models* are scattered all over the nation, but *the liberal media propagandists are the glue that holds the negative influence together.* Satan controls most of the media in the USA, as well as other countries around the world; *so it is no surprise that his demonic agenda is spread far and wide through all the liberal media outlets*—TV, radio, movies, newspapers, magazines, billboards, books, internet, etc. *The majority of the world's population is not of the liberal kind.* The problem: So Much of the media has been hijacked by liberals, *they have the loudest voice, and the most outlets*; making it *seem as though* they are in the majority, when in reality, *they are boldface liars about that and everything else they attempt to push on the average citizen.* (Satan's pawns!)

Truth is, *many of those celebrated celebrities are some of the stupidest people who have ever walked the earth. That is actually putting it mildly.* They might have an amazing voice, tremendous athletic ability, a voluptuous figure, astounding ability to make money, captivating acting ability, a hypnotic power in manipulating people, etc., *but they have absolutely no common sense.* Many seem to have convinced themselves that because they are *professional* actors, athletes, financial experts, etc. that they are automatically experts in all of life; and, therefore, *ought to be the moral yardstick for everybody living on earth.* (Ha, ha, ha, ha! But, not really that funny!) *I have observed that since they have no moral moorings, when they come into all that fame, and financial plenty, they have no idea about how to handle fame and fortune—Or how to be VALID ROLE MODELS to those influenced by their popularity.* That is the reason so many destroy their very own lives with that new lifestyle and its privileges. They are easily deceived by the politically-correct crowd, *and become themselves just additional pushers of demonic political-correctness lies.*

Since money can buy anything on the market, *and some things that are not available on the legal market*, then those who have *no moral moorings*, but do have some excess cash, and friends (?) who entice them to live it up, are going to be tempted to avail themselves of those dangerous things. That is why many of them die early of drug overdoses and worse.

*Sex is a powerful force.* Deity created that powerful force. But, He also instructed the human race as to its *proper* use. Those without such godly instruction are sure targets of the devil. *Having lots of opportunities to yield to sex-temptations, but, having NO MORAL MOORINGS against sex-temptations, celebrities often fall headlong into those temptation traps and are destroyed—If not in this life, later on in the Lake of Fire.* Money power *DOES NOT ALTER* God's judgment power!

Perhaps the most tragic result of the *celebrity-debacle* is: *Gullible young people are so powerfully influenced by those celebrities that they FOOLISHLY look to them as role models*; rather than to people who are not so good looking, talented, rich, or fleshly-favored in some other way. *Satan appeals to the flesh,* and celebrities are almost always readily available to Satan to do his dirty work. And of course, *common people practically worshipping celebrities appeals to their pride; and serves to increase their pride.* A never-ending demonic cycle. *Those annual celebrity AWARD SHOWS amount to little more than one dishonorable person honoring another dishonorable person.* True honor comes *ONLY* from God (John 5:44)!

# Chapter Eight

## Bible Interpretation I

*Bible interpretation, a hiding-place of the devil?* Certainly! One of his favorites. Why should it be such a shock to learn that the devil is behind Bible interpretation? *The Bible itself FORBIDS Bible interpretation!* Thus, all attempts to interpret the Bible must be of the devil. Have you ever noticed 2 Peter 1:20-21? "Knowing this first [One vital key: Just how many people—especially preachers and theologians—know that at all? Let alone first?], that *NO* prophecy of the Scripture is of *ANY PRIVATE INTERPRETATION*. For the prophecy came not in old time [from the beginning] by the will of man. But holy men of God spoke, [then wrote it down,] as they were moved [upon] by the Holy Ghost." *Human Bible-book-authors spoke and wrote just what God instructed them to speak and write. They did not attempt to explain what they thought He meant.* Thus, no man today has any right, or authority, to interpret the Scriptures—*to either speak or write what they think God MEANT to say in His Word*—NO PRIVATE INTERPRETATION! *Private interpretation is one's OPINION of the Bible message. And Bible commentaries are filled with interpretations, which CONTRADICT one another, and EVEN THE BIBLE itself!*

*VALID* Bible doctrines must be built upon more than one Scripture passage. So says the Scripture itself! *In the mouth of two or three witnesses* (out of the Bible) *must every word be established* (Deuteronomy 17:6, 19:15, Matthew 18:16, 2

Corinthians 13:1, Hebrews 10:28, etc.). Furthermore, "If we receive the witness of *MEN*, the witness of *GOD* is greater (1 John 5:9)." And, verse 10: "*He who does not believe God has made Him a liar.*" That is, accuses Him of being a liar. Deity does not actually become a liar. The Bible itself tells us that God cannot lie. *CANNOT LIE! The God of Truth does not lie!*

Titus 1:2 says it: "In hope of eternal life, which God, *Who cannot lie*, promised before the world began." Hebrews 6:18 says this: "That, by two *IMMUTABLE* things, in which it was *IMPOSSIBLE for God to lie*, we [believers] might have strong consolation, who have fled for refuge, to lay hold of the hope set before us." "*I have NOT written to you because you know NOT the truth, but because you DO know it, and that NO LIE IS OF THE TRUTH* (1 John 2:21)." (Bible Truth, that is!)

So, from where do lies come? And who is behind all lies? *Which would have to include distorted interpretations of the Bible! Because, that is exactly what Bible interpretations are: Lies—Distortions of Bible Truth, which God communicated to mankind through His faithful prophets, who told it just like it really is, and NOT how they thought it OUGHT to be. Amen!*

John 8:44 answers it clearly: "*YOU are of your* [spiritual] *father, the devil, and the lusts of your father YOU will do. He was a murderer from the beginning*, and *ABODE NOT IN THE TRUTH*, because, *THERE IS NO TRUTH IN HIM.* When Satan speaks a lie, he speaks from his own [resources]. For he is a liar, and [thus] the [spiritual] father of [both lies and liars]."

How does the devil spread his lies? *Does his voice fill the air, so that when people walk through it they get soaked? He is called the prince of the authority of the air* (Ephesians 2:2). No! Romans 1:25 says that "*MEN CHANGED THE TRUTH OF GOD INTO A LIE.*" Satan uses people to broadcast his lies!

Do they outsmart God? No! "The *WISE* men [of the world AND religion] *are ashamed, dismayed and taken. They have REJECTED the Word of the LORD. So, what wisdom do they really have (Jeremiah 8:9)?*" Their *WISDOM* is based on their interpretation of the Bible. Thus, "'*Through deceit they refuse to know Me,' says the LORD (Jeremiah 9:6).*" "*They hold fast to deceit* (Jeremiah 8:5)." *MANY*, even in the church, deceive themselves, then hold tight-fisted to their self-deception.

*Religious leaders have been JUST as guilty as the world's leaders in disobeying God, and deceiving and hurting people.* Not all, but many. Worse; *some of history's religious leaders have been even MORE deceptive and cruel than many world leaders.* If that seems too much to believe, look at Jeremiah 12:10: *"MANY PASTORS HAVE DESTROYED MY VINEYARD. They have TRODDEN My portion* [My own people] *under foot; and made My pleasant portion A DESOLATE WILDERNESS." Pastors destroyed God's people! They mutilated God's people with their private-interpretation-mutilations of God's Word.*

Our Savior faced the same opposition while He was here. And so did Stephen and Paul. *Stephen rebuked the religious bunch* in Acts 7:51-53: "You stiff-necked and uncircumcised in heart and ears, you always resist the Holy Ghost: Just as your fathers *DID* so *DO* you. Which of the prophets have not your fathers persecuted? *Slaying men who prophesied of the coming of the Just One: Of Whom you have NOW become the betrayers and murderers—You who have received the law by the disposition of angels, AND HAVE NOT KEPT IT."* How did they *KEEP* from keeping God's law? *They interpreted it!* That is the *ONLY HUMAN* reason for interpreting Scripture. *They INTERPRET THE BIBLE SO THEY CAN DISOBEY THE BIBLE!* "The time has now come for judgment to begin at the house of God: [Why? For interpreting and disobeying God's Word!] And, if judgment begins with us Christians, what will be the end of those who obey not the Gospel? And, if the righteous scarcely be saved, where will the ungodly and sinner appear (1 Peter 4:17-18)?" *Bible interpretation is disobedience!*

Remember, by two or three witnesses every word is to be established. So, we have to find more passages than 2 Peter 1:20-21 that forbid Bible interpretation. And, here they are: "You must not add to the word which I [God through Moses] command you, neither diminish anything from it [My word], so that you may keep the commandments of the *LORD* your God which I [Moses] command you (Deuteronomy 4:2)." The warning could not be any plainer. *Adding to God's Word is a forbidden form of Bible interpretation. Deleting anything from it is another.* Proverbs 30:6 also forbids Bible interpretation: *"ADD NOT TO GOD'S WORD, lest He reprove you and you be found a liar."* Satan lies; men lie. God's Word does not lie!

Paul addressed the issue this way in Romans 3:3-4: "For *WHAT IF SOME DID NOT BELIEVE?* Will their unbelief make the faith of God without effect? God forbid! Let God be true, but *EVERY MAN A LIAR*. As it is written: 'That You might be justified in Your sayings, and might overcome when You are judged.'" Bible interpretation is a *SLY FORM* of judging God: *Suggesting God could not have meant what He actually said in plain words*; *BUT had to mean something totally different*: *THE DIFFERENT INTERPRETATION BEING A PRIVATE ONE. BIBLE INTERPRETATION IS FORBIDDEN IN BOTH OLD AND NEW TESTAMENTS!* Numerous passages bear that out.

Consider 1 John 5:9-10 one more time: "If we receive the witness of men, the witness of God is greater: For this is the witness of God that He has testified about His Son. He who believes on the Son of God has that witness *INSIDE* himself. [But] *He who believes not God has made Him a liar*; because he believes not the record [in the Bible] that God gave of His Son." *Bible interpretation denies part or all of the redemption Jesus Christ wrought for us on the cross*. A prime example of that undeniable truth is the *Cessationism doctrine*; *invented by John Calvin, and then handed down from one generation to the next for the last 500 years by gutless theologians*; *who by preaching Cessationism are guilty of destroying countless lives, both physically, and spiritually*. God will hold all those men *fully accountable*; as is *plainly prophesied* in Revelation 22:18-19: "I testify to every man who hears the words of the prophecy of this book [Revelation]: 'If *ANY MAN* adds to the things [written in it], *God will add to him all the plagues that are written in it*. And if *ANY MAN* takes away from the words of the book of this prophecy, *God WILL TAKE AWAY his part from the Book of Life, and from the holy city, and from all the* [good] *things written in this book*.'" (And no exceptions!)

I needed to establish up front in this chapter the biblical truth that: *Interpreting the Bible is actually forbidden by the Bible itself*. I have never heard any teaching on that subject, but *my eyes have recently been opened to that Bible Reality*, and *the seriousness of violating the Bible warnings*. So, with that brief introduction behind us, let us investigate some of the really bizarre Bible interpretations. Brace yourself!

(But before that, I need to explain the difference between Bible *translation* and Bible *interpretation*. *Bible translation is transferring the message of the original Greek or Hebrew into English, etc. The translator has to be familiar with both those ancient languages, and the language he or she is translating the original into.* Thus, the translator must be knowledgable of both the *definitions of words*, and *peculiar idioms*, of each language. *I learned that when you perceive the PUNCH LINE of a joke in some new language you have a good grasp of the language. But, a problem that plagues even Bible translation is that THE PERSONAL BIASES of translators OFTEN BLEED INTO their translations.* So study different Bible versions.

Bible interpretation is: *THE DELIBERATE MANIPULATION OF BIBLE WORDS TO MAKE THEM FIT PERSONAL BELIEFS. The worst problem with PRIVATE Bible interpretations is that they rarely stay private, but go VIRAL throughout the church; spreading their death-dealing theological viruses everywhere they go. And, the NUMBER of theological viruses being great, it is difficult to know which one ought to be exposed first.* The job is almost overwhelming; but it must be done!)

And now we will begin. *I have written three books dealing with Calvinism, so I will not go into great detail on Calvinism here.* Yet, I must point out *SOME* of John Calvin's errors, *so that you will grasp what is meant by deliberate manipulation of word meanings, etc.* Just a few examples ought to suffice.

The first one exposes Calvin's deliberate manipulation of one word in Genesis 4:7. Every English Bible version of that verse I have read renders one of the Hebrew words as *"sin."* "*Sin* lies at the door, and *its* desire is for you. And you must rule over *it.*" The word *SIN*, not fitting into Calvin's doctrine of Total Depravity, *he contended that* (and get this) *it is more agreeable to the context that God meant NOT SIN, but Cain's brother ABEL.* So let us check that out and see if *Abel* better fits that context than *sin:* "If you do not well, *Abel* lies at the door, and *his* desire is for you, and you must rule over *him.*"

JOHN CALVIN'S PRIVATE INTERPRETATION *of that word in that verse completely altered the message of that passage. He deliberately manipulated that one Inspired Bible word, in order to stubbornly hold onto his Total Depravity doctrine!*

115

In order to maintain his Limited Atonement doctrine, the man manipulated *AN ENTIRE VERSE* in the New Testament. Romans 11:32 says: "*God has consigned all to disobedience, that He might have mercy on all.*" Paul's statement obviously includes *ALL mankind!* But Calvin smugly claimed: "*All Paul meant in that verse is that those who are saved,* [that is, the Elect only] *ought to ascribe their salvation to God's grace.*" It is very suspicious that *ONLY* those passages which posed a threat to Calvin's doctrines he insinuated had been *vaguely worded, so that he had to render the* "correct interpretation" *of them.* Calvin did not alter non-threatening passages. Paul meant what Paul said; not what Calvin said Paul meant!!!

Without going into the fine details, let me list a few more of *Calvin's deliberate distortions of particular Scriptures, as well as his castigation of some of the inspired writers. Calvin accused Moses of being demon-possessed by his asking that his name be blotted from the Book of Life.* Blotting not fitting into his "once-saved-always-saved" doctrine, Calvin accused Moses of "speaking *AS* one possessed." Possessed *BY* what? *Demon-possession* had to be what Calvin meant! *Jesus said that attributing to Satan the Holy Spirit's work is blasphemy: An unpardonable sin. But here, it was blaspheming the man of God who wrote by Holy-Spirit inspiration. Still blasphemy!*

Moreover, Calvin contended that King David and Ezekiel were *CONFUSED* over the possibility of names being blotted out of the Book of Life. *Names CANNOT be deleted from that book, Calvin taught!* He also accused Paul of being confused over the possibility of the Elect losing their salvation. Calvin *EVEN* accused the Almighty of lying! In Exodus 32:33, Deity said out of His own mouth that *He would blot from the Book of Life the names of all those who sinned against Him. So, in claiming that names cannot be blotted out of the Book of Life, Calvin accused Deity of lying.* Using complicated arguments to establish his point, Calvin still insinuated that God lied.

Let us look deeper into Calvin's contentions here: Moses, King David, Ezekiel, and the apostle Paul were all confused, but John Calvin was in-the-know about all the things those *HOLY-SPIRIT-INSPIRED* Bible-book-writers were ignorant of! (?????) *John Calvin was not only blasphemous, but stupid!*

And not only did Calvin low-rate certain Bible writers, he also scrapped some of the prominent Bible promises meant for the *entire church dispensation.* Calvin contended without offering even *ONE* Scripture passage proving his contention, that apostles, prophets and evangelists were only temporary ministries, whereas, pastors and teachers were given to the church permanently. *PRIVATE INTERPRETATION! BUT,* just as I said, *HIS private interpretations did not REMAIN private, but, were passed down from one generation to the next, until now;* and have done an undetermined amount of *DAMAGE* to the church over the last 500 years. *CALVINISM IS A CURSE!*

Not only did Calvin *CHEAT the church out of the apostolic, prophetic, and evangelistic ministries,* he also contended that God ended the supernatural healing-ministry *AFTER the first century. THAT GIFT TOO WAS TEMPORARY!* James 5:14-16 *was valid back in James' day, but was no longer valid in the 1500s.* And, of course, *if such WERE the case in the 1500s, then believers cannot expect healing-miracles today.* And no mere coincidence; *that is exactly what cowardly pastors and theologians teach today.* And you can thank John Calvin for that *UN-BLESSING! John Calvin was a deceived deceiver.*

Well, enough of that satanic theology. I had thought that I would never find any theology worse than Calvinism, but I have recently discovered one (not that I was looking for one) *that makes Calvinism almost seem tame in comparison.* But, let me begin with some erroneous teachings that seem a bit less threatening before getting into those more vicious ones.

While I am not familiar with all existing theologies, or all the gross errors they embody, *whether minor or major,* I am familiar with certain theologies which have *minor flaws,* and some that are *made up mostly of major errors.* I have written books on *SOME* of those errors. But, again, not to duplicate any of my books on any of those subjects, but just touching on some of the more glaring errors of some of the theologies I am familiar with, I will now *EXPOSE* some of those errors. *I do know something about the Word of Faith movement; and even though I am not aware of MANY MAJOR FLAWS in that theology,* I do need to expose *ONE INEXCUSABLE ERROR* in their doctrine—having to do with the subject of *authority.*

I researched several of the books on *authority* by several of the teachers in *the Word of Faith movement,* and saw that *they all teach the same basic tenets on that authority issue.* Their very first point is that Deity gave Adam authority over the earth and everything in it. *That point is biblically correct.* However, *from that point they botched the doctrine, adding to God's Word some CRAZY concepts. Some have said that God gave Adam the title deed of earth as well as authority over it; so that when Adam sinned, he relinquished to the devil both earthly authority and earth-ownership.* Just remember that. The next point is that *Satan held Adam's lost authority until Jesus died on the cross, and His Spirit descended to Hades, where He fought Satan, defeated him, and took back Adam's SUPPOSEDLY-LOST AUTHORITY; plus the keys of death and Hades.* Before Jesus ascended back to heaven, He gave that authority to the church. *Every one of their theological claims on authority from the second point on is an outright LIE; not only lacking any Bible-backing, but actually being refuted by many Scriptures.* And most amazingly; *even after decades of teaching those erroneous doctrines, they STILL do not see the unbiblicalness of their errors on the subject of authority.*

First of all, to be valid, a doctrine has to be supported by more than one clear Scripture passage on the subject. *Their entire authority-theology is based on just one passage*—Luke 4:5-7. Moreover, that passage recorded the words of *the one Jesus said has NO TRUTH in him—Satan. So, the foundation of the Word of Faith teachings on authority is ONE PASSAGE; which records the words of the only one Christ ever said has NO TRUTH in him.* An authority doctrine based mostly upon lies. Not much of a foundation to build a Christian life on!

In order to get the *full impact* of the biblical truth on that subject, you will need to read my book on authority. Here, I just want to point out a few Scripture passages which prove the unbiblical nature of their authority doctrine. It seems to me that, as much as they obviously study the Bible, at least one of them would have noticed that *in Daniel alone at least a half dozen verses tell us plainly that God gives authority to whomever HE pleases* (Daniel 2:37, 4:17, 25, 32, 5:18, 21; and Jeremiah 27:5-7). *God, not Satan, possessed authority!*

*Those passages refute their claim that Satan took Adam's authority when Adam sinned.* And their claim that God gave Adam ownership of this planet is blasted by Genesis 14:19, 22, Psalms 24:1, 50:10, etc. An additional flaw is that, in all of their books on authority, *I have found NO instance of any of those writers saying any more about Adam's ownership of the planet.* Surely, *if earth-ownership was lost when Adam's authority was lost, Christ would have taken earth-ownership back from Satan, along with that authority. It is strange that earth-ownership is never mentioned again. That leaves PART of their authority doctrine dangling.* BIBLE TRUTH is: Neither authority nor earth-ownership was lost when Adam sinned. *God has always been the owner of all creation, and He gives authority to whomever HE pleases!* In Luke 4:6, Satan lied!

And, as to Christ battling Satan in hell, *nothing could be further from Bible Truth. Hell is not the Adversary's domain. He walks upon the earth.* Hell is the devil's worst nightmare. Moreover, the Bible is clear that *Jesus crushed the serpent's head (authority over mankind) on the CROSS, where the heel of the woman's SEED was bruised.* Every salvation blessing was purchased on the *TREE* (Deuteronomy 21:23, Galatians 3:13, 1 Peter 2:24). Of course, *our Savior obviously suffered while in hell, but no passage implies that Christ fought Satan in Hades.* They use Colossians 2:15 to prove their case, but the Greek says Christ *unclothed Himself of principalities and powers.* He took nothing off them; as some English versions imply. *That Greek word being in the middle voice proves that Jesus acted on Himself, not on some other personality. And, it all occurred on the cross; not in hell.* Nor does *ANY* passage imply that the keys of death and Hades had been lost to the devil, so that the Savior had to get them back. He possessed those keys because His Father had given them to Him.

Another disturbing heresy I have encountered recently is by a man steeped in the Jewish feasts, and customs; trying to pull the church back under at least some Old Testament laws and practices. He wears the garb of the Jewish priests, and emphasizes the Jewish feasts, as though believers were still under that old system. *Paul blasts that lie in Colossians chapter two.* Read the entire chapter for the full impact.

119

*Michael Rood* hits the nail right on the head, as they say, by his exposure of modern church customs that have come from *the ancient Babylonian religious system*; blasting away all those heresies. *I commend him for that.* However, *when it comes to his teachings on last-days events, Rood is not only "out in left field," as the saying goes, but has soared beyond our solar system.* He gets WILDLY WEIRD AND HERETICAL!

First of all, he, like some other *deceived preachers* today, pushes *his opinion* that there will be *no rapture* of the saints before the Antichrist appears. More strange, the one who is holding back the Antichrist (2 Thessalonians 2:6-7) is Satan himself! (?) *Rood says Satan and Jesus have equal authority before God's throne, and that Satan will retain that authority until the archangel Michael and his angels cast the devil and his fallen-angel army from heaven* (Revelation 12). *Only then will the Antichrist come forth. Not one Scripture even hints of such absurdity.* In his book, Rood BLASTED Tim LaHaye for his teaching on the *pre-tribulation rapture of believers.* So in this book, *I blast Rood's unwarranted massacre of Scripture.*

(Such does not mean that I necessarily agree totally with Tim LaHaye on everything he believes and teaches. But I do biblically believe in the pre-tribulation rapture of the saints. Be patient, and I will give you a thorough explanation later.)

Michael Rood says that the man-child of the *sun-clothed woman* is Jesus (born about 2000 years ago), whereas both Revelation and Daniel prove that The Great Tribulation will take place in the *LAST* days of this age. *The woman will flee into the wilderness, where she will be protected for three and one half years* (Revelation 12:6) *at the END of this age.* That did not occur 2000 years ago! The man-child will be caught up into heaven, escaping Satan's wrath, whereas Jesus was crucified. Truth is: The male-child will be 144,000 first-fruit Israelite converts—*AFTER the rapture of the church.* And the woman—Modern-day Israel—will give birth to that 144,000; which is called a *male-child, children* and *a nation,* in Isaiah 66:7-8: "Before she travailed [as the nation accepting Christ as their Messiah], she brought forth; before her pain came, she was delivered of [or gave birth to] a *male child.* Who has heard of such a thing? Who has seen such a thing? Will the earth be made to bring forth in one day? Or may a *nation* be born all at once? For as soon as Zion travailed, she brought forth her *children*." That is a definite prophecy of Revelation 7:4-8, 12:1-6 and 14:1-5. *Just a little honest Bible study will totally annihilate all doctrinal heresies*; including Rood's!

(I need right here to remind the reader that the purpose of this book is to uncover the hiding-places of the devil, and that this chapter reveals that one of Satan's hiding-places is Bible interpretation. May sound strange; but *ANY* distortion of the Bible is an interpretation of it, and any interpretation of the Bible is a distortion of it—Deuteronomy 4:2, Proverbs 30:6, Romans 3:3-4, 2 Peter 1:20-21, Revelation 22:19, etc.)

Still more hard-to-believe *STUFF*: Stuff is the appropriate word, *for Rood is trying to STUFF the Body of Christ with his absurd lies*—His private interpretations of Holy Scripture.

Revelation chapter nine says that during the Tribulation of the last days, one of the hardships thrust upon humanity will be wrought by locusts (*obviously demons*) that come out of the abyss. Michael Rood contends that the passage really describes military weaponry, such as tanks and helicopters. It is my understanding that tanks and helicopters come out of factories, *NOT from the center of the earth*. Rood contends as well that smoke coming from the abyss is actually deadly radiation from an atomic blast. *He also says that the USA is the beast* (Antichrist), *and that Russia will nuke and destroy the USA, and afterwards the USA will revive as the wounded head of the seven-headed beast* of Revelation 13:3. (?????)

*ONE of his primary lies is that the church will go through the Great Tribulation.* Rood insists, just as do other deceived teachers, that when Christ descends with the trump of God, it is the *SEVENTH* trumpet of Revelation 11:15. Not so! *Most false doctrines are formed by what I call surface scanning of Scripture.* "Why, that sounds just like it is saying..." *Typical, private interpretation!* But consider this enlightening truth:

The *seventh trumpet* of Revelation 11:15 is a JUDGMENT trumpet. Its purpose is to *pronounce woe* on human beings, who sport the mark of the beast and worship his image. *The trumpet accompanying Christ's Coming will ANNOUNCE the resurrection of the righteous dead. Two different trumpets on two different occasions with two different functions.* Why not *LINK* every trumpet Scripture mentions with that *SEVENTH* trumpet, implying that they *ALL* speak of that future event? *SURFACE SIMILARITIES are not proper foundations to build doctrine on.* The trumpet accompanying our Lord will sound years *BEFORE* that seventh *JUDGMENT* trumpet is blown.

*Michael Rood says without flinching that no Christian will go up in the rapture to meet Jesus Christ in the air before the seventh trumpet is blown. That will occur when Christ comes to set up His Kingdom at the end of this age; so that is when the resurrection will occur, and NOT before. Rood also claims that the resurrection of our body is our ACTUAL NEW BIRTH. We are not truly born again until we get our glorified bodies.* You can surely see the devil behind that doctrine! He would love for us believers to think that we cannot take advantage of the fact that we are *"New creatures in Christ" NOW* in this life. Besides, *how could we be NEW creatures, if we have not been born again already?* Rood is a deceived deceiver.

(*Let me sandwich in right here another most enlightening truth.* Theologians lie! Wow! Tis true! *One of the purposes of Bible interpretation is to do away with the supernatural.* One example is this *educated comment* by a Calvinist theologian. Romans 11:29 tells us: *The GIFTS and CALLING of God ARE IRREVOCABLE—cannot be recalled. GIFTS is CHARISMATA, in Greek. CALLING is the Greek, KLASIS. There ARE* (plural) *Charismata—miracle-healing gifts.* Moreover, *Paul said that Israel was called as God's own inheritance—The CALLING of whom could not be recalled. But GIFTS and CALLING are not the same. Supernatural GIFTING enabled Israel to fulfill their GOD-CALLING; and empowers us to work miracles. The trick of that Calvinist theologian: HE SAID Paul meant THE GIFT OF CALLING* (singular); eliminating the miracle-power of the word Charismata. Interpreting Paul as *MEANING* the gift of calling, *the man made two entities one.* But, had Paul meant calling (singular), he would have said: *"The calling of God." There would have been no need to use Charismata too!* The verb being *"ARE,"* and not *"IS,"* Paul spoke of *TWO* entities.

The *tricky trick* of the *tricky tricksters*, and, the *deceiving deception* of the *deceived deceivers* goes something like this: "The Bible says this, but it actually means this!" And we are

122

supposed to believe what they say it means, instead of what it actually says? Such is at the same time an insult to all of us believers, and a slap in the face of our God. The audacity of all such educated idiots. And I did mean just what I said! They may be highly-educated, but educated in what? Trash! Lies are not what you could call a good education. *IDIOTS!*)

*I promised to explain the Bible explanation of the rapture*; so here it is: For the most part, even *rapture-preachers* miss the Bible message badly; for even they misunderstand what that *Great Tribulation* is all about. They get *HUNG UP* on *the seven trumpets, the man-child, the seven-headed beast from the sea, those ten kings with ten horns*, etc. *I have heard all kinds of speculations, which are actually refuted by the Bible itself.* But, when they get those *private interpretations* stuck in their heads, they will not listen to anyone; even the Bible.

Daniel's 70 weeks (seven years each) totals 490 years in prophecy. *And the KEYS to understanding that prophecy are in Jeremiah, Daniel, and Revelation.* Jeremiah 30:7 tells us what the Tribulation is *ALL ABOUT*: "*It is the time of Jacob's trouble.*" *The Tribulation is ALL about Israel and the Gentiles. Through it, Deity will convince Israel, AS A NATION, to accept Jesus as the Messiah. And at the same time, God will punish the Gentile nations for their historical mistreatment of Israel.*

The Tribulation has nothing to do with the church, *for it will be taken from the earth BEFORE that Tribulation begins.* Remember, *the Tribulation is the time of JACOB'S TROUBLE; NOT the church's trouble! The church will be out of here!*

In Daniel 9:24-27, Gabriel informed Daniel that "Seventy weeks [seventy sevens—490 years] are determined upon [or has to do with,] *your people* [Israel], and upon *your holy city* [Jerusalem]; *TO FINISH THE TRANSGRESSION*, to *MAKE AN END OF SIN*, and to *MAKE RECONCILIATION FOR INIQUITY* [reference to the Lord's sacrifice on the cross], and to *BRING IN EVERLASTING RIGHTEOUSNESS*, and to *SEAL UP VISION AND PROPHECY*, and to *ANOINT* the most Holy. Understand that *from the going forth of the* [first] *commandment* [by King Cyrus] *to restore and build Jerusalem, unto the Messiah, the Prince* [Jesus], *will be seven weeks* [49 years], *and sixty-two weeks* [434 years—total of 483 years—7 years short of 490]. The street will be rebuilt, plus the [Jerusalem] wall, even in troublous times [See Nehemiah.]. And, after sixty-two weeks [the second portion of time] will the Messiah be cut off [that is, crucified—Isaiah 53:8], but, not for Himself, [but for us]. And, the people [Romans] of the prince [Antichrist] who will come [*in the last seven years of this age*] will destroy the city [of Jerusalem] and the sanctuary [temple—in A.D. 70]...And [the Antichrist] will confirm a covenant with many [in Israel] for one week [seven year contract]. And, in the midst of that week [three and one half years into that seven year deal], he will cause the sacrifices and the oblation to cease [desecrate the temple, terminating the Jewish sacrifices]." That will all be centered in the Middle East, and concern Israel; *NOT* the church. Again in Daniel 10:14, Gabriel said: "I have come to make you understand what will befall *your people* [Israel] in the *latter days*. For yet the vision is for many days [from the days of Daniel]." Revelation 22:10 refers to that very time.

In both Daniel and Revelation, *three and one half years, 1260 days, time, times, and half a time* all refer to the same time period—the last three and one half years of this age. "I heard the man clothed in linen, who stood upon the waters of the river, and held up his right and left hands to heaven, and swore by Him, Who lives forever, that [the wrapping up of this age] will span *time, times, and half a time*; *and when he* [the Antichrist] *will have scattered the power of the holy people* [Jews], *all these things will be finished* (Daniel 12:7)." Time=1 year; times=2 years; half a time=6 months; or three and one half years. Then the Millennium will begin.

Between the time the Jewish Messiah was cut off (Isaiah 53:8) and His Second Coming to earth at the very end of the last seven years of this age, there has been a large time gap: Close to 2000 years. *All 490 years of Daniel's prophecy was about Israel!* But from A.D. 70 to 1948 there was no Israelite nation. *The first 483 prophetic years being about Israel, and not the church, then the last seven of the 490 years is about Israel, and NOT the church. That means the Church Age has been sandwiched between the year 483 and the last seven.* The church will have served its purpose, and will be gone.

Obviously, that means the church will not be present on earth during the Tribulation Period spoken of in Daniel and Revelation. One of the big, big hang-ups of those no-rapture heretics concerns that restraining entity of 2 Thessalonians 2:6-7. Michael Rood teaches that *the devil* is the Restrainer. Talk about a stretch of the imagination! And he bothers not to provide any *biblical proof* for his claim. Instead, he insists that Satan has an established position in heaven along with Jesus, *until the angel Michael casts him out. What Scripture even hints at such absurdity?* Actually, that is blasphemy!

There are *other guesses* as to who or what the *Restrainer* is; *so let us consider all the possibilities, then eliminate them one by one—until we reach the only valid biblical conclusion. The primary factor in the identity of the Restrainer is that he, she, or it, is to be removed from this planet!* Thus, whatever, or whoever it is, *its absence is what will allow the infamous Antichrist to come on the scene in the last days of this age.*

How many groups could possibly restrain the Antichrist, right up to the last seven years of this age? *What are all the possible entities?* One pick might be the Gentiles. However, the Gentile nations will obviously be on earth until the end. Deity is going to have them surround Jerusalem, in order to *PUNISH* them at the Battle of Armageddon (Isaiah 66:18-19, Zechariah 14:2). Moreover, *the Antichrist will rule over all of the Gentile nations in his regime.* So, the Gentiles are out as the Restrainer of the Antichrist. No question about that.

Next would be the Jews. *They might do some restraining. But, the Tribulation concerns the Jews, so they will obviously be on the earth during that time of Jacob's trouble.* Thus, the Jews cannot be the Restrainer—narrowing the possibilities.

Human governments would be another possible entity to hold back the Antichrist; but according to many Scriptures, *Antichrist will be attempting to rule the world through human governments.* Besides, human governments will be made up of Gentiles and Jews, both of whom we already eliminated.

Only two more possibilities I can think of: *The Holy Spirit and the church.* Of course, *the Holy Spirit is the main choice of many Bible teachers.* Let us ponder that possibility. *If the Holy Spirit, and not the church, is the Restrainer, would God remove the Holy Spirit from this planet and leave His church here defenseless?* Moreover, *how would anybody during the Tribulation Time GET SAVED without the Holy Spirit?* People have to be convicted of sin, righteousness, and judgment, in order to be saved (John 16:8-11). Some may argue that only the *restraining power* of the Holy Spirit will be removed, but *the Bible says plainly that the Restrainer himself, herself, or itself will be taken out of the way.* Do not add to the Bible or take away from it. *No private interpretation allowed!* Besides that, *the Holy Spirit cannot be removed from any place in the universe.* God—the Holy Spirit—is omnipresent. See Psalms 139:7-10. Therefore, *the entity holding back the Antichrist is not the Gentile nations, or human governments, or the Jews, or the Holy Spirit. Especially not the devil! Why would Satan want to restrain the Antichrist? He is the one who will invest all of his powers in that man of sin* (2 Thessalonians 2:3).

*That means the church is the Restrainer of the Antichrist: Which in turn means the church will be the one removed from earth before the Antichrist can be revealed. And that, in turn, proves that the church will be raptured before the last seven years of this age! We will be caught up TO CHRIST in the air before the Tribulation, then come back WITH HIM at the end.* Read 1 Corinthians 15:51-53, 1 Thessalonians 4:14-17 and Zechariah 14:3-5. The 7 year Tribulation concerns the Jews and Gentiles, not the church. Thus, the church will *NOT* be on earth during the last 7 years of this age. *That is Bible!*

Whereas many theologians and preachers claim there is *NO* Scripture teaching that the church will be removed from earth *before* Antichrist comes on the scene, *MANY Scripture passages prove beyond doubt that the church WILL be out of here before that time comes.* Jesus Himself said that just as it was in Noah's day, so will it be *THEN* (Matthew 24:37-39). Remember, Noah, his family, and all of the animals boarded the ark 7 days *BEFORE* that flood came and destroyed all of those outside the ark. Also remember that *Lot was removed from Sodom before the fiery judgment was rained on that city* (Luke 17:28-29). Therefore, neither Noah nor Lot was *IN* the water or fire during those divine judgments. So, neither will the church *GO THROUGH* that final Tribulation time!

One more *heretical theology* I have to expose in this book is the very *CORE* of another ministry, with a large following, and very popular, even around my neck of the woods. Being popular, however, does not necessarily *qualify* a ministry in God's estimation; because: "*What is highly esteemed among men is an abomination to God (Luke 16:15).*" *Ministries have to meet divine qualifications, which are plainly laid out in the Bible for all to see and heed.* And, a primary requirement is: "*No private interpretation of Scripture (2 Peter 1:20-21).*" The ministry I am about to expose has violated that *RULE* many times. *Even the theme of that television ministry is erroneous in claiming GOD'S LOVE AND GRACE ARE UNCONDITIONAL. NO Scripture even hints that either of those is true.* In fact, the opposite is taught throughout Scripture. For instance, *if Deity's love were unconditional, He would Not have expelled Adam and Eve from their Paradise!* The truth is: *Both God's grace and love have certain conditions attached*. I will not go into detail about that here, because I do go into detail about that in my book, "Are Christians Just Saved Sinners?".

But, I will say this: *UNconditional love would necessarily have NO conditions attached to it. It would require nothing on our part.* It would *JUST WORK AUTOMATICALLY in our lives.* Moreover, the word love implies that only good things ought to happen in our lives. Otherwise, God's love would actually be undesirable. *So many undesirable things happening in so many Christian lives today actually proves that God's love is not unconditional, and that most Christians have not met the Bible conditions to receive and enjoy His love*. Thus, pushers of that *unconditional-love-theory* do not know what they are talking about. *We had NOTHING to do with God's decision to love the world enough to offer His Son to save the world. But, now that Christ has been offered, it is up to us to receive the benefits of the loving salvation provided by God's love!*

Although numerous ministries teach that *false concept*, I will focus on one in particular—Andrew Womack Ministries. Womack teaches some really *WEIRD* doctrines; about which I will go into detail. *He goes far beyond privately interpreting the Scriptures to placing his doctrines ABOVE the Scriptures! That is an even worse crime.*

Obviously, Womack believing the concept that God's love and grace are both unconditional opened a demonic door to other, *even more diabolical,* doctrines. Let me start with this one. *And, the reader might possibly think it is correct! I have heard it come out of the mouths of some people whom I know personally.* However, we will consider what God's Word says about it. That should forever set the record straight.

The flawed doctrine: The very moment we got born again all of our sins were forgiven—*past, present and future.* What is wrong with believing that doctrine? *It SOUNDS like such a good deal.* It is one big lie! The Bible teaches *NO* such thing. You see, one flawed doctrine leads one into other erroneous concepts as well. The process is similar to drawing plans for some residence. If you move one wall you change what is on the other side of that wall. Once the plans have been drawn and approved, *the builder has no authority to alter the plans; thereby altering the planned product.* At a tool-and-die shop I used to work at, *the chief-engineer oversaw all of the work of the drafters, and made all final approvals. Nobody but he was authorized to alter any portion of the finalized blueprints for the product we were making for our customer. ANY KIND of alteration could render the project worthless, and cost both our customer, and our company, dearly.* If such carelessness was risky in industry, *think how much it could cost believers to tamper with the Master Blueprint*—God's Written Word.

It takes diligent study of the Scriptures to insure that we do not get deceived by deceived preachers. Not all preachers deliberately *PLAN* to deceive people, but many ignorantly do so, because they themselves have been deceived by others.

In addition to watching several of Andrew Womack's TV programs, I purchased some of his books and dvds, in order to learn his overall theology. *So, I am not merely speculating on his doctrinal stance, but have firsthand knowledge of it.*

*Womack teaches both on his TV program and in one of his books that even our future sins were forgiven the moment we were born again. And the very moment I heard him say that, the Holy Spirit immediately reminded me of what Peter wrote* in 2 Peter 1:9: "Who lacks these things has forgotten that he was purged from his PAST sins." Was Peter ignorant of what Andrew Womack claimed to be certain of? Think about this:

*If FUTURE SINS are forgiven BEFORE we commit them, then Peter would have included FUTURE sins.* Then I remembered James 5:15: "The prayer of faith will save the sick, and if he has committed sins, they *WILL BE FORGIVEN* him." Will be; not have been. I stick with God's Word! What will you do?

Remember, *one theological error will necessarily result in yet another, and then in still another.* If all of our future sins have been forgiven up front, when we do commit those sins, *we will not be required either to repent or confess them.* That is exactly what Womack teaches! So, I looked up *repent* and *confess* in the concordance, and found that *Womack was in error regarding those claims as well.* In 2 Corinthians 12:21, *Paul WARNED those Corinthian believers that when he came again to Corinth, he would deal with those who had sinned, and HAD NOT REPENTED OF THOSE SINS.* Furthermore, in Revelation chapters two and three, Jesus commanded some to repent. *Was Jesus Himself unaware of the supposed truth Andrew Womack was sure of? Womack versus Jesus Christ!*

In 1 John 1:9, John also made it clear that when we sin, we must *CONFESS* our sins, in order to be forgiven of them. What Bible did Andrew Womack use to form his theology? *It is obvious that Womack redrew the approved Bible Blueprint.* He has altered Holy Scripture to fit his *WARPED* theology.

*And talk about being warped*; consider Womack's twisted view of the Garden-of-Eden episode. *Whereas Isaiah chapter fourteen and Ezekiel chapter twenty-eight reveal the origin of the devil—Lucifer's fall—Womack rejects that clear scriptural evidence, and says he does not believe it happened that way at all.* Instead, Womack teaches that God sent the pre-fallen Lucifer to the Garden of Eden to help Adam. Help him how? Genesis 2:20-24 tells us that the woman was intended to be man's helpmeet. *NO Scripture backs that weird Womackism!* Remember, one error sets one up for another; then another. *Womack claims that God created Lucifer, but Adam made the devil! WHAT?* Womack put his twisted theological foot in his warped theological mouth in claiming that: *When Lucifer saw that Deity had granted Adam full AUTHORITY over all of the earth, Lucifer became jealous of Adam and plotted his fall.*

Thus, *even IF Lucifer was still innocent when he came to Eden, he SINNED FIRST by tempting Adam; while Adam was still innocent.* Adam did nothing to tempt Lucifer. Therefore, Lucifer fell before Adam did. So how did Adam make Satan? The truth is, Andrew Womack has been deceived by Satan!

*Womack having to convince himself that his theology was based upon God's Word, what Scripture did he use to put the supposedly-un-fallen Lucifer in the Garden of Eden? He took a New Testament passage out of context, and applied it to an Old Testament event.* Hebrews 1:14: "Angels are ministering spirits *sent to minister to heirs of salvation.*" Well, Adam had not sinned, so *he was not an heir of salvation.* He needed no salvation! Thus, *Andrew Womack rejected plain Scripture on one hand—Isaiah fourteen and Ezekiel twenty-eight—and on the other, took a Scripture out of context and applied it where it did not belong.* And all in order to build his theology!

*He did the same in his claim that our sins are all forgiven up front. Ignoring many clear passages that prove otherwise, Womack assumed that one Old Testament Scripture passage relating to God's future treatment of restored ISRAEL applied to the New Testament Church.* Isaiah 54:9 *prophesied that in Israel's future restored state, God would not be angry with or rebuke them! Womack contended that that Scripture passage referred to New Covenant Christians—discounting numerous New Testament passages that clearly teach that: Both Father and Son DO rebuke people they love, and Do require that we repent of our known sins, and that we MUST confess them.*

Womack also said that no matter what a Christian does, *it does not affect his new-born spirit, for it cannot be defiled*; whereas in 2 Corinthians 7:1, *Paul commanded us believers to cleanse ourselves from all defilements of flesh and SPIRIT!* Moreover, in one of his books, *Womack finally admitted that it is possible for a believer to fall away from God and be lost again*; thereby actually trashing his very own theology. How can anybody trust a man who is inconsistent, not only with God's Inspired Word, but even with his own theology?

# Chapter Nine

## Bible Interpretation II

Even though I am not in-the-know about *EVERY satanic doctrine that is propagated by deranged human beings, who have decided that their own personal, private interpretations of Scripture are the correct ones*, I am familiar with enough of them to keep me busy for some time; exposing them for what they actually are—DESTRUCTIVE, DEMONIC HERESIES!

Now I must uncover *the most ungodly, deceptive theology ever to plague any group of people who dares to claim to be a Bible-believing church*. After writing three books that expose the *unconscionable* Calvinist heresies, I never thought that I would run across any theology WORSE than Calvinism. But I have: *Shepherd's Chapel, located in Arkansas*. A Dr Arnold Murray was the obvious founder, *though he passed on some years ago*. Some of the man's deceived followers continue to *SPREAD HIS DEMONIC THEOLOGY* by books, cds, dvds, TV, and internet—*reaching millions of homes around the planet*. Shepherd's Chapel has a worldwide clientele; some of whom I know personally. Therefore, *I am aware of how detrimental THAT theology is. But even more alarming than the doctrines themselves is that people are so easily taken in by them!*

How do I begin to expose such a demonic theology? I will first list the basic elements of that *blasphemous* heresy, and then expand upon each element in the same general order.

Every facet of Shepherd's Chapel theology is not only not supported by Holy Scripture, but is *diametrically opposed* to Scripture. It is also difficult to determine which facet of that ultra-satanic theology is the *cornerstone*, upon which all the rest is built. *All is bizarre! None of it actually believable!*

The very first cd that I listened to being on the subject of the supposed *pre-existence of the human soul*, that is where I will begin to unmask that theology; after I compile a list of its errors. *Murray constantly taught that every human being pre-existed in SOUL form from the dateless past. Of course, we today cannot remember our pre-existence. (OF COURSE!)*

Perhaps, his most blasphemous contention is that Satan had *SEX* with Eve, *making Cain the actual physical offspring of the devil! Abel was his TWIN brother!* (?) Adam sired Abel, and Satan fathered Cain in Eve's *same* pregnancy! *How can any REAL Christian countenance that utter nonsense? It also being outright blasphemy! That untruth permeates the man's entire theology*—Satan being the physical father of Cain.

Such doctrine also *necessitated that Cain's family line be prominent throughout human history. So, Murray taught that some of Cain's descendants boarded the ark with Noah and his family, and so survived the flood. Cain's family line came to be known as the Kenites*, according to Dr Arnold Murray. He claimed as well that Kenites are still with us to this day.

The Russian communists are Kenites; and other Kenites in Europe and the USA are *we, who believe in the rapture of the church prior to the Tribulation period.* That *rapture theory* (???) is linked to the *mark of the beast* in Revelation. HUH?

The false church (those who believe in the rapture of the church) will be *Satan's bride,* just as the true church will be the *Bride of Christ*—the true church being Shepherd's Chapel and people of like doctrine. (???) Murray condemned all who believe in the church's *pre-tribulation* rapture; claiming that we are the devil's helpers. *We WILL FALL for every Antichrist deception, because we have already FALLEN for that satanic* (???) *falsehood.* Although Murray called it a mere THEORY, it was obviously a thorn in the man's side. He HARPED on that subject more than on any other in his weird theology. But, as we investigate Dr Murray's teachings, it will become obvious that his doctrines are the satanic falsehoods. All of them!

*Murray-ism also contains less-threatening errors; which I will deal with as we travel along. Most of them are intricately connected, but some seem to be dangling by themselves. Yet, ALL of them are opposed TO God's Word, so ALL of them are opposed BY God's Word. Not one agrees with Holy Scripture!*

Let us first investigate the supposed pre-existence of the human soul. Dr Arnold Murray was a deliberately-deceptive theologian. His primary proof of those *supposed pre-existent souls* was taken from the book of Job. Job 1:6 says that one day the *sons of God* came to present themselves before God, and Satan came among them. *Whereas, the overall Scripture picture PROVES that the sons of God were actually ANGELS, Murray contended they were pre-existing HUMAN SOULS.* A second assembly of the same beings is recorded in Job 2:1. And the same Bible Truth applies there as well.

Murray used Job 38:4-7 as further proof of his doctrine; *although the passage actually refutes his blatant contention.* Let me expose Murray's flaws. In verse four, God asked Job: *"Where were you when I created the earth?"* And verse seven adds: *"when all the sons of God shouted for joy?"* Bible Truth totally annihilates that Dr Arnold Murray tall theological tale. But, before we get to that, let me explain more of the man's biblically unfounded pre-existence doctrine. *Mind-boggling!*

Murray claimed that in the first earth age (and there was one; but not Dr Murray's version), some pre-existing human souls rebelled with Lucifer, while some remained true to the Creator. Those souls that remained true to God became the elect, who now have no free will (???); while those souls that rebelled retained a free will to get right with God in this age. *Those souls remaining true to Deity during Lucifer's rebellion EARNED their election.* (Leaving no place for God's grace!)

*Deity places our SUPPOSED pre-existing souls in our flesh bodies at our birth.* (I have not figured out why we elect ones must be tested again in this age, if we remained true to God in that earlier age. *Murray's theology leaves lots of questions unanswered.*) Murray had to have gotten that false doctrine from the devil, for he certainly did *NOT* get it from the Bible! Scripture clearly disproves his ungodly theological position.

In reality, *most of the Scripture passages Murray used to prove his point prove the very OPPOSITE.* In Job 38:4-7, God asked Job: *"Where were you when I created the earth?"* And then verse seven: *"when all the sons of God shouted for joy?"* Murray taught that those *sons of God* in Job 38:7, as in Job 1:6 and 2:1, *were pre-existing human souls. But if Job's soul existed then, why would Deity ask: "Where were you when I created the earth?"* Ponder with me the following set of Bible facts, which totally destroy Murray's demonic contentions.

When God *FIRST* created creation, Lucifer could not have rebelled already! So, if those *sons of God* were human souls, none of them could have rebelled with Lucifer against Deity. Job himself, then, would have been among the sons of God. Thus, *God would have no reason to ask: "Where were you at creation?" The fact that Deity asked Job that question during his trials IN HIS PHYSICAL BODY proves that Job's soul DID NOT exist prior to his bodily birth.* For Job to have existed at creation, he would have needed to be physically *BORN* then. Truth is, neither Job's, nor *ANY* soul, pre-existed! *Our souls come into existence when we are conceived within the womb; and at no time before!* Dr Arnold Murray lied, lied, lied!

One other Scripture passage Murray used to *supposedly* prove his questionable point was Ephesians 1:4, where Paul said that God chose us in Christ *BEFORE* the *FOUNDATION* of the world. The Greek word for *foundation* refers not to the creation of earth, but to its *overthrow.* Murray rightly points out that fact. However, *the man contended that Deity having chosen us at that time means that we existed back then.* Our bodies obviously not existing at first, Paul must have meant that our souls did already exist. Mere demonic speculation!

The Murray flaw: Paul said that Deity chose us in Christ *BEFORE the overthrow of the world.* That would have been *BEFORE Lucifer's rebellion. So, Deity's choice of us would be based on something other than our having been loyal to Him when Lucifer rebelled—for that had NOT YET occurred.* God's choice proves not our pre-existence, but His foreknowledge!

*The apostle Paul was NOT teaching arbitrary election. Nor was he teaching the pre-existence of the soul. WHERE* would salvation be located? In Christ! *WHO* would get into Christ? Those who *WOULD* believe the Gospel—Romans 10:9-10.

Job 38:4-7, 21, and Ephesians 1:4, *prove the opposite of Murray's theological absurdity. Murray contended that every Scripture mentioning the foreknowledge of God is proof of the pre-existence of the human SOUL. But Job 38:21 proves that Job did NOT EXIST in any form at creation, for God said that; for Job to EXIST then, he would have had to be BORN then.*

*The straw that broke the camel's back*, as that old saying goes: In Murray's *erroneous teaching* on the resurrection, he turned to 1 Corinthians 15:44: *"There is a natural body and there is a spiritual body."* I will expose his errors concerning our resurrection later. But here, let me expose not only that man's error regarding the pre-existence of the soul, but also his blasphemy regarding Paul's comment about the order of mankind's formation. Paul said: *"The spiritual IS NOT FIRST but the natural; AFTERWARD the spiritual* (verse 46)." Well, such not fitting Murray's *soul-existing-first doctrine*, he sort of lightly chuckled (on one of his cds I was listening to), and then said: *"Paul was just having a little fun there."* That was definitely the *theological straw* that broke that camel's back. *No longer could I give Murray any benefit of the doubt, as to whether he had just been deceived, or perhaps was suffering some degree of dementia. Obviously, he was DELIBERATELY DISHONEST in his handling of the Scriptures; and so was an obvious FRAUD!* "Paul was just having a little fun there," the man said. *Paul wrote under the inspiration of the Holy Spirit!* And what he said in that verse blew away Murray's doctrine of the *pre-existence of the human soul*. Thus, Murray had to somehow dismiss 1 Corinthians 15:46, because *Paul plainly taught that the NATURAL IS FIRST, THEN THE SPIRITUAL!*

What was Murray suggesting in saying "Paul was having a little fun"? He implied that Paul was just kidding around. *Paul really knew that our human souls pre-existed, BUT was teasing us in that passage. Ohhhhhhhh!* It is difficult to find the appropriate word or phrase to describe the *PUTRIDNESS* of such an accusation against the apostle Paul; and against God's Inspired Word. *Dr Arnold Murray was a FRAUD!* That means that *Shepherd's Chapel is a fraudulent ministry. NOT ONE Scripture backs even one of his or their errors. But most puzzling is the PRONENESS of some people to BELIEVE such garbage! And the worst of his errors comes up next. Ohhhh!*

One of the most *BIZARRE AND BLASPHEMOUS* of Arnold Murray's doctrines: *Eve had sex with Satan; the result being Eve becoming pregnant with Cain. But Eve also had sex with Adam, she becoming pregnant with Abel. Sex with SATAN is the blasphemous part of that FOUL doctrine. The bizarre part is that both boys were twins; born from the same pregnancy.* Many years ago, a Christian sister told me that she believed Eve had sex with the devil. It puzzled me that anyone could believe such; let alone a *Spirit-filled* church member. At that time, *I wondered where she heard such an unbelievable LIE. But now I know exactly where she got it: Shepherd's Chapel!* That *so-called Gospel ministry* has been around a long time.

*Let us investigate that illegitimate doctrine, and see what light Holy Scripture shines upon it.* First of all, Genesis says nothing about Eve having *SEX* with the devil. Nothing at all! Murray used Eve's confession that the serpent had *beguiled* her, then she ate of that fruit. Murray's contention was that *the TERM Eve used means to totally seduce sexually. That is Murray's ONLY argument. Truth is, sexual seduction is ONLY one of several uses of the word.* The primary meaning of the term Eve used in Genesis 3:13 is to *DECEIVE—lead astray.* The serpent (Satan's puppet) *DECEIVED* Eve with lies. In 2 Corinthians 11:3, Paul expressed concern that: *As the devil BEGUILED Eve by his craftiness, SO he might CORRUPT the minds of believers from the simplicity of the Gospel.* Did Paul fear that those believers would have sex with the devil?

Moreover, Genesis 4:1 says plainly that *ADAM knew Eve intimately* (*Bible terminology for sexual intercourse*), and *she conceived from Adam,* and bore Cain. Cain was the offspring of Adam, not Satan! Besides, the *beguiling* took place in the Garden *even before Adam and Eve sinned*, and the *knowing* and *conceiving* occurred outside the Garden, *after they were ousted*. But, to Arnold Murray, those details meant nothing. What *HE* himself wanted to believe, and what he wanted *US* to believe, was all-important to him (and the devil). Eve said in Genesis 4:1 that *she birthed Cain with THE LORD'S help; not with Satan's help. MURRAY failed to point that out!*

Let me mention something else: *Lucifer was an angel—A FALLEN ANGEL.* And in every case of fallen angels taking on human form, *and then cohabiting with female humans,* their offspring were giants. Look at Genesis 6:4, Numbers 13:33, Deuteronomy 2:11, 20, Joshua 12:4, 13:12, 17:15, 18:16, 2 Samuel 21:16, 18, 20, 22 and 1 Chronicles 20:4, 6, 8. If the devil (being a fallen angel) had had *SEX* with Eve, then their offspring (Cain) would have been a giant. Thus, according to the Scripture passages above, *Cain's descendants would be giants from generation to generation.* That would mean those *Russian Communists* would be giants; as well as *a multitude of us Christians who believe in the rapture.* (????) MURRAY'S ASININE DOCTRINES break down at every turn! *Why would any person voluntarily follow such blasphemy and stupidity?* Yet, many people fall into that very trap! (Shaking head!)

And one more telling biblical detail: "Those angels which kept not their *first estate [that is, remaining in angelic form],* but left their own [original] habitation, [God] has *reserved in everlasting chains* [Greek, *Tartarus*—part of the underworld] *under darkness unto the judgment of the great day.* Even as Sodom and Gomorrah, and other cities around them, in like manner [*to those fallen angels who took on human form and cohabited with human females; siring giant offspring*], giving themselves over to fornication, and *going after strange flesh, are set forth as an EXAMPLE, and suffering the vengeance of eternal fire* (Jude 6-7)." Therefore, *the devil would have been incarcerated in Tartarus, just like the other fallen angels who committed those sex crimes* (Jude 6-7, 2 Peter 2:4). It being obvious that that did not happen, *it is also obvious that EVE DID NOT HAVE SEX WITH SATAN. So Cain was the offspring of Adam; not the devil. DR ARNOLD MURRAY—THE LIAR!*

*One of Murray's arguments is that Adam is not mentioned in Cain's family line listed in* Genesis 4:17-24 (suggesting to Murray that Cain was not Adam's offspring). *One more point he makes is that Cain is not mentioned in Adam's family line starting in* Genesis 5:1. *HOW would that make Cain Satan's child? NOR was Abel mentioned in the Messiah's lineage, for Abel had no offspring. He was obviously killed before he had opportunity to marry, and have children.* Genesis 4:17 *starts Cain's family line with Cain just like other family lines began with a certain ancestor; not going back to Adam.* Genesis 5:3 *starts the genealogy of the Messiah with Seth. Luke chapter three takes the genealogy back to Adam through Seth.*

To Dr Arnold Murray, *Cain being the physical offspring of the devil was very important*; for Cain's influence permeated history—*according to Murray*. Thus, *Cain's descendants had to somehow SURVIVE the universal flood of Noah's day. Two arguments supposedly prove that supposed fact*. The first is: The term Kenite can mean offspring of Cain. But I question: *"Was there only one man in all human history named Cain?"* Moreover, *that is only ONE of the dictionary definitions of the term Kenite*. Murray's emphasis on one possible definition of one word is a flimsy foundation for a theological doctrine.

But, even more condemning is *the flimsiness of his claim that some of Cain's descendants boarded the ark along with Noah and his family; and thereby survived the flood*. Murray insisted that despite what Hebrews 11:7, 1 Peter 3:20 and 2 Peter 2:5 all clearly say, *Cain's offspring survived that flood, and were involved in repopulating the earth*. The Scriptures:

"By faith, Noah, *being warned of God about things not yet seen* [worldwide flood], *moved with fear, prepared an ark to the saving of his house* [his own family members and no one else]; *by which he condemned the world* (Hebrews 11:7)."

"By which also Jesus went and preached to the spirits in prison; which at sometime were disobedient, when once the long-suffering of God waited in the days of Noah, while that ark was being built; wherein few, that is, *eight souls* [and no more] were saved by [the flood] water (1 Peter 3:19-20)."

"God spared not the old world [Genesis chapters 6, 7, 8], but saved Noah, *the eighth person* [Noah and seven others], who was a preacher of righteousness, bringing that flood on the world of the *ungodly* (2 Peter 2:5)." Destroying them all!

How did Murray handle the truth in those passages? *He said they were referring to eight people in Adam's race. That number did not include Cain's kids; who, Murray INSISTED, boarded that ark*. He said: "I assure you that some of Cain's descendants were on that ark during Noah's flood!"

Let us go back to Genesis for details of that *fateful event*. "GOD saw that the wickedness of mankind was great in the earth; and EVERY IMAGINATION of the thoughts of his heart was only evil continually. It repented the LORD that He had made man on the earth; and it grieved Him at His heart. So, the LORD said: 'I will destroy mankind whom I created from the face of the earth; man, beast, creeping thing and fowl of the air. For it repents Me that I have made them.' *But, Noah found grace in the eyes of the LORD* (Genesis 6:5-8)."

"*The earth was CORRUPT before God, filled with violence. And Deity looked at the earth, and SAW that it was corrupt;* for all flesh had corrupted his way on the earth. God said to Noah: *'The end of all flesh has come before Me; for the earth is filled with violence.* Therefore, *I will destroy them, with the earth* [breathing beings on its surface] (Genesis 6:11-13).'"

"I, even I [God,] will bring a flood of waters upon earth *to destroy ALL FLESH, wherein is the breath of life*, from under heaven. Everything on earth will die. *But, with you* [Noah,] *I will establish My covenant.* You will come into the ark: You, your sons, your wife, and your sons' wives, with you. *And of every living thing of ALL* [animal] *flesh* [NOT human beings], two of every sort you will bring into the ark, to *KEEP THEM ALIVE.* They will be male, and female: Of *FOWLS*, after their kind, *CATTLE*, after their kind, *EVERY CREEPING THING* on the earth, after its kind; *two of every sort will come to you to keep them alive* (Genesis 6:17-20)." No Cain-kids on the list!

"In the selfsame day entered Noah, and Shem, and Ham, and Japheth, the sons of Noah, and Noah's wife, and those wives of his sons, with them, into the ark: *THEY*, and *every beast* after its kind, and *all cattle* after their kind, and *every creeping thing* that creeps upon the earth after its kind, and *every fowl* after its kind; *every bird* of every sort. *THEY* went into the ark, to Noah; two and two of all [non-human] flesh, wherein is the breath of life. They that went in went in male and female of all [animal] flesh, *just as God had commanded Noah.* And the *LORD* shut him in (Genesis 7:13-16)."

"*Fifteen cubits* [more than twenty feet] upward the waters prevailed; so the mountains were covered. And all flesh died that moved upon the planet, both of fowl, and of cattle, and of beast, and of every creeping thing which creeps upon the earth, and *EVERY MAN: All in whose nostrils was the breath of life*, of all that was on the dry land, died. And every living thing was destroyed which was upon the face of the ground; both man and cattle, and the creeping things, and the fowls of heaven; they were all destroyed from the earth. And *Noah only remained alive, and those who were with him in the ark* (Genesis 7:20-23)." (Only Noah, family, and the animals!)

"And God commanded Noah: *'Go out of the ark, you, your wife, your sons, and your sons' wives, along with you. Bring with you also every living thing which is with you of all flesh: Fowl, cattle and every creeping thing that creeps upon earth; that they may breed abundantly in the earth, and be fruitful and multiply on the earth.* So Noah came out, with his sons, his wife, and his sons' wives with him. And, every beast and every creeping thing that creeps upon earth, and every fowl, after their kind, left the ark (Genesis 8:15-19)." (*No one else un-boarded the ark, for no one else had boarded the ark!*)

All of these passages are what I call "clincher-passages." *Each passage is DEFINITE PROOF that Murray was not only in great error in his theology, but was also outright dishonest in his doctrinal stance*—Proving the man was a *FRAUD!*

But, what I deem the *clincher-clincher Scripture passage, which proves beyond doubt that none of Cain's descendants survived the flood,* is Genesis 9:18-19—which plainly states: "The sons of *NOAH,* who departed the ark, were Shem, Ham and Japheth. *These were the three sons of NOAH. And, by THEM was the WHOLE EARTH REPOPULATED.*" Cain's kids were *OUTSIDE THE ARK* during the flood. *So ALL drowned! No Cain descendants survived to REPOPULATE THE EARTH!* Thus, *Kenites were not Cainites; but came from either Shem, Ham or Japheth. Arnold Murray's theology bites the dust!*

Actually, I need to post this *POSTSCRIPT* on the subject: *The Creator said He regretted making humankind in the first place.* Moreover, 2 Peter 2:5 tells us *Deity brought that flood upon the world of the ungodly. Well, if God flooded the entire planet, in order to destroy all the ungodly* (corrupt mankind), *why would Noah allow Satan's own offspring—descendants of Cain—to come aboard the ark? THEY* would definitely be *UNGODLY!* Or, *if Noah KNEW NOT they were onboard, how did they get away with being stowaways all that time?* They would have to eat! Arnold Murray-ism bites more dust!

The truth in this case is that Murray had the audacity to accuse the Almighty of being either a liar or a fool. Whereas the Scriptures I provided reveal that *ONLY* Noah, his family, and some of every species of the animal world boarded that ark, *Murray "ASSURED" us that some of Cain's descendants were on it too.* No Scripture even hints of the possibility that

Cain's descendants survived that flood. Thus, either Murray or the God of the universe lied. The Bible says in more than one place that *GOD CANNOT LIE*. Where does that leave Dr Arnold Murray? *In the devil's dishonest garbage heap!*

A second post script: If Cain had been Satan's offspring, why would the Creator plead with Cain, and encourage him to *"do well"* in his offerings to the Lord (Genesis 4:6-7)? How could Satan's offspring do anything good anyway? By giving Cain a second chance, God would be giving Satan a second opportunity to defile the rest of creation as earlier. No way!

The next monstrosity Dr Arnold Murray unleashed upon the church was his unfounded rejection of the teaching that the church will be raptured before the *Antichrist* appears on earth. On every one of the 20+ cds I waded through, Murray had something negative to say about all of us who believe in the *Pre-Tribulation Rapture* of the church. *It was not a mere difference of opinion, but an outright castigation of everybody who believes that established biblical reality.* In the previous chapter, I laid out *the Bible stance* on that issue. This is one of Dr Murray's dangling doctrines—it not being necessary to *ANY* of his other demonic teachings. I can see *NO* necessary connection; although *it seemed to be a bur under his saddle*, as one old saying goes. Somehow the devil sneaked that bur under the man's theological saddle. What a false foundation to build doctrine upon. *Dr Murray was a theological FRAUD!*

Whereas Michael Rood insists that Satan is the Hinderer of the Antichrist, which is a s-t-r-e-t-c-h of the imagination, *Murray went not that route, but did teach that the Antichrist will appear and establish his kingdom BEFORE Jesus Christ comes to earth in any capacity. Bypassing Scripture, thereby essentially eliminating it, in order to enable one to push one's own doctrine, is an evil but common violation of the Bible rule of NO PRIVATE INTERPRETATION OF SCRIPTURE. Dr Arnold Murray was one of the worst violators of that Bible rule.*

As evil as are the Murray lies I have already covered, the one that most obviously reveals that his theology is of Satan is his claim that *passages that teach eternal suffering in hell are mere figures of speech. No eternal suffering for anybody!*

I am not God, so I am not Murray's judge. But he having left this life some years ago, I figure the man has learned by now that he was deceived by the devil about there being *NO* hell-fire. *One way or another, he now knows that hell-fire is real, hot, and eternal.* Feel free to speculate on my meaning.

Whereas Paul only once wrote that the natural was first, then the spiritual, *blasting Murray's claim that human souls pre-existed, which prompted Murray to slyly imply that "Paul was just having a little fun there," insinuating that Paul was just kidding around in that passage,* many Scriptures teach clearly that there *IS* a current hell, in which many departed souls currently suffer. One word or one short phrase might indeed be considered a figure of speech. *But, when Scripture after Scripture, not only plainly states that such an existence exists, but also describes with clarity the sufferings of those in Hades—and even records some of the responses of those in Hades—there is no way all of those Scriptures can be only figures of speech.* That would violate the rules of speech.

So, let us look at many of those clear Scripture passages that Murray contended did not reflect reality, but were mere figures of speech. The primary passage he blasted was Luke 16:23-24: "In hell he [the rich man] lifted up his eyes, *being in torments*, and saw Abraham afar off, and Lazarus in his bosom [a safe haven]. Then [the rich man] cried out: 'Father Abraham, have mercy on me and send Lazarus that he may dip the tip of his finger in water and *COOL* my tongue: *For I am tormented in this flame.*'" That is much too descriptive to be a mere figure of speech. *Only Murray's deceived followers believe such nonsense.* Again, *one word or one phrase might be taken as a figure of speech, but not an extended essay.*

Matthew 8:12: "*The* [intended] *children of the kingdom* [of God—unbelieving Jews] *will be cast out into outer darkness. There will be* [literal] *weeping and gnashing of teeth* [pain]."

Matthew 13:42: "[The angels] *will cast* [all sinners] *into a furnace of fire. There will be wailing and gnashing of teeth.*" Repeated again in Matthew 13:49-50: "*At the end of the age, the angels will come forth, and sever the wicked from among the just, and will cast them into the furnace of fire. There will be wailing and gnashing of teeth.*" (Not imaginary, but real!)

Matthew 24:50-51: *"The Lord of that servant will come in a day when he LOOKS not for Him, and at an hour that he is not aware of, and will cut him asunder, and appoint him his portion with the hypocrites* [for, he has become one himself]. *There will be weeping and gnashing of teeth." (LITERALLY!)*

Matthew 25:30: "Cast the unprofitable servant into outer darkness. *There will be weeping and gnashing of teeth."* The same recurs repeatedly. *TOO MANY AND TOO CLEAR TO BE mere figures of speech.* And the greater proof is yet to come.

If Dr Arnold Murray was right, Jesus Christ was wrong. Mark 9:43-48: "If your hand offends you [causes you to sin] cut it off. It is better for you to enter into life maimed, than to have both hands and go to hell; *into the fire that will NOT be quenched* [Murray contended that the fires of hell will go out.]: *Where their worm will not die, and the fire will NOT be quenched.* If your foot offends you [causes you to sin], cut it off. For it is better for you to enter halt into life, than having two feet, and be cast into hell; *into the fire that never will be quenched*: Where their worm dies not, *and the fire* [of hell] *is not quenched.* And if your eye offends you, pluck it out. For, it is better to enter the heavenly Kingdom with only one eye, than having two eyes, and be cast into hell-fire: Where their worm dies not, and *the fire is not quenched."* The Savior was quoting Isaiah 66:24—*Which plainly teaches that in the New Earth, when human beings leave God's presence to go home,* "They will go and LOOK [in the Lake of Fire] *on the carcases of those who sinned against Me*: WHERE THEIR WORM DIES NOT, AND THE FIRE WILL NOT GO OUT. *And those sufferers will be an abhorring unto all* [natural] *flesh* [people forever]."

And not only did our Lord quote Scripture about the fire of hell being a *present reality, and perpetual in duration*; He Himself experienced the suffering of hell. Acts 2:24: "Whom God raised up, having loosed the *pains of death*: Because, *it was impossible for Him to be held by it."* Acts 2:27 is Peter's quote of Psalms 16:9-10; a prophecy of Christ: *"You will not leave My soul in hell, nor allow Your Holy One to* [experience] *corruption* [decay]." Acts 2:31: "He, seeing this before, spoke of the resurrection of Christ; that *HIS SOUL was not left in hell; nor did His flesh see* [experience] *corruption* [decay]."

*"The pains of death" could NOT have referred to suffering experienced by the Savior in His body as it lay in the GRAVE three days.* It had to describe the suffering of His soul down in Hades—just like Luke 16:19-31 revealed. One more Bible Proof that Murray's *NO-HELL* doctrine is an outright lie.

Dr Murray's *unreasonable reasoning* was this: Since God is a God of love, *He would not be inclined to have any of His CHILDREN burn in a fiery furnace forever. Not even the devil!* But, *not EVERY human being is a child of God; and certainly not the devil!* Both John 8:44 and 1 John 3:9-10 tell us that *Satan himself has spiritual children. They cannot be Satan's kids and God's kids simultaneously.* (Satan is their spiritual daddy, not their physical father.) Besides, Deity is not *ONLY* a God of *LOVE*, but *JUDGE* of creation. And, eternal hell-fire is His ultimate judgment. And, that fire is already burning!

Revelation 14:9-11: "And the third angel followed, saying with a loud voice: *'If anyone worships the beast* [Antichrist] *or his image, and receives his mark in his forehead, or in his hand, the same will drink of the wine of the WRATH of God, which is poured out without mixture* [dilution] *into the cup of His indignation; and he* [the violator] *will be tormented with fire and brimstone in the presence of the holy angels, and in the presence of the Lamb. And, the smoke of their TORMENT ascends up for ever and ever. And, they have no rest day or night, who worship the beast, and his image, and whosoever receives the mark of his name."* (Bible versus Dr Murray!)

Revelation 19:19-20: "I [John] saw the beast [Antichrist], and all of the kings of the earth, with their armies, gathered together to make war against Him, Who sat upon the horse, and against His army. *And the beast was caught, and along with him the false prophet who wrought miracles before him, with which he deceived those who had received the mark of the beast, and people who worshipped his image. These both were cast alive into a Lake of Fire, burning with brimstone."*

Revelation 20:10: "The devil who deceived them was cast into *the Lake of Fire and brimstone, where the beast and the false prophet are* [and have been for 1000 years], *and* [they] *will be tormented DAY AND NIGHT forever and ever."* Murray said they will burn up quick; then the fire will go out. (???)

Dr Arnold Murray so fiercely fighting biblical truth about rebels suffering for eternity in hell *strongly suggests that he had a secret fear of going to hell.* So if he could somehow rid his mind of Bible Truth on hell, he would rid himself of that fear. *The solution he supposedly found was to call that Bible Truth a figure of speech; which would remove the reality of it.* But look up "figure of speech" in an English dictionary, and see if you are convinced its definition agrees with his use of that phrase—applying it to his fear. "Figure of speech" does *NOT* do away with the reality of what it is a figure of. *Hell is real! People are in it now! And it will endure for all eternity!*

Murray also TACKLED the issue from this angle. *He tried to convince himself and others that the word destroy means to annihilate—to make something go out of existence; so that it exists no more. He said the eternal part of destruction was that one would just exist no longer. He would forever not be. Murray persuaded his followers to live right by warning them that: If they served the devil, rather than God, they would be annihilated. They would be incinerated in an INSTANT in the Lake of Fire; and then that fire would go out. He taught such in the face of multitudes of Scripture passages revealing the very opposite*—many more than the ones I have presented.

Now I invite you to think with me on this: If annihilation is the ultimate punishment for enjoying the pleasures of sin for a lifetime—Let us eat, drink, and be merry, for tomorrow we die—then what is so scary about being annihilated when life is all over? *You will have neither good nor bad memories; nor any ongoing unpleasant experiences.* So, even if you lie, steal, rape and murder, you will only have to suffer what all *OTHER* sinners will experience—annihilation. What a *WEAK* deterrent that would be to thieves, murderers, rapists, etc!

*You can be assured the devil wishes it were so! He would be overjoyed to know HIS punishment would be annihilation.* Revelation 12:12: "Woe to you inhabitants of earth, and sea. *The devil has come down to you, having great wrath because he knows he has only a short time* [before he is locked in the abyss for 1000 years, then is loosed for a little season, then will be cast into the Lake of Fire to burn for ever and ever]."

*Murray did find a passage in Jeremiah which supposedly solidified that no-eternal-suffering doctrine.* Jeremiah 51:39: "'In their heat I [God] will make their feasts, and I will make them drunken, that they may rejoice; then *sleep a perpetual sleep and not awake,*' says the LORD." The same is repeated in verse fifty-seven. "*Sleep a perpetual sleep and not awake*" is much closer to being a "*figure of speech*" than all of those passages that clearly confirm and describe eternal suffering in the Lake of Fire. The context of that chapter reveals that Deity was prophesying a swift demise of Babylon. He would help them get drunk (literally). Then, when they passed out, their enemies would come in and *kill them in their sleep;* so that they would not awake from their drunken state. That is all God meant in that statement. *It certainly does not negate all those passages which definitely teach eternal suffering in the Lake of Fire.* But to Murray, those two verses did negate all others; for they fit his doctrine, and the others did not.

Remember, *the prophecy was about Babylon,* and Daniel 5:30 records the fulfillment of it. Daniel chapter five tells us about King Belshazzar throwing a drinking party, and when he and his guests were drunk, *a hand appeared, and wrote a message of judgment on the wall.* And, it was "In that very night that Belshazzar, the King of the Chaldeans, *was slain* [obviously in his sleep]." But to Murray, those two Jeremiah passages which SEEMED to fit his doctrine, voided all those other passages that clearly teach ETERNAL suffering in hell.

That man's lies never ceased. *One more of his seemingly dangling doctrines is that the devil is "The Son of Perdition"; and that the term "perdition" was NEVER applied in the Bible to anyone, except the devil.* In Murray's attempt to prove the term had nothing to do with Judas Iscariot, he made claims that were truly outlandish. Let me show you what I mean.

In Strong's concordance, "perdition" *NEVER APPEARS in connection with the devil! It almost ALWAYS refers to people! That is a direct contradiction of Murray's argument.* Consider this passage. In His prayer to the Father in John 17:12, the Savior testified: "*While I was with THEM in the world, I kept THEM in Your name. THOSE You gave to Me I have kept, and not one of THEM is lost* [literally, perished] *except the son of perdition; that THE SCRIPTURE might be fulfilled.*" (Satan?)

146

*Murray claimed Ezekiel chapter twenty-eight prophesying the devil's FUTURE DEMISE was THE SCRIPTURE our Lord referred to when He spoke of the "son of perdition." However, it was JUDAS, one of the twelve, who had perished, NOT the devil. There was just ONE devil. But it was one of THEM who had perished.* Furthermore, "had perished" indicated a past event; not a future one. Now the perdition passages:

Philippians 1:28 encouraged the believers in Philippi: "In nothing be terrified by your adversaries: *Which is to them an evident token of* [their] *perdition...*" (People, not the devil.)

Second Thessalonians 2:3 says: "Let no man deceive you by any means [including the lies of Dr Arnold Murray]. For, that [Judgment] Day will not come about except there come first a falling away, then *that MAN of sin* [Antichrist] will be revealed, *The Son of Perdition.*" (Again a man, not the devil.)

First Timothy 6:9: "But, *they* [people] *who will* [to] *be rich fall into temptation, and a snare, and into many foolish, and hurtful lusts, which drown men in destruction and perdition.*" (Once again, *perdition* applies to *MEN*, not the devil!)

Hebrews 10:39: "*We are not of them who draw back unto perdition; but of them who believe to the saving of the soul.*" (One more passage connecting the word *perdition* to people.)

Second Peter 3:7: "But, *the heavens and the earth, which NOW EXIST, by the same word* [of God] *are kept in store and reserved unto fire against that day of judgment and perdition of ungodly men.*" (Ungodly men, not the devil—once again!)

Revelation 17:8: "The beast that you saw was, and [now] is not; and will ascend out of the bottomless pit, and go into *perdition.*" Satan will not ascend out of the bottomless pit. It will be one of the fallen angels, who ruled over a kingdom in the past—*Most likely the prince of Greece*—Daniel 10:20 and Revelation 17:10-11: "These [seven beasts, which John saw] are seven kings [actually, seven kingdoms]. Five have fallen, one is, and the other [seventh] has not yet come. And, when he comes, he will continue only a short time. And, the beast which was, and is not, even he is the eighth, and is *OF* the seven, and *goes into perdition* (Revelation 17:10-11)." This is an angel, but not the devil. Greece was one of the five fallen kingdoms. *Rome was the kingdom that then was.* The eighth will be the Antichrist's version of a previous kingdom.

147

*ONE OF THOSE WHOM GOD HAD GIVEN TO JESUS HAD PERISHED.* Those given were twelve apostles—not the devil! *And the one of the twelve who perished was Judas—a man, not the devil.* In Acts 1:16, Peter was reminded of a passage prophesying that *the office of a follower* would be given unto another; *REPLACING* the betrayer of the Messiah. Well, who was that betrayer? *JUDAS!* And the passage? Psalms 109:8. So, both Peter and Christ were evidently referring to *JUDAS*; and Psalms 109:8 was *THE SCRIPTURE* Christ was referring to; *NOT* Ezekiel twenty-eight, as Dr Arnold Murray claimed. *Did the devil perish? No! Was he replaced? No! Who perished and had to be replaced to fulfill Scripture? Judas! SETTLED!*

Murray sharply contended that the term *Son of Perdition* referred only to Satan, and never to a human being. He was obviously trying to get away from admitting that both Jesus and Peter were speaking of Judas and not the devil. *Murray even went so far as to claim that Judas did not hang himself.* The Jewish religious leaders hanged Judas; *for he had been converted (????), and might testify that Jesus had risen from the dead, and so had become a THREAT to them. Thus, they did away with Judas.* (??) (Matthew 27:3-5 *says that Judas hanged himself!*) Murray insisted that Acts 1:18, *saying that Judas fell, his body burst open, and his entrails gushed out, backs his claim that someone else hanged him; then hacked him to pieces.* However, *dead bodies decompose quickly; and Judas' rotten body having fallen loose from the noose, would have hit the ground and burst open. Reasonable explanation!*

We discovered from those Scriptures I presented that *Son of Perdition NEVER EVER refers to the devil, but is connected to people (with one angelic exception), the very opposite of Dr Murray's claims.* Will we believe Dr Murray or the Bible?

*The entirety of Dr Arnold Murray's theology is a big farce!* To confirm my exposure of Murray's heresies, blasphemies and utter stupidity, you will need to obtain some of his cds and listen to them for yourself. *I do not recommend that you wade through them; but if you are so inclined, click on Shepherd's Chapel on the internet.* The message on those cds you listen to should be the same as what I listened to. Just be sure you are not taken in by those lies.

According to Dr Arnold Murray, *our human souls existed from forever past, although we have NO MEMORY of our past existence.* (?) When God created Adam and Eve, *He put their pre-existing souls within their flesh bodies.* Sometime later, *the devil talked Eve into engaging in sex with him, resulting in the birth of Cain;* who was half-human, half-angel. *Satan having gotten his SEED* (Cain) *into the world, he would need to preserve his posterity, so Murray contended that when the flood of Noah came, at least some of Cain's offspring found a place on the ark, and therefore survived that universal flood.* Cain's descendants became known as *Kenites, who are still with us even today.* Kenites brought *communism* to Russia. (*He also claimed that the Russians are descendants of Esau,* whereas Jeremiah chapter forty-nine places them southeast of Palestine.) The *ten Northern Israelite tribes* were dispersed into Europe, *then migrated to these United States. According to Murray, then, Americans are both Jews and Kenites.* (???)

*Two vague verses in Jeremiah chapter fifty-one outweigh a dozen or more clear passages elsewhere, as to whether or not rebels will burn up quickly, or suffer for all eternity. Even Satan will be annihilated, NOT SUFFER FOREVER and ever; for God is a God of love, and therefore would not be so cruel as to punish His own children throughout eternity. For, even the worst of sinners—including the devil himself—are God's creatures—His own children.* Those are Murray's teachings; not Bible Truths. His entire theology is thoroughly satanic!

Interspersed throughout Dr Arnold Murray's *teachings* is his *HANGUP* over the *Pre-Tribulation Rapture* of the church. *Murray condemning everybody who believes and teaches the Pre-tribulation Rapture Bible Truth, he condemns multitudes.*

I have already explained the Bible Truth on the rapture, but let me reiterate this much: Jesus said plainly that *JUST as it was in the day Lot left Sodom, and just as it was in the days of Noah, when he, his family, and the animals boarded the ark, so will the Coming of the Son of Man be.* Well, those angels informed Lot that they could rain *NO* fire down until he was out of there; and *NO* wet stuff fell until Noah and his family were safe on the ark. Neither suffered the judgments.

*Christ comparing those TWO events to His Second Coming SETTLES the argument about whether or not THE CHURCH* (Symbolized by *LOT AND NOAH*) *WILL BE REMOVED FROM EARTH BEFORE THAT SEVEN-YEAR TRIBULATION BEGINS.* Second Thessalonians 2:7 also teaches that a present entity will hold back the Antichrist from appearing on earth—*Until that hindering entity is REMOVED from the earth. That entity cannot be the Gentiles, or the Jews, or human governments, or the Holy Spirit. And certainly not the devil.* So, it must be the church—*the only other entity capable of holding back the Antichrist. Indisputable Bible evidence settles all arguments.*

Connected to Dr Murray's denouncement of the *Rapture Theory*, as he named it, is his claim that that theory is part of the *mark of the beast* spoken of in Revelation 13:16-17. It is not an actual visible mark, he said, but rather a mind-set based upon believing in the rapture of the church. However, it makes *NO BIBLE SENSE* to say that the mark is not really a physical mark, but is instead a *theological mind-set*, when John said that mark will be either on the *FOREHEAD*, or on the *RIGHT HAND. HANDS HAVE NO MIND-SETS!* The details John provided prove Murray's claim to be the theory.

More *mind-set* theology: Murray insisted as well that *the pregnant women fleeing when Jerusalem comes under siege in the Tribulation will not literally be pregnant with child, but instead, will be mentally pregnant with confusion because of that rapture theory.* Murray was obviously the confused one. And his confusion affected his teachings on the *resurrection* of the physical body. That man messed with every pertinent Bible doctrine. He distorted everything. *He had no honesty!*

Murray claimed that our physical bodies will deteriorate in the grave, and therefore simply cease to exist. Who would want those rotten flesh bodies again anyway? Therefore, *our original flesh bodies will NOT be resurrected. When Paul said there is a natural body, and a spiritual body, he was talking about two different entities, rather than two forms of a single entity*—according to Murray's argument. Thus, *Murray either revealed GROSS ignorance of Bible Truth, or his animus—his deep-seated resentment and hostility—toward God's Word.*

In 1 Corinthians 15:42-49, speaking of the natural body, Paul said *IT* (our body) will be *sown in one condition*, and *IT* will be *raised in a totally different condition*. *IT* is sown; *IT* is raised. Paul gave no indication of exchange of one entity for another, but rather *the same entity entering into a different condition—A vastly improved condition! The word IT refers to the same body, not a different body.* Jesus told His disciples to observe the nail prints in His raised body. *SAME BODY!*

Moreover, *every Scripture that speaks of the resurrection plainly proves that what is being raised is the DEAD!* Murray attempted to throw us believers OFF TRACK by arguing that *dead bodies rot, stink and disintegrate; and therefore cannot be what God will raise up*. Rather, *it will be a spiritual body, that we ALREADY have, that will REPLACE our disintegrated flesh body!* But 1 Corinthians 15:54 says that *CORRUPTION* (*which even Murray would have to admit describes our flesh*) must *PUT ON incorruption. And the corruptible will TAKE ON an incorruptible condition. Mortal will BECOME immortal.*

A kindred Murray-error insists that the word mortal refers ONLY to the soul; NEVER to one's body. But in my studies, *I found the VERY opposite. The word mortal ALWAYS refers to the body, and NEVER to the soul!* Which means Murray was either *grossly ignorant*, or *deliberately dishonest*. It must be the latter, because he was dishonest in all of his theology.

For instance: *To hold to his anti-resurrection lies*, Murray totally distorted Daniel 12:2; which plainly says: "*Many who SLEEP IN THE DUST will awake, some to everlasting life and some to shame and everlasting contempt.*" The dust refers to the devil, *whom God condemned to crawl in the dust*, Murray said. *Sleeping in the dust means being deceived by the devil. Sleep is deception, and Satan is the dust eater*, said Murray: Claiming Daniel 12:2 *is not about the resurrection*. However, *not Satan, but the Eden serpent was a SNAKE. And snakes, NOT LUCIFER*, are *dust-eaters* (Genesis 3:14; Isaiah 65:25).

Daniel 12:2 actually destroys that and one other Murray lie. Not only does Daniel 12:2 talk about *actual resurrection, but proves as well that some will enter everlasting life, while others will face everlasting shame and contempt. If the life is EVERLASTING, the SHAME IS EVERLASTING!* He who exists no more would not be affected by shame. *Hell is forever!*

*One more Murray error*: The Bible teaches that there is a *second* death, meaning there must be a *first* death. The flaw in Murray's doctrine concerns *WHAT* the *first death* and the *second death* consist of. *He contends that the FIRST death is physical death, and the SECOND death is the annihilation of the soul at the end of the Millennium.* That overlooks the fact that *Paul repeatedly taught that as sinners we were already dead in sins and trespasses* (2 Corinthians 5:14, Ephesians 2:1, 5, Colossians 2:13). That has to do with our spirits, not our bodies. *Paul said the sinner's spirit is dead, although he or she is still alive physically.* So, *spiritual death must be the FIRST death.* Revelation 20:14 and 21:8 teach that *the Lake of Fire (which burns eternally) is the SECOND death.* Sinners will be resurrected, and *their reunited body and soul will be FOREVER TORMENTED in the Lake of Fire* (Matthew 10:28). *The Second Death, then, lasts for all eternity! The sinner who is still alive during this age can repent, and get saved, so can avoid that Second death.* Both Revelation 2:11 and 20:6 *say plainly that Christians will NOT be hurt by the Second Death. Murray maligned the resurrection like he did everything else. His theology is made up of non-explanatory explanations!*

Murray also reasoned: *When Jesus Christ told John there will be no more sorrow, pain, or death* (Revelation 21:4), *that had to mean nobody would be suffering in that Lake of Fire. Murray developed a keen ability to overlook or outright avoid those passages that exposed his erroneous position on many Bible subjects.* Revelation 21:4 obviously refers to the saints in the New Earth, because Revelation 21:8 says plainly that sinners will have their *PART* in that Lake of Fire. Revelation 22:15 also proves that *sinners will still exist.* Using the word *PART* suggests not immediate annihilation, but an assigned place. In Matthew 24:51, *Christ taught that the faithful who FALL AWAY will be assigned a PORTION with the hypocrites.* Isaiah 14:15 prophesies that *Lucifer will be brought down to the LOWEST pit.* Those words, *PART, PORTION* and *LOWEST* all point to a permanent location; *not immediate annihilation.* Matthew 8:29 agrees, for those demons pleaded with Christ: "Have you come to *TORMENT* us before the time?" Torment; not annihilate! Instant annihilation could not be counted as torment. *This also proves Dr Arnold Murray was a FRAUD!*

I could go *ON* and *ON*; and I think I will. However, I will not go into all of Murray's many errors, but will concentrate on the more inconsistent, stupid, and deadly of his heresies and blasphemies. Next is one of his more *stupid* ones.

Dr Murray taught on the 70 years spoken of in Jeremiah 25:12 and Daniel 9:2. However, Murray taught not that the 70 years referred to Israel back then and in these last days. Instead, he said they referred to the 70 years between 1917, when communists took over Russia, and 1987, the year the Berlin wall came down. *He said the 70 years were over, and that everything is going to be okay now.* (Okay for whom?)
*That within itself ought to be a red flag to Christians. For, even Christians must believe God, and obey His Word, to be okay during this age.* History is neither over nor okay!

*In Jeremiah and Daniel we find that those 70 years have to do with Jews, Jerusalem, and the Gentiles; both back then and in these end-times. This age did not end in 1987.* Where was Murray's mind? *How could he think he had authority to YANK Scripture passages, or parts of passages, out of their contexts, and make them say something totally different from the actual biblical wording?* Did he replace the Holy Spirit?
That brings up this problem: *If we cannot trust the literal biblical message for the TRUTH about God, Satan, the world, or the church, then we are at the mercy of people like Arnold Murray* (the devil's very mouthpiece) *to gain the truth.* Thus, the needed exposure of Murray's demonic lies by this book.

Concerning those seven churches of Revelation chapters two and three, *Murray said Jesus condemned five out of the seven; and would have no Christian to be a member of either of those congregations.* Of course, *Murray linked those Jesus called the synagogue of Satan with the Kenites, Cain's kids, who believe in the rapture.* In truth, *Christ condemned none of the seven churches, but did rebuke some of their practices that were less-than-godly.* Moreover, Jesus assured the last of the seven churches, which had the worst reputation, that *He rebukes and chastens those whom He LOVES. That truth blasts Murray's outright untruths. Murray seemed compelled at every turn to splice in his hatred of the rapture teaching.*

*Murray said Satan will become a MAN, and look just like JESUS, and we Rapture Theorists will worship SATAN as our Messiah.* But instead of there being two Messiah's, the Lord said there will be *MANY* claiming to be the Christ. Moreover, *Satan will not become a man. He will energize the Antichrist, who is a man, to deceive the multitudes. Murray himself was actually AN antichrist!* The apostle John said that in his days many antichrists were ALREADY present on the planet. So, it ought not be surprising that antichrists are on earth today.

A few other Murray inconsistencies: The 144,000 spoken of in Revelation 7:4-8 *will all be priests, Murray said.* Truth is, all twelve tribes will make up that 144,000, and of those twelve tribes, only the Levites are priests. Murray also failed to point out that the 144,000 will be Jews. *He said they are Christians*—part of the church, which he insists will still be here during that time. On top of all of that, Murray claimed that the 7,000 faithful men Paul said lived back in Elijah's day will instead be faithful Christians in the end-times. (??)

Murray also insisted that the chain which that one angel will use to bind the devil will not be literal, but symbolic. He also contended that the mark in the forehead of believers in the end-times will not be an observable body mark, but will instead be the Gospel truth in the minds of believers. (???)

The sea that gives up the dead (Revelation 20:13) will be the sea of people as in Revelation 13:1, Murray said. Not so! *It instead refers to the seven oceans in which countless dead bodies have been planted since death entered this world.*

Dr Arnold Murray left practically *NO* Scripture intact. *He perverted passage after passage in building HIS THEOLOGY.* Within this chapter, I have dealt with what I deem his most dangerous and stupid doctrines. *Rather than being the voice of God, as he claimed, Murray was the devil's mouthpiece!*

# Chapter Ten

## Bible Interpretation III

I thought Bible Interpretation would be one chapter, but as I proceeded, I realized the chapter was getting just a little long; so I started Bible Interpretation II, *which covers only a portion of the Shepherd's Chapel heresies.* And now, in order to do the subject justice I need to do Bible Interpretation III, because there are additional heresies out there that need to be exposed; *which proves once more that Bible interpretation is one of the devil's most favorite hiding-places.*

A big flaw in one other minister's theology, whose name I opt not to divulge, is that *when the Roman soldiers whipped Jesus, with each STRIPE they laid upon His body, His Father placed upon Jesus some disease, infirmity, sickness, or pain. The supposed thirty-nine stripes Christ bore at that whipping post supposedly match the supposed thirty-nine categories of sickness suffered by the human race.* Of course, that man is not the only one who teaches that unbiblical doctrine. Some others I respect also ignorantly preach that false theology.

I have personally met that *ELDERLY MINISTER*, one who is *well-educated in both Hebrew and Greek*, and has written Bible study books. Thus, that scholar should know from his *OWN* Bible studies that in both Hebrew and Greek the word translated *STRIPES* in both Isaiah 53:5 and 1 Peter 2:24 is *SINGULAR*; not plural. That word does mean stripe, wound, or bruise; but it is *SINGULAR; NOT PLURAL.* Big difference!

Let me enlighten you about that big difference. In Isaiah 53:10, we learn that *GOD* made Jesus Christ sick—literally, *"crushed Him with disease." Not man but God!* The only way man can make someone sick with disease is to contaminate them with germs or viruses. But, there are maladies that no human can contaminate others with—those not transmitted by germs or viruses. So how could the Roman soldiers place upon our Savior *ANY* such infirmities. Moreover, why would God need some human activity to make Jesus sick? Did He use men to put our sins upon Christ? Men had no access to either our sins or diseases. *So, men could put neither sin nor sickness on Jesus. Only His Heavenly Father could do that!*

*WHO* made our Lord sick? His Father! *WHERE* did Jesus bear our sicknesses and diseases? On the cross! *NOT* at the Roman whipping post. *That also answers the question about WHEN our Lord bore our infirmities: While hanging upon that cross; not before.* Galatians 3:13 states: *"Christ redeemed us FROM the curse of the law BY BECOMING A CURSE FOR US, for cursed is everyone who HANGS ON A TREE [cross]." The curse of the law included sickness, poverty and other painful conditions.* First Peter 2:24 tells us that Christ bore our sins and diseases *ON THE TREE*. Men did put stripes on Christ's body at the whipping post, but those actions had nothing to do with Jesus Christ bearing either our sins or sicknesses.

I have not discovered just when the word stripes (plural) was injected into the Isaiah 53:5 and 1 Peter 2:24 texts. *Nor why the translators of more recent translations felt compelled to continue that dishonest theological tradition. I can tell you why the devil maneuvered them to do so—to distort the Bible message so the readers would get a distorted understanding of Gospel Truth about DIVINE HEALING.* Stripes were laid on Jesus by men. Our diseases were placed upon Christ by the Father of Christ: *And that happened on the cross, not at the whipping post. Every portion of our salvation was purchased by what God did to Jesus Christ while He hung on the cross.* Men did nail our Lord to the cross, where He purchased our redemption, *but the redemption itself was WROUGHT by the activity of Almighty God*; not devil-controlled human beings! *Faith comes by hearing God's Word, not by distortions of His Word. Faith diminishes through human Bible interpretations.*

*I will name one popular preacher, because he deserves to be exposed and rebuked for his GROSS DISTORTIONS of the Bible message.* Just because he was the pastor of a famous church in England for many years, he could write a book on any Bible subject, and say anything in the book he wanted, and it would be published as Bible Truth; then devoured by multitudes of *gullible church members* all around the world. In 2004, R. T. Kendall wrote a blasphemous book, which he titled *"The Thorn In The Flesh."* Of course, it was supposedly based on Paul's thorn, mentioned in 2 Corinthians 12:7-10. However, the occasion for the writing was his wife's negative experience of a temporary physical ailment. From that base, the man expanded his erroneous discourse to blasphemous proportions. It is hard to believe that people actually believe what he wrote in that book—error from cover to cover.

To summarize his pack of lies: First, he contends that all of us have some kind of thorn in our flesh—in most cases a physical infirmity. *Not only did the apostle Paul have a thorn in his flesh, but every Christian either HAS a fleshly thorn, or at least OUGHT TO have one. Thorns are good for Christians. If we do not have a personal thorn making us miserable, we are missing out on a great blessing.* (R. T. Kendall theology!)

That man is quite obviously a Calvinist, which he proves by his *DEMONIC THEOLOGY* in his thorn-book. John Calvin suffered multiple infirmities most of his life, and taught that whatever comes our way we just have to suffer; *because if it were not GOD'S WILL, it would not have come our way.* Such an attitude persuades Christians to just lie down and let the devil walk all over them. However, *the Bible commands us to RESIST the devil* (1 Peter 5:8-9)! And sickness is of the devil! *"Our Lord went about healing all who were oppressed* [made sick] *by THE DEVIL* (Acts 10:38)." God commanded believers to resist sickness; not accept it as God's thorny will!

*Kendall said we ought to pray to be healed, BUT if we are not healed, God evidently wants us to stay sick; both for His glory and for our spiritual good.* (???) *Sicknesses He does not heal we must accept as our God-ordained flesh-thorns.* That man's pride is almost unbelievable! Brace yourself.

The most *unreasonable* part of R. T. Kendall's theology is his brash boast that HE PERSONALLY GUARANTEES that: *If we pray for deliverance from wheelchair confinement, or any other infirmity, and God does not heal us, WHEN WE STAND BEFORE GOD IN THE NEXT WORLD, WE WILL THANK GOD FOR NOT DELIVERING US FROM OUR FLESH-THORN.* (???) R. T. Kendall *GUARANTEES that we will actually thank God for our thorn-suffering during our earth-life.* What blasphemy by that famous preacher! *And how many Scripture passages did Kendall provide to back that theological farce? NOT ONE! Why? Because there are none! Who does he think he is?*

All of my Bible versions teach that *the prayer of faith will SAVE the sick* (James 5:14-16). Whereas, *God commands us to use our faith to RESIST THE CURSES Christ bore for us on the cross* (every kind of sickness and disease—Isaiah 53:5, Matthew 8:16-17, Galatians 3:13, 1 Peter 2:24—all poverty and lack—2 Corinthians 8:9, Galatians 3:13), R. T. Kendall teaches that we ought to *cave in to those curses, and accept as God's will for us the very CURSES our Savior delivered us from by His bearing them in our behalf upon the cross!* John Calvin taught the very same demonic lie to the church. And R. T. Kendall obviously accepted that Calvinist falsehood.

Kendall used the apostle Paul's account of a thorn in his flesh as a mere springboard into his *heretical* teaching on it. He honored neither Paul nor Scripture in his entire book on the thorn issue. For one thing, Kendall said Paul did not tell what *HIS* thorn was. Well, Paul *DID* describe what his thorn was. In 2 Corinthians 11:22-33, Paul listed many sufferings he bore because of his testimony for Christ. That list ranged from beatings to jail sentences; from shipwrecks to stoning; from hunger to exposure to the elements. *His thorn was the many persecutions and hardships he endured because of his miraculous and EFFECTIVE MINISTRY of filling the church up with Gentile believers! The devil sent one of the fallen angels to harass Paul at every turn.* In fact, *Paul said his thorn was a messenger of Satan to buffet him.* So, Paul did identify his thorn; regardless of what R. T. Kendall or anybody else says about it. *If they can convince themselves and others that we cannot really know what Paul's thorn was, that leaves them wiggle-room to speculate and teach their theological garbage.*

Denying Bible information that Paul provided about that *THORN IN HIS FLESH, Kendall and many other theologians and preachers have speculated many kinds of ailments Paul never mentioned as his thorn in the flesh.* That way they can teach believers that any of those things could be their thorn in their flesh. *It is a control-theology based on fear.* And, it is founded upon *NO* Scripture; but upon *demonic* speculation.

Actually, the apostle Paul identified not only *the source of that flesh-thorn*—the devil; not God—*he also bore witness to the PURPOSE of the thorn. Paul had been caught up to the third heaven, where he saw things that earthlings would not understand. He received freedom-giving truths from the Lord, and then TAUGHT them to the church* (Acts 26:16-18). *Satan tried to put a stop to Paul's ministry through persecution. The thorn,* then, *was the devil's idea; not God's.* That messenger of Satan, a fallen angel, tried to put so much *PRESSURE* on Paul that he would *forsake his ministry and go home.* Satan, however, *underestimated* Paul's commitment to the Gospel; and *overestimated* the potential of his evil plan to stop Paul.

Paul plainly stated that *the thorn was given him because of those visions, and that heavenly trip* (2 Corinthians 12:7). Did R. T. Kendall have heavenly visions? *Have any readers of his book been caught up to the third heaven?* How can any person claim to need a flesh-thorn for the very same reason Paul had one? Moreover, *if Paul's thorn was persecution, not sickness or disease, then how come modern flesh-thorns are almost always physical ailments? The devil has to be behind such degrading and suffering theology!* You ought to obtain my book titled "*Christian Suffering?*". And read it, of course. Many believers suffer many unnecessary hardships. *And so much of that is accepted as God's will because of the FALSE teachings of theologians and preachers such as John Calvin, R. T. Kendall, Arnold Murray and many others.*

*What causes Bible teachers to fall into satanic deception?* I am endeavoring to help as many people as I can to get out from under such *demonic influences.* The Bible tells us how: *STUDY* to be approved by God (2 Timothy 2:15); because, *all Bible Scripture is God-breathed, and therefore, profitable for doctrine, reproof, correction, and instruction in righteousness* (2 Timothy 3:16). How dare anybody take a man's word over the Bible about anything? *We will be judged by God's Word, not by man's interpretation of God's Word* (John 12:47-50)!

I am sure there are many other *DANGEROUS HERESIES*, both in the world and in the church. But, I cannot deal with them all. Yet, *what you LEARN from the lessons in this book will help you detect such errors, plus enable you to avoid the heartaches accompanying all satanic lies.* It will certainly be worth the effort on your part. This book should be a keeper. Refer to it as often as necessary. *Truth does not get old!*

Heretics do not realize the tremendous danger they draw to themselves by teaching their demonic doctrines; let alone the incalculable damage they cause others who fall for their deceptions. Consider the following scriptural warnings:
"As also in all of his [Paul's] epistles, speaking in them of these things; *in which there are some things that are hard to understand, which unlearned and UNSTABLE people WREST [TWIST], as they do also the other Scriptures TO THIER OWN DESTRUCTION* (2 Peter 3:16)." TAMPERING *with God's Word CURSES both the tamperers, and their blind followers. Also, the farther down that road they travel, the WORSE their final judgment will be.* Romans 2:5 says that *people who continue to harden their hearts, and continue in their rebellion, STORE UP FOR THEMSELVES WRATH, that will be meted out on the day of wrath. They deceive themselves into thinking they are getting away with their rebellion, whereas they are actually making their final judgment EVEN MORE UNBEARABLE.*

God simply will not tolerate *ANY* private interpretation of Scripture (2 Peter 1:20-21). *That means many preachers are in trouble.* That includes current theologians, preachers and teachers; and all of those throughout history who have been so foolish as to try to *ALTER THE BIBLE* in their own minds, as well as in the minds of their foolish followers. Ephesians 5:11 commands believers to have *NO* fellowship with works of darkness (*such as private Bible interpretation*), but rather, to expose such works: Exactly what I am doing in this book. Please join me in this godly endeavor. Thank you!

# Chapter Eleven

## Money

While few would be surprised that the devil hides behind earth's money systems, *most are likely unaware of the many ways he uses that power to accomplish his dirty deeds*. I am sure you have heard the term *dirty money*. But what makes money dirty? Is *ALL* money dirty? We will allow Scripture to validly answer both of those valid questions. But now this:

First of all, *money has a lot of power in the earthly realm, and Satan is always on the prowl for whatever has power he can use to his advantage*. You see, *no matter your character, money has the same purchasing power*. Money may be used for *good* purposes, and *not-so-good* purposes. But one thing is certain: *Not everything good may be obtained with money*; despite what King Solomon said in Ecclesiastes 10:19. Most English versions translate Solomon's words in that passage: "Money answers everything." I do not know if King Solomon was mocking others who thought so, or, if Solomon himself, in his fallen state, came to believe that lie. But it is certainly *NOT* true; if the rest of the Bible *IS* true. *Money has limits!*

Consider this *three-pronged lesson* that will answer many questions, and dispel much confusion. In respect to money: First ask yourself *WHY* you are going after money; secondly, *WHAT MEANS* will you use to get money; and thirdly, what do you plan to *USE* money for after getting hold of it. Those honest questions demand honest answers. So keep reading.

*Let us consider the different ways the devil HIDES behind that great necessity called money.* Matthew, Mark and Luke all record our Lord's words about *the deceitfulness of riches* (Matthew 13:22, Mark 4:18-19, Luke 8:14). Consider Mark 4:18-19: "These are people [*in whom Gospel Word seeds are*] sown among thorns: Such as hear the Word, then the cares [worries] of this world, and *the deceitfulness of riches* [what they are persuaded money can buy for them], plus the lusts of other things, entering in, choke the Word, and it becomes unfruitful." *Just like weeds and other non-productive plants take moisture and nutrients from productive seeds, so do lies about money deprive Word-hearers of nutrients they need for Gospel productivity in their lives. Word-seeds planted in their hearts get trashed, and so do their lives. Many remain lost!*

One reason riches are deceitful is that they are uncertain. For one thing, money cannot relieve people of every problem they have. *Money being from the lower earth realm, it cannot solve problems originating in the spirit realm.* Money may be used for trading stuff and services, but money cannot touch one's inner self—where many problems have their origin.

Moreover, money may be here today and gone tomorrow. *Money can provide no REAL security, for money itself has no security.* It cannot guarantee its own perpetuity! We will see that truth in upcoming Scriptures. And here is one of them:

First Timothy 6:17-19: "*Charge those* [believers] *who are rich* [have a lot of money] *in this world* [age], *that they be not high-minded, nor trust in uncertain riches,* but in The Living God, Who gives us richly all things to enjoy. [But,] that they do good; that they be rich in [performing] good works; ready to distribute [some of their money, and not hoard it]; willing to communicate [share]. Laying up in store for themselves a good foundation against the time to come, so that they may lay hold on eternal life [instead of accumulating money]."

*Because cash is so vulnerable*: "Lay not up for yourselves treasures on earth, *where moth and rust corrupt and thieves break through and steal. But, lay up for yourselves treasures in heaven, where NEITHER moth nor rust corrupt, and where thieves DO NOT break in and steal* [because they cannot get to what you have stored in heaven]. For where your treasure is, there will your heart be also (Matthew 6:19-21)."

The bottom line is: "No man can serve two masters...*You cannot serve both God and mammon* (Matthew 6:24)." Thus, *money-grubbers are NOT God-worshippers*. However, money is a necessity on this planet, and *there are legitimate uses of money*; and God demands that we Christians use money for those legitimate needs. Paul wrote in 1 Timothy 5:8: "*If any provide not for his own, and especially for those of HIS OWN HOUSE, he has denied the faith and is worse than an infidel* [unbeliever]." Wow! If such were not possible, then Paul was wasting his breath, and his paper and ink. Some Christians (at least some church members) treat people, even members of their own household, worse than the world treats them.

The bottom line, one more time: *The purpose of money is to meet the needs of human beings.* Money is *NOT* printed to be hoarded. Stored away for long periods of time, it mildews and rots. *And if thieves find out where you have your money stored on earth, they will make plans to un-store it for you!*

Luke 12:16-21: "Jesus spoke a parable to them, saying: 'The ground of a certain rich man brought forth plentifully. And he thought within himself: "*What will I do, for I have no room where to bestow my goods?*" He decided: "This is what I will do: I will pull down my barns, then build greater ones; and there *I WILL STORE* all my fruits and goods. Then, I will say to my soul [myself]: 'Soul, you have many goods, laid up for many years; take your *EASE*, eat, drink, and be merry.'" But God said to him: 'You *FOOL*, this night your soul will be required of you. Then whose will those things be, which you have provided?' So is he who lays up treasures for himself, and is not rich [in his use of those treasures] toward God."

Thus, *money is NOT to be used for personal consumption alone; using it all for one's own needs and desires*—although *that is a valid use of it*—but also to honor God, Who blesses us with money, *by sharing its buying power with people who cannot meet their own needs*—Giving to the *GENUINE POOR AND NEEDY*; both in our own family, and out in the world.

But, I must make a *distinction* between the genuine poor and con-artists—those who make their living (and a copious one too) by begging and scamming. We are not to waste the cash God has given us by putting it right back into Satan's hands—that is, the con-artist's hands. A thief is a thief!

John 10:10: *"The thief* [Satan] *comes not except to steal, kill and destroy. But I,* [Jesus Christ,] *came that they might have life, and have it more ABUNDANTLY." POVERTY IS NOT ABUNDANT LIFE; NOR IS SICKNESS! Jesus came to bring us material and financial prosperity, as well as abundant life in both our SPIRITS and our BODIES.* The Lord became poor on the cross, so that we might become rich (2 Corinthians 8:9, 3 John 2). *The POVERTY He suffered on the cross bought us material and financial PROSPERITY.* (Also see 1 Peter 2:24.)

*How does the devil use money as a hiding-place?* For one thing, *he clouds people's perceptions about both the purpose of money, and the right and wrong ways of obtaining money.* Worst of all, *letting money be one's god.* Remember Matthew 6:24. *Today, money is the master of most human beings.*

God created the *supply* of man's needs before He created man (Genesis 1:3-31). Therefore, God knows human beings *NEED* material things (Matthew 6:32). Satan knowing it too, our needs become one of his hiding-places. Remember that Satan played on our Savior's need for food, in tempting Him to turn a stone into bread, in order to supply that need. *The devil takes advantage of our need for material things, and/or the money which buys those things that supply those needs.* He uses material and financial pressure to control people.

One of the 7 churches in Asia had succumbed to Satan's temptation to give money a place in their lives that it should not have. And so doing, they had become lukewarm in their faith-walk—*proving the truth of Jesus' words that one cannot serve both God and mammon* (money and stuff money buys) *simultaneously* (Matthew 6:24). *"Because you are lukewarm, and are neither cold nor hot, I will spue* [vomit] *you out of My mouth* [not confess you before God and His angels—Matthew 10:32-33 and Luke 12:8-9]. *Because you say: 'I am rich and increased with goods, and have need of nothing'; and know not that you are* [in reality] *wretched, miserable, poor, blind, and naked* (Revelation 3:16-17)." Those believers had fallen for the temptation *to place a VALUE on money that was both deceptive and destructive. They let money become a WEDGE between them and Christ*; occasioning that stern rebuke.

The Lord did not order them to burn or throw away their money, but rather to adjust their evaluation of it. Instead of their trusting in the *false security of money,* He told them to go for the true riches: "I counsel you to buy of Me [spiritual] gold tried in the fire, that you may be [truly] rich; and white [spiritual] raiment, that you may be clothed [properly on the inside], so the shame of your [spiritual] nakedness does not appear; and anoint your eyes with [spiritual] eye-salve, that you may see [as God sees, with spiritual eyes]. As many as I love I rebuke and chasten. Be zealous, therefore, and repent (Revelation 3:18-19)." *Money cannot provide spiritual riches!*

That Bible principle is plainly spelled out for us by Paul: "*Godliness with contentment* [peace of mind] is *GREAT GAIN* [Money CANNOT buy contentment!]. *For, we brought nothing into this world* [when we were born], *and it is certain we can carry nothing out* [when we die]. [*And, since we can use only so many things while we are here,*] *having food and raiment, let us be therewith content.* But those who will to be rich will fall into temptation, and a snare, and into many foolish and hurtful lusts; *which drown men in destruction and perdition: BECAUSE, THE LOVE OF MONEY IS THE ROOT OF ALL EVIL* [not money in itself]. *Some having coveted after money have STRAYED FROM THE FAITH and pierced themselves through with many sorrows* (1 Timothy 6:6-10)." Thus we Christians *MUST* properly prioritize our financial priorities.

It is not that Deity wants to deprive us of the purchasing power of money. *He just does not want Satan to be in control of our attitude toward money; or our means of getting money; or our use of money after we get it.* In fact, on the cross, our Savior provided a godly way to gain cash. "*For you know the GRACE of our Lord Jesus Christ,* that, *although He was rich, yet for your sakes He became poor, so that you, through His poverty, might be rich.* So herein I [Paul] give my advice: For, this is *PROFITABLE FOR YOU* who began before, not only to do, but also to be forward a year ago. *Now therefore perform the doing of it;* so that, as there was a readiness to will it, so there may be a performance also out of that [money], which you have. For if there be *FIRST* a willing mind, it is accepted according to what a man *HAS;* not according to what he has not (2 Corinthians 8:9-12)." *God multiplies money-seeds!*

In 2 Corinthians chapters eight and nine, *Paul speaks of money, not spiritual riches; as biased theologians teach, and deceived and deceiving preachers preach. Jesus bore on that cross what Deity does NOT want us to bear! Poverty is one of the CURSES brought upon humanity by Adam's sin* (Genesis 3:17-19, Deuteronomy 28:47-48, Galatians 3:13, etc., etc.): *FROM which Jesus Christ DELIVERED us by His sacrifice on the cross. And Paul taught that the way we believers release God to release those cross-bought riches our way is to GIVE.*

However, we also have to give with the right attitude, not with wrong motives. "Peter said to Ananias: *'why has Satan filled your heart to LIE to the Holy Ghost, and keep back part of the price of the land* (Acts 5:3)?'" Ananias tried to give the impression he had given the *TOTAL* amount he had received from the sale of some land. *But he did NOT give all of it; and that deceptive act proved that he was still trusting in money, and not in God—Who promised in His Word to meet all of his needs* (Proverbs 19:17, Matthew 6:33 and Philippians 4:19). Ananias lied about it, which was his crime against the Holy Spirit, and the church. *The man did not have to give all of it; nor any of it.* He evidently wanted to gain a REPUTATION *for being a generous giver*, like other believers during that time, but was not willing to give as freely as the others had. Mark 12:41-44 tells about the poor widow's giving, and the Lord's *POSITIVE* comment about her giving. Also see Luke 21:1-4.

Probably, the paramount passage dealing *IN DEPTH* with the *trusting-in-money-rather-than-trusting-in-God* subject is Luke 18:22-25: "But, when Jesus heard these things [which the rich young ruler had said], He said to him: 'Yet you lack one thing. Sell all that you have, then distribute to the poor, and you will have treasure in heaven. Then come follow Me.' And when he heard that, he was very sorrowful. For, he was very rich. And when Jesus saw the man was very sorrowful, He said: *'How hardly will they who have riches enter into the Kingdom of God!* For, it is easier for a camel to go through a needle's eye than for a *RICH MAN* to enter into the Kingdom of God.'" A real camel and a real needle! His disciples lost it. Luke 18:26: "And those who heard it said: *'Who then can be saved?'*" Their comment proves they were not dirt-poor!

So, the Lord explained: *"Those things that are impossible with men are possible with God.* [Salvation is a supernatural commodity. And responding to the Lord's words to that rich man,] Peter said: 'Behold, *we have left all and followed You.'* [Jesus answered back:] 'Truly,' I say to you, *'No man has left his house, parents, brothers, wife, or children, for the sake of God's Kingdom, who will not receive manifold MORE* [except for wives] *in the present time,* and life-everlasting in the next world (Luke 18:27-30).'" Sacrificing unto God and the needy pays off. Withholding from either costs in the long run.

Remember that foolish farmer Luke 12 told us about. He was not rich toward God or his poor neighbors. Neither was that rich man in Luke 16. "There was *a certain rich man* [So this was *NOT* a fictional character, but a real person.], who was clothed in purple and fine linen [the best of everything], and *LIVED sumptuously* every day: And, there was *a certain beggar* named Lazarus, who was laid at the rich man's gate, [being] full of sores; just desiring to be fed with crumbs that fell from the rich man's table [*but obviously did not get any*]. Rather, *dogs came up and licked his sores* (Luke 16:19-21)." Eventually, that poor, sick, starving man died. But not long after that the rich man died as well. Therefore, *riches are no guarantee of long life!* The secret to a long and blessed life is revealed in Psalms 91. *Money cannot give life, for money has no life!* Money is manufactured by man, and man is not the source of life. *Life comes from the Living God.* That rich man not only forfeited a long, truly blessed earth-life, but landed himself in hell as well. Thus, once again we see a scriptural example of how the misunderstanding and misuse of money is detrimental to all parties involved—Lazarus and the rich man. *Oh, the deceitfulness of riches!* And, we know the devil is behind all deceit. An additional significant passage:

"*If therefore you have not been faithful in the unrighteous mammon* [money and things wrongly used], *who will commit to your trust the TRUE riches* [risking your misuse of them as well]? *And, if you have not been faithful in what belongs to some other man, who will give you that which is* [to become] *your own? No servant can serve TWO* [opposing] *masters* [at the same time]. *Either he will HATE one and LOVE the other; or else, he will hold to one and despise the other.* [Thus,] *you CANNOT serve BOTH God and mammon* (Luke 16:11-13)."

One Old Testament case of falling for the *deceitfulness of riches*: After the prophet Elisha refused payment for healing the Syrian officer, Naaman, of leprosy, the young servant of Elisha, Gehazi, decided that the man's deliverance ought to cost him something, so he set out after Naaman and caught up with him and told him that the prophet had changed his mind, and wanted some money after all. "And Naaman said: 'Be content; *take two talents.*' *And he urged him, and bound two talents of silver, in two bags, along with two changes of garments, and laid them on two of his* [Naaman's] *servants; and they bare them before Gehazi. And when he came to the tower, he took them from their hand* [before coming to where Elisha was, so Elisha should never know about his actions], *and bestowed* [the goods] *in that house.* Then he let the men go, and they departed. Then he went in and stood before his master, Elisha. Elisha said unto Gehazi: 'Whence came you, Gehazi?' And he said: 'Your servant went nowhere.' Then he [Elisha] said to him: '*Went not my heart with you, when that man* [Naaman] *turned around in his chariot to greet you?* Is this the time [for you by means of shady shenanigans] to go after money, garments, olive-yards, vineyards, sheep, oxen, menservants and maidservants? *The leprosy of Naaman will CLEAVE to you and your seed forever.*' And Gehazi went out from Elisha a leper; as white as snow (2 Kings 5:23-27)." *Oh the deceitfulness of riches!* Gehazi haphazardly TRADED his health for money, which cannot buy health. *It can purchase all kinds of medical help; just not health. Medical services do not guarantee health! People can die of disease with a pocket full of money. Or, starve to death with a pocket full of money. God wants us to have both money and health!* His will for us in that regard was recorded in 3 John 2, where John wrote: "I pray that you *prosper,* and *be in health,* even *as your soul prospers.*" And John wrote that by Holy-Spirit Inspiration!

The reverse: "*Because you served not the LORD your God with joyfulness, and gladness of heart, for the abundance of all things* [He divinely provided], *you will serve your enemies which the LORD will send against you, in hunger, and thirst, and nakedness, and in the lack of all things. And He will put a yoke of iron on your* [stiff] *neck, until He has destroyed you* (Deuteronomy 28:47-48)." *Poverty for rejecting prosperity!*

*One of the many falsehoods regarding money is that God does NOT want us to have MONEY—or at least, not a lot of it. The supposed reason: It automatically draws us away from Deity. But, if money keeps people from serving God, why did God make Abram VERY RICH (Genesis 13:2)? Moreover, why did God call Abraham His friend (Isaiah 41:8, James 2:23)? Religious traditions are outright lies, designed by the devil to keep us Christians poor, sick, confused, and depressed. The DECEITFULNESS OF RELIGION lies about money; giving the devil a most convenient hiding-place in many churches—One more weapon our enemy uses to steal from, kill, and destroy believers and their families. It is time to expose and eliminate that satanic hiding-place—One purpose of this unique book.*

You may have heard the complaint: *"He has just a nickel too many!"* What does that mean? How many nickels are too many? Of course, it is not about nickels anyway. It is MERE jealousy. *"He has more nickels* (dollars or stuff) *than I have, and therefore I am envious of him and his stuff."* "Keeping up with the Joneses" is one more way the practice is articulated. Thus, money takes on a *function* it was never meant to have in society. *And Satan is behind all deceitful functions.*

One of many deceptions regarding riches: Money being a necessity, how can going after money be evil; no matter how one gets it? Well, *DESTROYING YOURSELF AND OTHERS in your pursuit of money defeats the purpose of having money!* Ruining your health by working three jobs is asinine. In the process of *adding to* your wealth, you *subtract* your health. Moreover, damaging others in your pursuit of money invites divine judgment. Actually, *losing your health in the ungodly pursuit of financial gain is judgment you bring upon yourself.* Money-grubbers are NOT that smart! Look at Luke 12:20-21; then carefully ponder its message regarding money.

Let us consider some Bible examples of *HOW* money has been misused. Matthew 28:12-15 is a prime example: "They gave a lot of money to the soldiers [*bribing them to say:*] 'His disciples came by night, and stole him away while we slept.' If Pilate hears of this, we will persuade him and secure you. *So they took the* [bribe] *money, and did as they were told."*

Isaiah 56:10-11 is another: "[God's] watchmen are blind: They [Israel's religious leaders] are all ignorant. They are all dumb dogs that cannot bark; sleeping, lying down, loving to slumber. They are *GREEDY* dogs, which never have enough. *They are shepherds that cannot understand. They all look to their own way* [making up their own idea of ministry]; *every one for his gain* [using ministry as a means of personal gain, rather than helping people], *from his own quarter* [territory; keeping all other preachers away from those who financially support him]." *Still happening in some churches today!*

Paul warned against such attitudes and practices among church leaders, commanding: "A bishop must be blameless [blamelessness consisting of being] the husband of only one wife [being a monogamist, not a polygamist], vigilant, sober, of good behavior, given to hospitality [opening your house to visitors], and apt to teach. Not given to wine, no striker, *not greedy of filthy lucre* [dishonest gain], patient, not a brawler, *not covetous* (1 Timothy 3:2-3)." "Likewise must the deacons be honorable, not double-tongued, not given to much wine, *not greedy of filthy lucre* [money gained by unsavory means] (1 Timothy 3:8)." *Covetousness must have been a problem in the churches*, or Paul would not have mentioned it so much. And Satan uses the same temptation in every generation.

*Another money deception*: "When Simon the sorcerer saw that by the laying on of the apostles' hands, the Holy Ghost was given, *he offered them money,* saying: 'Give me also this power, so that on whomever I lay *MY* hands, he may receive the Holy Ghost.' But, Peter said to him: 'Your money perish with you, because you thought that the gift of God could be purchased with money. You have neither part nor lot in this matter [word]. *Your heart IS NOT RIGHT in the sight of God.* Repent therefore, of your wickedness, and pray unto God, if perhaps the *thought of your heart* may be forgiven you. For I perceive that you are yet in the gall of bitterness, and in the bond of iniquity [although Simon himself had believed (Acts 8:13) and had been baptized] (Acts 8:18-23).'" *DIVINE GIFTS* cannot be bought with money. *Simon tried to use the power of money from this lower realm to purchase a gift which may be received ONLY from above* (the spirit realm) *by faith.*

Still another misuse of money is to *MAKE IT* off of things promoting devil-worship. "A certain man named Demetrius, a silversmith, *who made silver shrines for Diana, brought no small gain unto the craftsmen*: Whom he called together with *the workmen of like occupation,* saying: 'Sirs, you know that *by this craft we have our wealth* (Acts 19:24-25).'" *That craft served the devil's EVIL purposes by manufacturing idols that kept the worshippers BLIND to the truth about the True God, Who MADE all things, including the silver those shrines were made from.* Metal images did not create the universe!

"Woe unto them! For they have gone in the way of Cain, and have run *greedily* after the error of Balaam, *for reward,* and perished in the gainsaying of Core (Jude 11)." Woe unto those who pursue money in the WRONG WAYS, and for the WRONG REASONS! The Bible cure for that selfish practice:

"Let him who stole [before he became a believer] steal no more: But rather, let him labor, *working with his hands that thing which is good, so he may have something to give to him who is in need* (Ephesians 4:28)." See the difference? *People who have been born again, and have become NEW creatures in Christ, stop living as heartless getters, and become loving givers.* For, "God loves a cheerful giver (2 Corinthians 9:7)."

In fact, *true believers want to help others just as much as they want to help themselves.* Paul testified that he was: "As poor, yet making many others rich [through the Gospel]; as having nothing, and yet possessing all things (2 Corinthians 6:10)." Paul knew who he was and what he had in the Lord Jesus Christ, *and he assured others through the Gospel that they could have the same* (as proven in the next passage).

"Brethren, *we would have you to know about the grace of God bestowed on the churches of Macedonia: In a great trial of affliction, by the abundance of their joy and OUT OF DEEP poverty, they abounded to the riches of liberality.* For to their power, I bear record, yes, and even *beyond their power, they were willing of themselves; praying us with much entreaty to receive their* [financial] *gift, and take upon us the fellowship of ministering to those POOR saints* [who lived in Jerusalem] (2 Corinthians 8:1-4)." *The possessions of Jewish Christians in Jerusalem HAD BEEN CONFISCATED by religious leaders,* and Macedonian believers wanted to help them financially.

Early on, *some women, whom Jesus had helped, wanted to help Him help others, and so contributed financially to His ministry.* "Certain women, *who had been healed by Jesus of evil spirits and other infirmities*, one called Mary Magdalene, out of whom went seven demons, and others also, *provided for Him out of their* [financial] *substance* (Luke 8:2-3)."

And one other positive case: "You Philippians know also, that, in the beginning of the Gospel, when I [Paul] departed from Macedonia, *no church communicated* [shared] *with me as concerning giving and receiving*, but you only. For even in Thessalonica, you sent once and again to my necessity. Not because I desire a gift: But I desire fruit that may abound to your [financial] account [with God]. I have all and abound. I am full, *having received by Epaphroditus those things which were sent from you*; an odor of a sweet smell, and a sacrifice acceptable, well-pleasing to God. *And my God will supply all of your needs according to His riches in glory by Christ Jesus* (Philippians 4:15-19)." Divine sowing-and-reaping principle!

Faith has its riches: "By faith, Moses, when he had come to years, refused to be called the son of Pharaoh's daughter; *choosing rather to suffer affliction with God's people, than to enjoy the pleasures of sin, for a season. Moses esteemed the reproach of Christ greater riches than the treasures in Egypt: For he had respect to the recompence of the reward* (Hebrews 11:24-26)." Money is temporary. Faith-rewards are eternal.

"Come on you rich men, *weep and howl for your miseries that will come upon you. Your riches are corrupted, and your garments are moth-eaten. Your gold and silver are cankered; and the rust of them will be a witness against you, and will eat your flesh as it were fire.* You have heaped up treasures for the last days. Behold, *the hire of the laborers who reaped your fields, which you have kept back by FRAUD, cries. And, the cries of those who have reaped have entered the ears of the Lord of sabaoth. You have lived in pleasure on this earth, and have basked in luxury, and fattened your hearts as in a day of slaughter. You have* [even] *condemned, and killed, the just* [for money]; *and he does not resist you* (James 5:1-6)." I think all of this is enough to persuade the persuadable.

# Chapter Twelve

## Sex

Of course the devil uses sex to destroy people, but where is the deception? How can he hide behind the God-ordained sex-drive? *SEX DRIVE! Human feelings do not detect what is moral or immoral.* Feelings merely know what feels good and what feels bad. *So those who have no spiritual morals easily fall into the devil's SEX-TRAP. How can something that feels so good be bad?* I think those very words were in some song written decades ago. However, *not everything that feels good turns out to be good. There is a way that seems right to man, but it ends in death* (Proverbs 14:12 and 16:25). That has to include certain sex attitudes, as well as certain sex acts.

*The book of Proverbs has a LOT to say on the sex-subject.* For starters: *"A whore is a deep ditch; and a strange woman is a narrow pit (Proverbs 23:27)."* The warning is *NOT* about legitimate sex within a marriage, but *going outside marriage to enjoy the experience in a way the Creator never intended.* God has provided *adequate instructions* regarding sex in His Word—The Holy Scriptures. And, for this purpose:

*"To deliver you from the STRANGE WOMAN* [a woman not your spouse]; *from the stranger, who flatters with her words: Who FORSAKES the guide* [the godly instructor] *of her youth* [as well as her own husband; her protector], and forgets the covenant of her God. [Thus, marriage is a covenant between the husband, wife and Deity.] *Her house inclines unto death;*

*and her paths* [lead guys] *unto the dead. NONE who go unto her return again* [They lose their innocence.]; *neither do they take hold of the paths of life* [but death] (Proverbs 2:16-19)." Proving that: "*He who commits adultery* [has illicit sex] *with a woman lacks understanding: He who does so destroys his own soul* (Proverbs 6:32)." One cannot MIS-understand that!

*This more detailed warning:* "The lips of a strange woman drop as a honeycomb, and her mouth is smoother than oil. But, her end is bitter as wormwood [poison], and sharp as a two-edged sword. *Her feet go DOWN to death. Her steps take hold on hell* [taking men with her]. Lest you ponder the path of life, her *WAYS* are moveable, that you cannot know them. Hear me now, therefore, you children [you boys], and depart not from the words of my mouth. Remove your way far from her. Come not near to her house; *lest you give your honor to others, and your productive years to the cruel. Lest strangers be filled with your wealth* [the kids you sired]; *and, all your labors* [child-support] *be in the house of a stranger. And you mourn at the last, when your flesh, and body, are consumed* [by overwork to support all of them; and possibly dying with some venereal disease]. You will also say: '*How have I hated instructions; AND my heart has despised reproof; AND I have not obeyed the voice of my teachers; nor inclined my ear unto those who instructed me* [or at least tried to, about the true facts of life and death] (Proverbs 5:3-13).'" *Ample warning!*

Now, this observed case: "With her much fair speech she caused him to yield; with the flattering of her lips she forced him. He goes after her straightway; *just as an ox goes to the slaughter. Or, as a fool to the correction of the stocks. Until a dart strikes through his liver. As a bird hastening to a snare, and knows not that it is for his life* [Deception of illicit sex!]. Hearken to me now therefore, oh you children [young boys], and, [pay close attention] to the words of my mouth. Let not your heart *DECLINE* to her ways. And go not *ASTRAY* in her paths. *For she has CAST DOWN many wounded. Yes, strong men have been slain by her* [THE WHORE]. *Her house is the way to hell; going down to the chambers of death* (Proverbs 7:21-27)." However, Proverbs also prescribes the prevention of such illicit sexual attitudes and actions. Consider this:

"Drink waters from your own cistern [have sex with your spouse only], and running waters from your own well [your marriage partner]. Let not your fountains [*the offspring from your semen*] be dispersed abroad [by having sex with many women], and rivers of waters [your many kids] in the streets [by many women]. Let them be only your own [from you and your marriage partner], and not strange women's kids with you. Let your fountain [your semen planted in your spouse] be blessed. *Rejoice with the wife of your youth! Let her be as a loving hind, and a pleasant roe. And let her breasts satisfy you at all times. And, be ravished always with her love! Why should you, my son, even want to be ravished with a strange woman, and embrace the bosom of a stranger? THE WAYS of man are before the eyes of the LORD, and He ponders ALL of man's* [attitudes and actions] (Proverbs 5:15-21)." *Got that?*

In the New Testament, the rules got even stricter! Jesus Christ said: "You have heard that it was said by those of old time: 'Do not commit adultery.' But I say to you: '*Whosoever looks upon a woman to lust after her has committed adultery with her already in his heart* (Matthew 5:27-28).'" *Pay heed!*

Sexual immorality has been a big problem right from the beginning of man's sinful history; because *the devil perverts everything he touches in society (and all the rest of creation)*. Romans chapter one tells that story: "Professing themselves to be *WISE*, they *BECAME FOOLS*; changing the glory of the incorruptible God into an *IMAGE* made like unto corruptible man, and birds, and fourfooted beasts, and creeping things. Wherefore, Deity also gave them up to uncleanness *through the lusts of their own hearts, to DISHONOR their own bodies between themselves. They CHANGED the truth of God into a LIE*, and worshipped and served the creature more than the Creator—Who is blessed for ever. Amen! For that cause *God gave them over to VILE affections*. For, even their women did change their natural *USE* into that which is against nature. And likewise men, leaving the *NATURAL USE* of the woman, *burned in their* [sexual] *lusts one toward another—men with men committing IMPROPER acts; and receiving in themselves repayment, which is PROPER for their* [moral] *error* (Romans 1:22-27)." *That obviously refers to venereal diseases, etc!*

Of course, the devil endeavors to invade the church with every evil he can; including sexual immorality. It happened in Corinth: "It is *reported commonly* that there is fornication among you [believers at Corinth], and such fornication as is not so much as named among the Gentiles; that one should have [sexual intercourse with] his father's wife [stepmother]. And you are puffed up, and have not instead mourned, that he who has done that [demonic] deed should be taken away from among you (1 Corinthians 5:1-2)." *So, not only was the man living in sin a stumbling-block to unbelievers outside the church, the attitude of the rest of the Corinthian congregation gave the Gospel a black eye in the eyes of outsiders as well.*

*Paul had to straighten out that moral mess.* He dealt with that mess in 1 Corinthians 5:9-13 by saying: "I wrote to you in an epistle not to company with fornicators. Yet, [I meant] not altogether with the fornicators of this world; or with the covetous, extortioners, or idolaters; *for then you must needs go out of this world.* But now, I have written unto you not to keep company; *if any who is called a brother be a fornicator,* or covetous, or an idolater, or a railer, or a drunkard, or an extortioner; *with such a one not even to eat!* For what have I to do to judge people who are outside [the church]? Do you not judge those who are within [the church]? *But those who are outside* [the church] *God Himself judges.* Therefore, *put away from among yourselves that wicked person."* Why?

"Do you not know that the unrighteous will not inherit the Kingdom of God? [*Fornication is SIN for Christians, just as it is SIN for the lost.*] Be not deceived: Neither fornicators, nor idolaters, nor adulterers, nor effeminate, nor the abusers of themselves with mankind [*that is homosexuals*], nor thieves, nor covetous, nor drunkards, nor revilers, nor extortioners, will inherit the Kingdom of God. *And SUCH WERE SOME OF YOU!* But [now] you are washed [from all such sins]; you are sanctified; you are justified; in the name of our Lord Jesus, and by the Holy Spirit of our God (1 Corinthians 6:9-1)."

Another group was similarly guilty: "You adulterers, and adulteresses, *know you not that friendship with the world is* [actually] *enmity with God?* Whosoever, therefore, wills to be a friend of the world is the enemy of God (James 4:4)."

Why is that true? *"Know you not that your bodies are the members of Christ?* [Is it right to] *take the members of Christ and make them the members of a harlot?* God forbid. What? Know you not that he who is joined to a harlot is one body? 'For two,' says God, 'will be one flesh.' But, the one joined to the Lord is one spirit. *Flee fornication!* Every sin a man does is outside the body. But the one committing fornication sins against his *OWN BODY*. What? *Know you not that your body is the TEMPLE of the Holy Ghost*, which is in you, which you have of God, and you are not your own? For you are bought with a price [God's own shed blood—Acts 20:28]. Therefore, glorify God in your body, and in your spirit, which are God's [possession by virtue of the *extreme price* He paid for you on the cross] (1 Corinthians 6:15-20)." Believers belong to God!

Just as Proverbs 5:15-21 reveals God's plan for husband and wife, *eliminating the need and desire for either one to go outside marriage to experience a fulfilling sex-life,* Paul gives us the New Covenant version: *"To avoid fornication, let every man have his own wife, and let every woman have her own husband.* [Within that arrangement,] *let the husband render to his wife her DUE benevolence* [conjugal rights]. *Likewise, the wife to her husband. For the wife has not authority of her own body* [for, the *TWO* have become *ONE*], *but the husband* [has sexual rights]. *Likewise, the husband has not authority of his own body,* but the wife [has her rights]. *DEFRAUD* not one another [withhold not sexual activity from one another], except it be with [mutual] consent for a [short] time, so that you may give yourselves to fasting and prayer; and so, come together again, *lest the devil tempt you for your incontinence* [lack of self-control] (1 Corinthians 7:2-5)." Therefore,...

"*Let not fornication, uncleanness, or covetousness be once named among you, as is proper for saints. Neither filthiness, foolish talking, nor jesting, which are not convenient.* Rather, giving thanks. For you know that no whoremonger, unclean person, or covetous person, who is actually an idolater, has any inheritance in the Kingdom of Christ and of God. Let no man deceive you with *VAIN WORDS. Because of these things the wrath of God comes on the children of disobedience.* [Sex sins fall into the category of disobedience.] Be not partakers with them (Ephesians 5:3-7)." *God issues ample warnings!*

Colossians 3:5-7: "Mortify, therefore, your members that are on earth; *fornication,* uncleanness, *inordinate affection,* evil *concupiscence,* and covetousness—which is idolatry. *For which things' sake the wrath of God comes upon the children of disobedience*: [the same as in Ephesians 5:6] *In the which you also walked sometime, when you* [used to live] *in them."*

Paul did not say that those Christians were plagued with those sins in their *PRESENT* Christian life. He did not teach here that Christians are still sinners; or that every day they must crucify their flesh, as many modern preachers preach.

Rather, Paul taught plainly that: *"Those who are Christ's have* [already] *crucified the flesh with its affections and lusts* (Galatians 5:24)." *That happened when we were born again. We who are in Christ are new creatures; not those old sinful creatures we used to be.* When you get born again,...

*"You put off regarding your former conversation* [lifestyle] *that old man, which is corrupt according to the deceitful lusts* (Ephesians 4:22)." "[Then] *put on the new man* [Christ], *Who after God* [in His image,] *is created in righteousness and true holiness* (Ephesians 4:24)." (We discarded our sinner-ship!)

"For this is the will of God: *Even your sanctification* [from the sinful practices of your old life]; *that you should abstain from fornication. And that every one of you should know how to possess his VESSEL* [his body] *in sanctification and honor. Not in the lust of concupiscence* [deviant sexual desire]; *even as the Gentiles, who know not God* (1 Thessalonians 4:3-5)."

Touching on both the positive and negative: *"Marriage is honorable in all,* and the *BED* undefiled. But, whoremongers and adulterers God will judge (Hebrews 13:4)." *Even among His own people!* Hebrews 10:30 tells us: *"The Lord will judge His own people."* So even for Christians, "It is a fearful thing to fall into the hands of the Living God (verse 31)." *Sobering!*

The apostle Peter also had words on that subject. "When they [sinners the devil uses to lure Christians back into sin] speak great swelling words of vanity, *they allure through the lusts of the flesh* [Believers do live in bodies!], *through much wantonness* [the assumption that one may do whatever one desires to do sexually], people who were clean escaped from those who live in error. But while they promise them liberty, they themselves are the servants of corruption. *For of whom a person is overcome, of the same is he brought into bondage* (2 Peter 2:18-19)." So-called *free-sex* is actually bondage!

The primary deception Satan uses concerning sex is that it is both *natural,* and *necessary.* Sex being God's idea, how can it be evil? Moreover, *SEX is the WAY some women make their living.* "*The adulteress eats, wipes her mouth, and says 'I have done nothing wrong* (Proverbs 30:20).'" She sees it as the *ONLY WAY* she can avoid starving. However, "The whore works for a price, but the adulteress goes after a man's very life (Proverbs 6:26)." Both passages are most instructive.

The subject is dealt with again in the book of Revelation. "I [Jesus] have a few things against you [believers], because you have there those who hold the doctrine of Balaam, who taught Balac to cast a stumblingblock before the children of Israel, to eat meat that is sacrificed to idols, and, to commit *fornication* (Revelation 2:14)." Satan is always trying to lure God's people into sex sins. *Has occurred throughout history! Also notice that idolatry is always somehow connected to sex sins; and sex sins always lead to some form of idolatry.*

Another church was rebuked for that very same error: "I [the Lord] have a few things against you, because you allow the woman Jezebel, who calls herself a prophetess, to teach and to seduce My servants [believers] to commit *fornication; AND* to eat things sacrificed unto idols. [See that connection between idolatry and sex sins?] I gave her space to repent of her fornication; but, she repented not. Behold, I [Jesus] will cast her into a bed, and all those who commit adultery with her into great tribulation; unless they repent of their deeds. *And I will kill her children with death. Then the churches will know that I am He Who searches the reins, and hearts.* And, I will give unto each of you according to your works [*be they good or bad*—2 Corinthians 5:10] (Revelation 2:20-23)."

"There came unto me one of those seven angels who had the seven judgment vials, and talked with me, saying to me: 'Come here and I will show to you the judgment of the great whore who *SITS* upon many waters: *With whom the kings of the earth have committed fornication, and the inhabitants of earth HAVE BEEN MADE DRUNK WITH THE WINE OF HER FORNICATION.' He carried me in the spirit to the wilderness. And I saw a woman sitting on a scarlet-colored beast, full of names of blasphemy, that had seven heads, and ten horns. And the woman was arrayed in purple and in scarlet colors, and was decked with gold, and precious stones, and pearls; and had a golden cup in her hand, full of abominations, and filthiness of her fornications.* Upon her forehead was a name inscribed: *MYSTERY BABYLON, THE GREAT, THE MOTHER OF HARLOTS, AND ABOMINATIONS, OF THE EARTH. And I saw the woman drunken with the BLOOD of the saints*; even with the blood of the martyrs of Christ. And when I saw her, I wondered with great admiration (Revelation 17:1-6)."

"And the angel said to me: 'The *WATERS* which you saw, where the whore *SITS*, are peoples, multitudes, nations and tongues. And, the ten horns which you saw upon the beast, *these* [kings] *will hate the whore, and will make her desolate and naked, and will eat* [or destroy] *her flesh, and burn her with fire. For, God has put in their hearts to fulfill His will, to agree, and to give their kingdom to the beast* [the Antichrist], *until the WORDS of God are fulfilled. And, the woman whom you saw is that great city, which reigns over the kings of the earth* (Revelation 17:15-18).'" That city is a *religious system*, and a *literal city*—Babylon. To get a complete explanation of the final days of this evil age, get a Dake's annotated Bible. *I can only explain that THE WHORE REPRESENTS RELIGION throughout history, and that SEXUAL misconduct is ALWAYS connected to manmade religions, which were invented by the devil; and that Satan always tries to take down God's people with sex sins. LIES* about *SEX* is one of his hiding-places.

From Genesis to Revelation, we see the devil's use of sex in destroying people's lives. However, *the devil does not own sex.* He owns nothing of his own, except lies (John 8:44). *So the devil has to use what God created to tempt people to sin! The devil has to use God's stuff to destroy God's stuff! If God had not made sex such a powerful force in men and animals, both the animal and human populations would dwindle fast.* And Satan makes use of that intense sex-drive in nature.

# Chapter Thirteen

## Prayer

*The devil hides behind prayer? How can that be?* Hold on for another ride down Scripture lane. For starters, one more time: Remember, *Jesus Christ exposed the falsehoods of the much-speaking-syndrome* (Matthew 6:7)! *The Lord said such prayers are vain—worthless.* And Satan is obviously behind all worthless things; including prayers. In fact, references to *worthless prayers* are scattered throughout the Bible. Satan hides behind all falsehoods, and many prayers fall into that category. Numerous believers act like prayer is some kind of amulet—A magic charm that supposedly wards off evil. *That opens the door for Satan to bring even more evil into the lives of those who see prayer as such.* But, *no magic in prayer!*

I have often had people come to me and tell me that they need prayer. *Which sounds good!* I normally tell them *THEY NEED TO BELIEVE GOD.* That sounds calloused on my part. However, things are not always as they appear. *People often have more faith in a preacher's prayers than they do in God.* And Satan hides behind that form of unbelief. Yes, unbelief! *It is the prayer of FAITH that SAVES the sick*; or brings relief in other situations. Prayer is *OFTEN SUBSTITUTED* for Bible faith. *What gives prayer power? Faith! And from where does faith come? The Word of God! No preacher's prayers can take the place of real Bible faith. And EVEN BIBLE FAITH WORKS ONLY for people who live a righteous life!* Consider this:

Jeremiah 7:16: *"PRAY NOT for this people, neither lift up a cry, nor prayer for them; neither make intercession to Me, for I will NOT HEAR you."* The prayers of those who refuse to obey God go unanswered! *Such prayers are offensive to Him.*

Jeremiah 11:14: *"Pray not for this people, neither lift up a cry or a prayer for them. For I will not hear THEM [OR YOU if you pray for them]* when they cry unto Me for their trouble."

Jeremiah 14:11-12: "Then said the LORD unto me, *'Pray not for this people for their good.* [Even] when they fast, I will not hear their cry. *And even when they offer burnt offerings and an oblation I will not accept them; but will consume them by the sword, by famine, and by pestilence.'"* Moreover,...

"The LORD said to me: 'Even if Moses and Samuel stood before Me, yet My mind could not be toward this people. So, cast them out of My sight (Jeremiah 15:1).'" *So much for the preacher's prayer-power. Genuine prayer is much more than mouthing words.* Thus, no PRAY—ER can con the Creator.

More of the same in Ezekiel: "'Although these three men, Noah, Daniel, and Job were in it [the city of Jerusalem, and the land of Israel], they would deliver but their own souls by their righteousness,' says the Lord GOD (Ezekiel 14:14)."

Plus, Ezekiel 14:20: "Even if Noah, Daniel, and Job were in it [Jerusalem]: 'As I live,' says the Lord GOD, *'they would deliver neither son nor daughter; but their own souls by their own righteousness.'" Righteousness is the very foundation of effective prayer!* That truth resonates throughout the Bible.

Speaking of Judas, the psalmist said: "Set a wicked man over him. And, let Satan stand at his right hand. And, when he will be judged, let him be condemned. And, *let his prayer become sin.* Let his days be few. And so, let another take his office (Psalms 109:6-8)." *Prayer can actually BECOME SIN!*

Because: *"The one who turns away his ears from hearing the law* [of God], *even his prayers will be an abomination* [to God] *(Proverbs 28:9)." Some prayers evoke divine judgment!*

And this: *"Your new moons and appointed feasts My soul hates. They are trouble to Me. I am weary of them. When you spread your hands* [to pray], *I will HIDE My eyes from you.* Yes, when you make many prayers, I will not hear. For your hands are full of [innocent shed] blood (Isaiah 1:14-15)."

*Not all prayers are to Jehovah. "The residue of a TREE he has cut down, he makes into a god, even a graven image. He falls down to it, worships it, and prays to [a chunk of wood]: 'Deliver me; for you are my god (Isaiah 44:17).'"* Seriously? *"Can one [actually] make gods for himself? Which are not gods (Jeremiah 16:20)?"* Good question. And one more good question: *"Where are your gods that YOU made for yourself? Let them rise and save you in your time of trouble, if they can (Jeremiah 2:28)." Man-made gods are powerless—Except to deceive those who make them and worship them.* (Unsmart!)

But, *many who think they ARE praying to the TRUE GOD are often in error as well.* The Lord warned: *"When you pray, BE NOT as the HYPOCRITES. For, they love to pray standing in the synagogues, and on the street corners, that they might be SEEN by men. 'Truly,' I tell you, 'They have their reward!' But, when you [believers] pray, enter your closet, and when you shut the door, pray to your Father, Who is in secret; and your Father, Who sees you in secret, will reward you openly (Matthew 6:5-6)." Nobody can con God (Galatians 6:7)!*

Thus, in many cases, even those who pray not to a dead stick, but think they are impressing Deity, merely pray with or unto themselves. Luke 18:11 reports one such case: *"The Pharisee prayed thus with himself."* Nobody else listening to that Pharisee, nothing could be accomplished by his prayer. Was the man his own God? *Did he answer his own prayers? Satan can hide behind prayers, which God will not hear, and which will naturally go unanswered—and even become sin!*

Worse is this case: *"Woe unto you scribes, and Pharisees; you hypocrites! For you [by religion] devour widows' houses, and then for pretense make long prayers. Therefore, you will receive the greater condemnation [in the judgment] (Matthew 23:14)."* PRETENSE PRAYERS! *People who pray that way do not expect to get answers to their prayers. Such praying is a mere cover-up for their otherwise ungodly lifestyle!*

*"WHEN you stand, praying, if you have anything against anybody, FORGIVE THEM, so that your heavenly Father also may forgive your trespasses. For, if you do not forgive them, neither will your Father forgive your sins (Mark 11:25-26)!"*

You surely perceive that there is more to prayer than the mere mouthing of words. *Prayer has to come from the heart, and be in line with God's Word, in order to be legitimate, and to get God's attention. Only real prayer has real power!*

"Confess your faults one to another, and [THEN] pray one for another, so that you may be healed. The effectual fervent prayer of A RIGHTEOUS MAN avails much (James 5:16)!"

"Beloved, *IF* our heart [spirit] *condemns us not, then have we confidence toward God. And whatever we ask we receive of Him, because we keep His commandments, and do those things that are pleasing in His sight* (1 John 3:21-22)." Here, we see the connection between prayer, faith, obedience, and *actually getting our prayers answered. That is God's system.*

One more facet of prayer truth: "Likewise, you husbands, dwell with your wife according to knowledge; giving honor to the wife, as to the weaker vessel [referring to her body], *and as being heirs together of the grace of life; that your prayers be not hindered* (1 Peter 3:7)." The way we treat other people affects the effectiveness of our prayers! So, *it definitely pays to make sure our prayers are in line with God's Word—Which takes into account the way we treat other people. No one can fool Deity.* Yet, *many people fool themselves by thinking they can make up their own prayer rules.* (Satan's hiding-place!)

"*The eyes of the Lord are over the righteous, and His ears are open to their prayers. But, the face of the Lord is against all those who do evil* (1 Peter 3:12)." *An evil lifestyle renders one's prayers worthless; because our life is not DIVIDED into different compartments.* Everything affects everything else!

Finally, Revelation 5:8 and 8:3 tell us that *God considers genuine prayers of genuine believers to be incense; giving off a sweet aroma which is well-pleasing to Him.* Therefore, our prayers are stored in heaven, *and are often stirred to release that aroma for His pleasure.* (RIGHTEOUS PRAYERS, that is!)

(P.S. Pray not to discover God's will. *FIND* His will, which is already revealed in Scripture; then pray that will in faith. *God only promises to answer faith-prayers that are based on His Word; not so-called blind-faith prayer shots in the dark.*)

# Chapter Fourteen

## Fear

I am sure that few Bible-believers doubt that fear is one of the devil's hiding-places. And *ONLY Scripture can fill us in on how fear works;* thus enabling us to overcome the devil's fear-tactics. *Just a little of the right kind of knowledge goes a long way toward giving us believers victory over that enemy.* And the book of beginnings—Genesis—is where we first find that vital knowledge. God's Word always settles all issues.

*FEAR was the initial sinner-response to God. After Adam sinned, on the Creator's next visit to Eden, when He called to Adam, he answered: "I heard Your voice in the garden, and I WAS AFRAID, BECAUSE I WAS NAKED; and so, I hid myself (Genesis 3:10)." WHEN SINNERS' SINS ARE EXPOSED THEY BECOME AFRAID; and that fear prompts them to HIDE from God, and hold to fear, instead of asking God for forgiveness. That is the opposite of what they need to do. Neither fear nor the devil, either can, or will, forgive. Forgiveness is a DIVINE GRACE.* Sin, coupled with fear, dominates *God-avoiders.*

One confusing fact about fear is that there are two basic kinds of fear. *And it seems that MANY believers do not know the difference.* Thus, *they are confused about how to conduct themselves in the presence of DIFFERENT KINDS OF FEAR. This one chapter provides many answers to many previously unanswered questions on the controversial subject of FEAR!*

One example of the *blessed kind of fear*: "Then the angel said [to Abraham], 'Lay *NOT* your hand upon the lad [Isaac], neither do anything [damaging] to him. For *now I know that you FEAR GOD, seeing that you have not withheld your son, your only son, from Me* (Genesis 22:12).'" The godly fear that Abraham exhibited in that incident set it up for God to send the Messiah into the world. He would offer His only Son just as Abraham had done. *Only godly fear would move a man to take such risk. Fake-fear makes no genuine sacrifices!* Thus, the *godly fear* Abraham displayed was *the good-kind of fear*.

One more example of that *GOOD* (God-)kind of fear: "The LORD said to Satan: 'Have you considered My servant Job? That there is *NONE* like him on the earth; [who is] a perfect and an upright man, one who *FEARS GOD* and despises evil (Job 1:8)?'" Job 2:3: "The LORD [again] said to Satan: 'Have you considered My servant Job, that there is *NONE* like him on the earth, a perfect and an upright man, one who *FEARS GOD* and despises evil? And still, he holds fast his integrity, although you moved Me against him in order to destroy him without cause.'" To *fear God and hate evil* demonstrates the very words of our Lord in Matthew 6:24: "*NO MAN* can serve two [opposing] masters, for he will favor one over the other." Genuine God-fear holds onto God, and opposes the devil.

Psalms 19:9 explains why *GODLY FEAR* is a good kind of fear. "*THE FEAR OF THE LORD IS CLEAN, enduring forever.*" The Hebrew word rendered *clean* means *pure. God-fear has nothing to hide; is not hypocritical; and so endures forever.*

It ought not be surprising, then, that *the genuine fear of God is not only beneficial to Deity Himself, but also provides many benefits for God-fearers as well.* Notice how many!

For starters, let us consider Psalms 25:14: "*The secret of the LORD is with them who fear Him*; and He will show them His covenant." *Deity grants to God-fearers inside information and revelation on everything contained in the covenant!*

Next, Psalms 31:19: "*How great is Your goodness, which You have laid up for* [all] *them who fear You; which You have wrought for them who trust in You before the sons of men!*" If you want benefits, then you must take some risks. God did!

*More good news about the benefits of fearing God with an honest heart*: "Oh fear the LORD, you His saints. *For there is NO WANT* [no lack of anything good] *to those who fear Him.* The young lions [*which are good at hunting*] lack, and suffer hunger. But those who seek the LORD [because they have a genuine fear of Him] will *NOT LACK ANY* good thing (Psalms 34:9-10)." Thus, *lack is NOT God's will for anyone who truly fears Him with godly fear.* Those who teach otherwise either do not know these Scriptures; or just do not believe them.

"*His SALVATION is near all those who FEAR Him* (Psalms 85:9)." *Salvation is BOTH a CURRENT and ETERNAL benefit!* So: "*God is GREATLY TO BE FEARED IN THE ASSEMBLY OF THE SAINTS; and TO BE HAD IN REVERENCE of all who are about Him* (Psalms 89:7)." "*The LORD is great, and greatly to be praised. He is to be FEARED ABOVE ALL gods* [which are demons] (Psalms 96:4)." Leviticus 17:7, Deuteronomy 32:17 and 1 Corinthians 10:20 expose what false gods really are.

More God-fearer goodies: "*As heaven is HIGH ABOVE the earth, SO GREAT IS HIS MERCY toward those who fear Him. As far as East is from West, SO FAR HAS HE REMOVED our transgressions from us. Like a father PITIES HIS CHILDREN, so the LORD pities those who fear Him* (Psalms 103:11-13)." Thus, *abundant mercy, absolute sin removal, and comforting compassion are divine benefits of TRUE God-fearers.* The flip side of that coin: "*There is forgiveness with You, so that YOU MAY BE feared* (Psalms 130:4)." Receiving divine forgiveness does not gender haughtiness in the one forgiven, but rather holy reverence toward the Forgiver of trespasses. Therefore, "*The LORD takes PLEASURE in those who FEAR HIM; those who hope in His mercy* (Psalms 147:11)." *Good kind of fear!*

Now some *proverbial wisdom* about fear from the book of Proverbs. "*The fear of the LORD is the beginning of* [genuine] *knowledge. But fools despise* [godly] *wisdom and instruction* (Proverbs 1:7)." More truth: "*The fear of the LORD is to hate evil.* Pride, and arrogance, and the evil way, and the froward mouth do *I HATE* (Proverbs 8:13)." "*The fear of the LORD is also the beginning of wisdom. And the knowledge of the holy is understanding* (Proverbs 9:10)." How many Christians are *FAMILIAR WITH* all of these promises to God-fearers today?

Those God-fearer-benefits *keep piling up. "The fear of the LORD prolongs days* [of God-fearers, that is]. But, *the years of the wicked will be shortened* (Proverbs 10:27)." (Contrast!)

And not only does Deity expect people to have a reverent fear of Him personally, but also to have that same reverence for His Word *(whether written or spoken)*: "Whoever despises the Word [of God] will be destroyed [eventually]. But *he who fears the commandment will be rewarded* (Proverbs 13:13)."

More rewards: *"In the fear of the LORD* [there] *is STRONG CONFIDENCE* [in the God-fearer that God is for him and not against him]. *Even his children will have a place of REFUGE. The fear of the LORD is a fountain of LIFE, to depart from the snares of death* (Proverbs 14:26-27)." So who would not fear God? *Only those who have been deceived by the devil! Satan also lures people into evil. But,* "BY THE FEAR OF THE LORD MEN DEPART FROM EVIL (Proverbs 16:6)." *Right motivation!*

Can there be more benefits? *"The fear of the LORD tends to life. He who has it* [the fear of God] *will abide satisfied; he will NOT be visited with evil* (Proverbs 19:23)." *People search this world over their entire lifetime, hoping to obtain both life and satisfaction; both blessings being found only in the Lord.* Therefore, *only people who genuinely fear God have promise of both life and satisfaction; plus divine protection from evil.*

And can you accept this? *"By humility and the fear of the LORD are* [actual material and financial] *RICHES, and honor, and life* (Proverbs 22:4)." That one verse would surely upset the poverty-preachers. *True God-fear gleans many blessings which unbelievers, and even many believers, seek after their entire lives. And such blessings are right at our fingertips,* so to speak, *if we only develop a willingness to truly fear God.*

"Those who feared the *LORD* spoke often one to another. *The LORD heard it. And a book of remembrance was written before Him for those who feared the LORD, and who thought upon His name* (Malachi 3:16)." Plus: *"Unto you who fear My name will the Sun of righteousness* [Jesus Christ] *arise with healing in His wings* (Malachi 4:2)." *Divine healing benefit!*

Two New Testament Scriptures: "Then, had the churches rest in Judaea and Galilee and Samaria; and were *EDIFIED. And, walking in the fear of the Lord and in the comfort of the Holy Spirit they were MULTIPLIED* (Acts 9:31)." This passage refers to THE TEMPORARY REPRIEVE FROM PERSECUTION begun by Saul of Tarsus. *It proves that church growth DOES NOT depend on persecution.* Believers were both *edified* and *multiplied* during that time of peace. So the church ought to fear God at all times; not just during times of persecution!

Peter also testified: "Of a truth, I perceive that God is not a respecter of persons. But in every nation, *HE WHO FEARS GOD AND WORKS RIGHTEOUSNESS IS ACCEPTED BY HIM* (Acts 10:34-3)." *God welcomes all true God-fearers; desiring to fill His Kingdom with such people.* Look at John 4:23-24.

In light of all these positive passages, how can we believe that the devil hides behind fear? How does he do it? I know of three ways. Of course, *the devil cannot hide behind actual God-fear. It has to be some kind of perversion of it.* There are three varieties of that perversion I can think of. First, *since he cannot hide behind real God-fear, the devil HIDES FROM PEOPLE all of those God-fear-blessings; SO THEY WILL NOT BE AWARE that God-fear itself is a blessing.* If that fails, he *DISTORTS people's concepts of God-fear; making them either MAKE LIGHT OF God-fear or BECOME AFRAID OF God-fear. Satan's first trick could not work on Eve, since there was not at that time a multitude of Scripture passages relating all the advantages of God-fear TO HIDE FROM EVE.* Adam and Eve had only that one warning by their Creator to avoid one tree in the Garden. *So the devil went straight to that second ploy: DISTORTING GOD-FEAR in Eve's mind.* Questioning Deity's Word sowed within Eve doubt about whether Deity could be trusted. *If God's Word could not be depended upon, then His warning was not to be feared.* The second TRICK worked on Eve. And third, if the devil fails to deceive people by his first attempts, *he just sells them on a FALSE God-fear.* Scripture recorded this case of *FALSE God-fear*: "The *LORD* said: 'This people draw near Me with their mouths, and, with their lips they honor Me. But they have removed their hearts far from Me; *and their fear toward Me is taught by the precept of men* (Isaiah 29:13).'" MANMADE, FALSE, GOD-FEAR!

Numerous Scripture passages tell us what (or Whom) we are *supposed to fear*, while numerous others warn us about what (or whom) we are *not supposed to fear*. So now, we will consider some of those *characters* and *circumstances* we are *NOT* supposed to fear. One Old Testament case in point:

"Moses said to the people: 'Fear not [the Egyptian army], but stand still, and see the salvation of the LORD, which He will show you today. For those [armed] Egyptians whom you have seen [coming after you] today, you will see them again no more forever (Exodus 14:13).'" Well, *Israel did not see the Egyptian army again on that day alive, but they did see their DEAD bodies wash up on the shore of the Red Sea*. Although that happened under the Old Covenant, *divine protection is the same in the New Testament, because the New Testament God is the same as the Old Testament God* (Malachi 3:6). He does not change, so He is the same today as He was then!

*Whereas Moses told God's people NOT to fear the army of the Egyptian nation they were now leaving, when they came to Canaan, they were told NOT to fear the inhabitants of the heathen nations they were about to enter and take over*. This time, Joshua and Caleb issued the warning: "*Only rebel not against the LORD, NEITHER FEAR the people of the land; for they are bread for us. Their defense has departed from them, and THE LORD IS WITH US Israelites.* [Therefore,] *fear them not* (Numbers 14:9)!" To refuse to lay hold of those blessings our Redeemer has promised and provided is to rebel against Him! *All rebellion against the Creator is based on fear of the enemy. The only reason Israel might refuse to enter that land of milk and honey, which God had promised to Abraham and his descendants, would be fear that what God had promised Israel being in the hands of others, it would be too dangerous to GO FOR*. Today, believers *FEAR TO GO FOR* the blessings that were both promised and provided in the *New Covenant*, which Jesus purchased on the cross, *for fear of what people may say about them if they FAIL to get the blessings! Or fear of what they may say if they SUCCEED!* Satan has invented every kind of fear; except the kind that genuinely fears God. Unable to duplicate it, he can *ONLY* distort it; *OR* substitute something for it; *which convinces people they genuinely fear God, when what they have is not even a good counterfeit of the God-kind of fear*. True God-fear allows no other fears!

One of the benefits of God-fear is: *"All people of the earth will see that you [or we] are called by the name of the LORD; and they will be afraid of you [us] (Deuteronomy 28:10)."*

The *WRONG KIND OF FEAR*, and the *ABSENCE OF TRUE GOD-FEAR*, are akin; both resulting in *unwelcome results* in one's life. One more Old Covenant case in point: *"If you will not observe to do all the words of this law, which are written in this book [Moses' law], so that you may FEAR this glorious and FEARFUL name, THE LORD YOUR GOD; then, the LORD will make your plagues wonderful [very difficult to bear], and the plagues of your seed [children], even great plagues, and of long continuance, and sore sicknesses of long continuance [continual misery] (Deuteronomy 28:58-59)."* The absence of the God-kind of fear is actually caused by *having the wrong kind of fear—fear of the enemy instead of God. The two fears are not isolated from one another, but are in constant conflict with each other. Satan sows his kind of fear into the mindset of God's people* (and the thoughts of those potentially God's people) *to make them AFRAID to fear God! Why would people risk exposing themselves to the plagues Moses mentioned by NOT FEARING GOD, unless the devil had LIED to them about the advantages of God-fear, and the dangers of not having a genuine God-fear? Obedience being the product of God-fear, it is understandable why the devil pressures people to avoid God-fear! God-fear spells the end of Satan's devilish control.*

Those who refuse to fear Deity voluntarily will eventually find themselves on the unpleasant end of the fear of God: "I [God] will send *MY FEAR* before you, and I will destroy all of those people to whom you come. *I WILL MAKE your enemies turn their backs to you* [in fear] (Exodus 23:27)." So, to avoid the *FORCED* version of God-fear, voluntarily fear Him now!

"The fear of man brings a snare (Proverbs 29:25)." Thus, the *fear of man* is one of the devil's most powerful forces he uses to *steer people away from fearing God*. The divine cure: "*You* [judges] *must not respect persons in judgment. And you are to hear the small as well as the great. And, you must not be afraid of the face of man; for, the judgment* [you mete out] *is God's* [not yours] (Deuteronomy 1:17)." So fear not man!

People who choose to *NOT* fear God will eventually suffer from a kind of fear that is far worse than what they thought God-fear would be like: *"Your life will hang in DOUBT before you; and you will FEAR both day and night, and will have no assurance of your life. In the morning you will say: 'Would to God it were evening!' And at evening you will say: 'Would to God it were morning!' Because of FEAR in your heart, which you will fear* [in your expectation of the evils you may suffer next], *and for the* [fearful] *sight of your eyes, which you will see* [getting close to you] (Deuteronomy 28:66-67)." Now that warning was first applied to Israel, but the principle applies in truth to the entire human race; *for in the end-time, rebels will beg rocks and mountains to fall on them, and hide them from the wrath of God, and the Lamb, Whom they refused to FEAR and obey voluntarily* (Revelation 6:16). *God-fear gives victory over all deceptive, counterfeit fears, whereas the lack of God-fear opens the door to other kinds of fear that produce detrimental results.* Thus, our choices are, either voluntarily *FEAR DEITY UP FRONT*, and enjoy the *DIVINE BENEFITS*, or eventually run into *the negative side* of God-fear later in life; or in eternity—reaping *no benefits*; but the very opposite.

Let us look at some Bible examples of the outcome of the fear of man, which replaced God-fear. "Saul said to Samuel, 'I have sinned, for I have transgressed the commandment of the *LORD*, and your words, because *I feared the people, and obeyed their voice* (1 Samuel 15:24)." This passage presents a perfect example of Satan's purpose of scaring people with man-fear—*To motivate them to heed human voices instead of the divine voice.* Remember, *God had commanded King Saul to totally destroy every Amalekite, and all of their stuff.* Well, *Saul's soldiers did destroy everything that was INFERIOR IN THEIR ESTIMATION, but spared everything THEY THOUGHT would be good to offer to the LORD once they got back home.* Their human estimation of the value of certain commodities over others *OVERRODE* their evaluation of Deity's command to destroy all of those commodities. However, the real issue here is that Satan used the pressure of majority rule in this case *to move King Saul into disobedience to God's command. Saul feared what the people might do to him, if he carried out God's orders. Fearing with that fear, he fulfilled Satan's will!*

*The fear of man is obviously designed by Satan to replace God-fear in every case.* That must be the way it is, for *Deity would never replace His own fear with man-fear! Thus, it is evident that the devil is behind all fear of man.* Consider this case: "*[Certain treasonous Jews of Nehemiah's day]* reported his [Tobiah's] good deeds to me; then they uttered my words to him. And, Tobiah sent letters *to put me in fear* (Nehemiah 6:19)." Some Jewish traitors in high positions fed Nehemiah falsehoods about how *GOOD* Tobiah was on one hand, and then Tobiah endeavored to frighten Nehemiah with repeated written *THREATS* on the other; *and all to shake Nehemiah's integrity to the point that he would drop his God-fear, and do something really stupid*—like going into the holy place in the temple to hide from his supposed-murderous-pursuers, and *thereby dishonor God, and FALL into the hands of his haters* (Nehemiah 6:10-14). And, of course, *behind all of those evil actions of Nehemiah's enemies was the devil; who wanted to thwart the efforts of the returning Jewish exiles in rebuilding Jerusalem, and restoring true God-worship, based upon true God-fear.* The devil desires to be in control, and *he exercises that control chiefly through people who use fear of man to put pressure on other people to disobey God; and get themselves into trouble with God.* Nehemiah refused to fall for it!

However, another famous Bible character did fall for one of Satan's intimidating fears: "*For, that thing I greatly feared has come upon me, and that which I was afraid of has come unto me* (Job 3:25)." This passage proves that *any fear other than God-fear actually causes the thing feared to manifest in the fearer's experiences. Such fear DRAWS to the fearing one the very UNWANTED CONDITIONS that fearer is afraid of.* A New Covenant case corroborates that scriptural truth. Refer to Matthew 14:28-31. Acting in faith on just *ONE* word from Jesus, Who was walking on the sea, *Peter also got out of the boat and started walking on water to meet Jesus.* But, *when Peter began to FEEL THE WIND BLOWING on his face, and to OBSERVE THOSE WATER WAVES LASHING OUT AT HIM, he suddenly became afraid, and began to SINK in the water he had just been walking on.* As long as Peter focused upon the command of Jesus to come to Him on the water, *by faith he DEFIED gravity, and did what was impossible in the natural.*

*But, when he began to observe the natural circumstances, he stepped off that gravity-defying faith, and sank back into his natural fisherman-reasoning;* thinking: "What am I doing? I cannot walk on water!" *Peter being a professional fisherman, he was well-acquainted with the DANGER of drowning in the turbulent sea in a wind storm; and let his natural knowledge take over.* Both Job and Peter fell for the wrong kind of fear!

But, just as the wrong kind of fear draws toward one the very circumstances one does not desire, *the God kind of fear draws one toward God and His blessings.* Both kinds of fear have DRAWING POWER—the wrong kind toward unpleasant experiences; and the right kind toward blessedness.

The *TRUE* faith-walk, stemming from *GENUINE* God-fear, SHIELDS BELIEVERS from wrong kinds of fear: "Yea, though I walk through the valley of the shadow of death, I will FEAR NO EVIL: Because You [God] are with me. Your rod and staff COMFORT ME (Psalms 23:4)." Shepherds protect their sheep from wild animals and other hazards by their rod and staff. Sheep *being confident* that the shepherd is there to feed and protect them, *they thus are FREE from the fear of starvation, and ALL other dangers.* As Chief Shepherd, our Savior takes care of all of His believing sheep. (Proverbs 28:1 talks about the *temerity* of sinners, and the *boldness* of believers.)

Another goodie: "The *LORD* is my *light* and my *salvation*; so, whom will I fear? The *LORD* is the *strength* of my life; so, of whom will I be afraid (Psalms 27:1)?" Light, salvation and strength coming from God protect me from my enemies; so I have no reason to be afraid of my enemies. *Praise God!*

*Only the Almighty can deliver us from the wrong kinds of fear.* And, He obviously desires to do just that: "I sought the LORD, and He heard me, and *delivered me from all my fears* (Psalms 34:4)." *God tells us to FEAR ONLY HIM; for God-fear delivers us from ALL other fears; and does us ONLY GOOD.*

"When I am afraid, I will [choose to put my] trust in You. In God, I will praise His Word. In God, I have put my trust; *I will not fear what flesh can do to me* (Psalms 56:3-4)."

And the *CLASSIC* Old Testament passage on the subject: Because you have put your trust in the Lord, "You will *NOT BE AFRAID OF* any terror by night; or the arrow that flies by day [stray bullets]; or the pestilence [either animals, snakes or insects] which walk in the darkness; or destruction [war] that wastes at noonday. A thousand will fall [dead] at your side [right there beside you], and ten thousand at your right hand; *but it will not come near you!* Only with your eyes will you *SEE* the [unwanted] reward of the wicked [*WHO CHOSE NOT TO FEAR THE LORD by trusting Him*] (Psalms 91:5-8)." Exodus 15:26, 23:25, Deuteronomy 7:15 and Psalms 103:3 also speak of *divine deliverance* from sickness and disease.

And one more Psalm: "He will not be afraid of evil tidings [bad news]: [For,] His heart is fixed [unchangeable], trusting in the *LORD*. His heart is established. He will *NOT* be afraid, until he see his desire upon his enemies. [Moreover,] He has dispersed [his money and goods]. He has *GIVEN* to the poor. [Trusting that Deity will multiply the financial and material seeds he has sown, *he will NOT BE AFRAID of starving.*]. His righteousness endures forever; and his horn [authority] will be *EXALTED WITH HONOR* (Psalms 112:7-9)." *Now that is a mouth-full of blessings; all of them stemming from a genuine God-fear that refuses to be intimidated by any other fear.*

Now this passage from Proverbs, *which reveals the result of refusing to have genuine God-fear*: "Then, they will call on Me, but I will not answer. They will seek Me early [after they get in trouble], *but they will not find Me, because they hated knowledge and did NOT CHOOSE the fear of the LORD.* They would have none of My counsel. And they despised all of My reproof [correction and instruction in right living] (Proverbs 1:28-30)." *Such arrogant people tend to reject Deity up front, when they think they do not need Him, but then, expect Him to be lenient on them when they get into trouble. But, nobody can con God. Those who try only deceive themselves.*

One more blessing to those who honor God by genuinely fearing Him: "*Whoever hearkens unto me* [wisdom from God] *WILL DWELL SAFELY, AND BE QUIET FROM FEAR OF EVIL* (Proverbs 1:33)." God-fear delivers us from all other fears!

Because you received God's wisdom: "*When you lie down you will not be afraid* [that something will harm you in your sleep]. Yes, you will lie down and your sleep will be SWEET. [Moreover, you will] *Be NOT afraid of sudden fear, neither of the desolation of the wicked when it comes* [upon them]. *For the LORD will be your confidence* [because of your God-fear], *and will keep your foot from being taken* [caught in a snare] (Proverbs 3:24-26)." *Powerful promises to God-fearers!*

So, "Let not your heart envy sinners [because it appears that they get away with a lot of evil stuff]. But, *be in the fear of the LORD all the day long* [that is, continuously] (Proverbs 23:17)." *Sinners cannot expect divine protection, but God has sworn to shield the God-fearer from all harm* (Psalms 91).

The Proverbs lesson: "*The fear of man brings a snare, but WHOSOEVER PUTS HIS TRUST IN THE LORD WILL BE SAFE* (Proverbs 29:25)." *Trusting God and fearing God are the very same.* Therefore, nobody can fool God with some fake-fear.

And Isaiah has given us *more light* on the subject of fear. "*Neither fear their fear, nor be afraid.* [Instead,] *Sanctify the LORD of hosts Himself; and let Him be your fear, and let Him be your dread* (Isaiah 8:12-13)." Other fears are false-fears.

Refusing to fear God is not wise. "*The sinners in Zion are afraid*: FEARFULNESS HAS SURPRISED THE HYPOCRITES. Who among us [Jews] will [be able to] dwell with [or survive] the devouring fire [of Deity's wrath against those who refuse to fear Him]? Who among us will [be able to] dwell with the everlasting burnings (Isaiah 33:14)?" The answer is given in verses 15-16—Those who walk uprightly in true God-fear.

"Fear not! For, I have redeemed you. I have called you by your name. So, you are Mine (Isaiah 43:1)." Knowing we are redeemed quells all illegitimate fears. *WE ARE REDEEMED!*

"Hearken to Me you who *KNOW* righteousness; people in whose heart is My law [of God-fear]; fear not the reproach of men, neither be afraid of their revilings (Isaiah 51:7)." That clash between God-fear and man-fear once again! *Man-fear is forbidden! God-fear is both commended and commanded!*

And the contrast one more time: "I, even I, [Deity] am He Who comforts you [not frightens you]. *Who are you, that you should be afraid of a man who will die*; or of the son of man who will be made as grass [and wither fast] (Isaiah 51:12)?"

Jeremiah was instructed to: "'*Be not afraid of their faces*: For, I am with you, to deliver you,' says the LORD (Jeremiah 1:8)." *God is with us who FEAR HIM; to deliver us from every facial and verbal threat of the man-fearers. Moreover,...*

Concerning man-made idols, Jeremiah was commanded: "Be not afraid of them; for, they cannot do evil. Neither is it in them to do good (Jeremiah 10:5)." Therefore, *we cannot trust ANY god other than THE ONE TRUE GOD to do us good.* Nor should we fear any threat of idol-worshippers, or their idols. Rather, *we fear and trust God, Whose purpose is not to harm us, but to help us against all of our man-fearing enemies.*

Ezekiel too! "And you, son of man, *be not afraid of them, neither be afraid of their words*; though briers and thorns be present with you [threatening you], and you do dwell among scorpions. *BE NOT AFRAID OF THEIR WORDS nor dismayed at their LOOKS, although they be a rebellious house.* You will speak My words to them, whether they will hear, or whether they will forbear [*to listen to My words; which is more likely*]. *For they are* [a] *most rebellious* [people] (Ezekiel 2:6-7)." This passage in *Ezekiel provides even more details of the contrast between God-fear and man-fear.* We find here that man-fear not only *FLINGS* threatening words toward those they hate, but also gives them *"THE LOOK."* Frowning eyebrows! *I have been on the receiving end of both UNFRIENDLY WORDS, and THE LOOK.* So I know a little about what Ezekiel faced.

Haggai 2:5 relates this reason we ought to reject the fear of man and all other *UNGODLY* fears: "*According to the word that I covenanted with you WHEN you came out of Egypt, My Spirit REMAINS among you*: [Therefore,] *Fear not!*" Israel left Egypt hundreds of years before this was written in Haggai's prophetic book, yet Deity said that *both the covenant and its benefits were STILL in force.* Thus, *those under the covenant DID NOT HAVE TO FEAR ANYTHING coming against them or their covenant blessings.* Same for New Covenant believers!

Now, this much-misunderstood Scripture passage: "Fear not [anyone] who is able to kill the body, but not able to kill the soul. Rather, fear *HIM* who is able to destroy *BOTH* soul and body in hell (Matthew 10:28)." *Some CLAIM that he who destroys both body and soul in hell is the devil. But the devil does not reside in hell. Nor has he any power over the spirits residing in hell.* Actually, *an eternal future in the Lake of Fire is his own worst nightmare. Neither can he cast anyone into hell. Only God has that power.* Satan's trick is to talk people into committing sin, so that they fall under God's wrath (the wages of sin is death—Romans 6:23), and are cast into hell upon their death. *THE ONLY ONE ABLE TO DESTROY BOTH BODY AND SOUL IN HADES IS GOD ALMIGHTY!* Satan does not have that ability. Luke 12:4-5 further explains it.

Moreover, another *misunderstanding about this passage, and many others, is the belief that the Greek word DESTROY here and elsewhere means to annihilate a thing, or a person; causing it or them to cease to exist.* Looking up *DESTROY* in a concordance, you will find that *it basically means to RUIN; not go out of existence. The prodigal son became lost, but did not cease to exist. Nor did the woman's lost coin cease to be. Neither did the leftover bread and fish from the feeding of the thousands lose their existence. The lost boy and the lost coin were found, and the leftover food was gathered into baskets.* The Greek word rendered *DESTROY* or *LOST* in those cases means *to be diverted from God's ORIGINAL purpose. Adam's race became LOST—The very opposite of God's original plan for its reason for being.* Mankind did not go out of existence!

(Let me sandwich in a few passages that reveal that fear of man is common among humans. When one of the Herods jailed John the Baptizer, and "would have put him to death, *he feared the multitude* [of the common folks], *because they counted him* [John] *as a prophet* (Matthew 14:5)." Of course, Herod *DID* later execute John at the request of his unlawful wife. He obviously feared her more than he did that crowd.

Religious leaders *CAVED IN* to that man-fear, just as did Herod. When the Lord answered one of their questions with another question that put them on the spot, they reasoned: "*If we say* [John's baptism was of] *men; we fear the people; for, all hold John as a prophet* [who would have received his commission from God and not men] (Matthew 21:26)." Once again that religious bunch chickened out when they wanted to arrest the Lord Jesus: "*When they sought to lay hands on Him, they feared the multitude, because they took Him for a prophet* (Matthew 21:46)." Oh, the power of crowd pressure!

Some believed Jesus was a good man and deserved to be heard, "Howbeit, no man spoke openly of Him for *fear* of the Jews (John 7:13)." What did they fear? Being cast out of the synagogue. *The religious leaders back in that day* (just as in many cases today) *used fear to keep their members in line. It is sad, but true. Church membership is considered by many in our day to be necessary to one's salvation; and synagogue membership was obviously deemed JUST as important to the general Jewish population during that time. Being cast out of the synagogue back in those days, or today, one losing his or her church membership, both was and is equated with losing one's salvation—in the estimation of certain religious leaders and many church members. I have encountered some people who believe that LIE. I told them their names being written in THE LAMB'S BOOK OF LIFE is what gets them TO HEAVEN; not being recorded on a church file. Their names being inked on some roll book will not stop their lost soul from rolling into hell. One has to be born again to be saved and go to heaven.*

More religious fear: The Lord told a parable, then quoted a related Scripture, which incriminated the religious leaders of Judaism. And, of course, that infuriated them: "And they sought to lay hold on Him [to arrest Christ], but they feared the [crowd of common folks]. For, they knew He had spoken that parable against them. And, [angry and frustrated,] they left Him and went their [religious] way (Mark 12:12)."

And this case: "After this, Joseph of Arimathaea, being a disciple of Jesus, but *secretly for fear of the Jews*, besought Pilate that he might take away the body of Jesus. And Pilate gave Joseph [permission to take away] the body of Jesus [so that He would be buried with some respect, and not abused or just forgotten] (John 19:38)." Joseph faced his fears, and *risked ridicule and worse so that Christ's body would not be thrown in the Jerusalem dump; and everyone just go back to their useless way of living, as though nothing had happened to remedy their useless way of living.* Sandwich finished.)

"And Peter said to Jesus: 'Lord, if it be You, bid me come to You on the water.' And Jesus said: 'Come!' *So when Peter had come down out of the boat, he walked on the water to go to Jesus.* But when he saw the wind was boisterous, he was afraid; and, *beginning* to sink, he cried: 'Lord, save me.' And immediately, Jesus stretched out His hand and caught him; and said to Peter: *'Oh you of little faith, why did you DOUBT* (Matthew 14:28-31)?'" MORE than one lesson resides within this passage. One: *"When launching out on a FAITH mission, do not change your mind or your commitment about half way through. If it took faith to begin that mission, it will take faith to complete it."* Deity demands of believers nothing that does not require faith. Lesson two: *"If we cannot walk on water in a wind or rain STORM, then we cannot walk on water when the wind and water are CALM."* What enables one to walk on water; calm conditions on the water, or supernatural faith? If it is FAITH, then wind and water conditions have NO bearing on supernatural projects. Lesson three: *"Faith and fear being opposing forces, then they have opposing sources.* God being the Source of THE FAITH WHICH OPPOSES FEAR, and kept Peter from drowning, *Satan has to be the source of the kind of fear which challenged Peter's faith, and threatened his life on that turbulent lake.* Peter being a professional fisherman, when he saw those contrary weather conditions, he fell back on his natural knowledge of the dangers of a wind storm out on a lake; which he had gained from his experiences on past fishing expeditions. What Peter was sensing through his five PHYSICAL SENSES challenged the FAITH he had received by hearing that one word "Come!" from the Lord. FEAR ALWAYS CHALLENGES faith. Bible faith ALWAYS CONQUERS fear!

But, people who are steeped in the sense realm, *thinking it is the only dependable source of knowledge*, will fear more and more toward the *END* of this age: *"Men's hearts* [spirits] *failing them for fear; and for LOOKING after those things that are coming on the earth. For* [even] *the powers of heaven will be shaken* (Luke 21:26)." Therefore, those who believe *ONLY* in what they can see, hear, feel, taste, and smell—those five physical senses—*will have a tough time in the end-time.* The only weapon that will work against those end-time fears will be *Bible faith*; which originated in the heavenly realm.

Our Lord addressed just that kind of *heart* (spirit) *failure* when He assured His disciples that: *"Peace I leave with you. My peace I GIVE to you. Not as the world gives, give I to you.* [Therefore,] *LET NOT your heart be troubled. Neither let it be AFRAID* (John 14:27)." Christ's words "Let not" *being a clear command, then resisting fear is the clear responsibility of us believers, not our Lord:* That proving as well that peace is the opposite of fear, and that the two cannot co-exist. Plus, *fear causes turmoil on the inside; taking away one's inner peace.* One more Bible truth residing in this passage is that peace, real peace, just like faith, does not originate in this world. *It comes from above. Peace is of DIVINE origin.* Everyone wants peace, *but few are interested in Divine Peace.* So all that talk about world peace is a delusion in the minds and mouths of those who reject the Source of peace—Deity (Hebrews 13:20).

One more proof of that truth: "That same day at evening, it being the first day of the week [Sunday—The Lord's Day], the doors being shut where the disciples had assembled, *for fear of the Jews*, came Jesus, and stood in their midst; then said to them: 'Peace be to you (John 20:19).'" So here again, peace and fear are proven to be opposed to each other. Fear dominated the disciples before the Day of Pentecost, so they were hiding from the religious bunch, who might come after them just as they had Jesus. *Fear robs people of peace.* Yet, *Jesus soothed their present fears with a salutation of peace.*

Another *Bible evidence that real peace comes from above*: "For you [believers] have not received [from God] the *spirit of BONDAGE again to fear* [*You already had that in the world.*]. But, you have received [from above] the *SPIRIT* of adoption, whereby we cry, 'Abba, Father (Romans 8:15).'" Worldly fear binds people. *Peace is NOT the product of slavish fear. Peace comes from knowing Deity is our daddy! The SPIRIT of peace obviously comes from above; not from this lower realm!*

Even believers may fall for the wrong kind of fear, if they become careless: *"Before certain people came from James* [in Jerusalem], *Peter ATE with the Gentiles.* But when they had arrived, *Peter withdrew and separated himself; fearing those who were of the circumcision* [party] (Galatians 2:12)."

*FEAR produces cowardice, but FAITH produces boldness. So they are always in conflict with one another; especially in believers!* Therefore, *believers need to encourage one another to fear not but be bold; just as the apostle Paul's example did for the Christian believers in Rome*: "Many of the brethren in the Lord, *becoming confident by MY BONDS* [imprisonment], *are NOW MUCH MORE BOLD to speak the Word without fear* (Philippians 1:14)." *Paul NOT caving in to fear of suffering for his Christian testimony encouraged other Christians in Rome to be bold in the face of the same threats against them.*

Another example of the *right kind of fear*: "Wherefore, my beloved, as you have always obeyed [God's Word], not in my [Paul's] presence only, but now, much more, in my absence; *work out your own salvation with fear and trembling.* For, it is God, Who works *IN* you, both to will and to do of His good pleasure (Philippians 2:12-13)." *Deity works salvation IN us Christians. We work it OUT.* God works it in: We work it out. *We cannot produce salvation. ONLY God can do that!* Yet, He commands us to work out the salvation He puts in us when we believe. *We cannot do for ourselves what only He can do; and He will not do for us what He commanded us to do.* And part of His command is that we work out our salvation with *fear and trembling.* We better not treat our salvation lightly; but as a sacred trust. Moreover, our being saved brings God pleasure! *Fear and trembling simply MEANS that we respect the fact that while Deity does have the ability to harm us, He instead wants us to be saved. Satan is the one who wants to harm us; whereas the redemption Christ provided both saves us from any damage the devil has already done in our lives, and protects us from any future damage he would like to do.*

And that helps to explain Paul's words in 2 Timothy 1:7: "God has *NOT* given us [believers] the *spirit of fear;* but [the Spirit] of power, and [the Spirit] of love, and [the Spirit] of a sound mind." *The spirit of fear is not of God; not from above!*

Deity having given us such an advantage over fear, then: "*Let your conversation* [LIFESTYLE] *be without covetousness; and, be content with such things as you have.* For, [God] has said: 'I will never leave you nor forsake you.' *So that we may BOLDLY SAY*: 'The Lord is my Helper; *I will NOT FEAR what man can do to me* (Hebrews 13:5-6).'" See Psalms 56:4, 11.

Even Christ had to have the right kind of fear. "*WHO, in the days of His FLESH, when He had offered up prayers and supplications, with strong crying and tears, to Him Who was able to save Him from death, was heard in that HE FEARED* (Hebrews 5:7)." *God-fear was required even of Jesus, for,...*

*The godly kind of fear* (reverence) *has been a major factor in the lives of godly people since the days of Adam.* "By faith Noah, being warned of God of things not seen as yet, *moved with fear,* prepared an ark to the saving of his house; *by the which he condemned the world* [those things that died], *and became heir of the righteousness which is by faith* (Hebrews 11:7)." We Christians today are to have that same God-fear: "If you call upon the Father, *Who without respect of persons JUDGES, according to every man's work, then pass the time of your sojourning here in* [God-]*fear* (1 Peter 1:17)."

While Peter was obviously referring to *God-fear,* John, in 1 John 4:18, recorded another *Bible Truth about the kind of fear we are commanded to reject:* "*There is NO* [slavish] *fear in love*; *but perfect love* [which comes only from God, and is then redirected toward God] *casts out fear: Because, fear* [of Satan's sort] *has torment.* [God-fear does not cause torment in ANY God-fearer, but it does cause God-haters to tremble. Therefore,] *He who fears* [with the wrong kind of fear] *is not made perfect in* [the God-kind of] *love* (1 John 4:18)." Thus, *the forbidden kind of fear is contrasted with the God-kind of love—Which means that one cannot fear with the wrong kind of fear and love with the God-kind of love at the same time.*

But how may we gain that perfect love, by which we may overcome all of the wrong kinds of fear? "*Whoever keeps His Word, in him truly is the love of God perfected* (1 John 2:5)."

Wrapping up with a few more passages: "These are spots [speaking of false brethren who somehow sneaked into their midst] in your love-feasts, when they feast with you; *feeding themselves without* [any God-]*fear.* Clouds they are without [rain]water, carried about by winds [of false doctrines]; trees whose fruit *WITHERS* [because, there is *NO LIFE IN THEM*]; [and others are even] without fruit, [because they have] *died twice,* [and so are] *plucked up by the roots* (Jude 12)." To die twice (spiritually) means they were once alive in Christ! And that means *THEY LOST THEIR SALVATION.* They did not die twice physically. They were still alive; and feasting with real Christians. Jude had to mean that those false brethren had died spiritually two times. All sinners are *DEAD* in sins and trespasses (Ephesians 2:5, Colossians 2:13). So, in order for such people to have *died twice* they had to have been *saved once. Further proof of that is that, they had been plucked up by the roots.* What roots? *Redemption roots! Sinners have no LIVING ROOTS to be plucked up!* Therefore, it is obvious that they had *LOST BOTH* their God-fear and their salvation!

James 5:19-20: "If anyone among *YOU* Christians strays from [Gospel] truth, and one turns *HIM BACK,* let him know that, *he who turns that SINNER from the error of his way will SAVE HIS SOUL from death,* and cover a multitude of sins."

Why does God desire that both unbelievers and believers have genuine God-fear? *"It is a fearful thing to FALL into the hands of the Living God* (Hebrews 10:31)." So, by voluntarily fearing God up front, out of genuine reverence, we will *NOT FALL* into the *JUDGMENT HANDS* of the Living God later!

Revelation 21:8 puts the final cap on the fear issue: "The *fearful, unbelieving,* abominable, murderers, whoremongers, sorcerers, idolaters, and all liars, will have their *PART* in the lake which burns with *FIRE* and *BRIMSTONE*—Which is the *SECOND DEATH."* So, *the fearful (cowardly) and unbelieving are put in the same PILE with raunchy sinners! Which means THE WRONG KIND OF FEAR IS SIN! The only cure for such a sin is to repent of that fear and lay hold of genuine God-fear.*

Notice one more *sobering truth* in that passage: Of all the disgusting sins mentioned on that list, *fear and unbelief are at the very top of the list.* Therefore, *the wrong kind of fear is quite obviously the basis of ALL those other sins. Wrong-fear is entertained FIRST;* then it leads the wrong-fearers to other disgusting sins. Thus, *wrong-fear* is the *wrong foundation* to build one's life upon: For it actually leads to death (*Which is the subject-matter of the very next chapter.*). To get right with God, and to avoid eternal death, we must build our life upon the only fear that blesses human beings—Genuine God-fear. Satan will not like it, but that is his problem! God-fear totally destroys the devil's fake-fear dominion!

# Chapter Fifteen

## Death

Death is one of the devil's hiding places? Absolutely! One of his favorites. *But how can he HIDE behind what we know he is the very AUTHOR of?* The devil has deceived the world, *and many church members*, about both the *seriousness* and *finality* of death; and has actually trained the great majority of this planet's population, *and most church members*, to be *constantly conscious of death!* One proof of that truth is that people's mouths, including *many church members*, are filled with *death-oriented expressions*—such as *death-cliches* like: *"That just thrills me to death!"* Or, *"That nearly scared me to death!"* Or, *"I am just dying to go!"* Or, *"I will just die, if I do not get to go!"* Or, *"That is to die for!"* Etc., etc., etc. And, the queen-mother of them all: *"I just love you to death!"* Huh?

It is astonishing that even Christians are death-oriented; *in light of the fact that God's Word says plainly that death is an enemy*: "The LAST ENEMY that will be destroyed is death (1 Corinthians 15:26)." John 10:10 explains it well, stating: "The thief comes for no other purpose than to *steal, kill and destroy*. I [Jesus] have come that they might have *LIFE*, and that they might have life more abundantly." Satan being the *CHIEF THIEF*, John 10:10 obviously refers to *HIM*. The devil *STEALS* (things that are necessary to life). And *KILLS* (death certainly *ROBS* people of life). And *DESTROYS* (lures people into sin, *LEADING them to DESTRUCTION; both on earth and in hell*). Steal, kill, destroy—All take life from people's lives.

*Steal* and *kill* speak of the *seriousness* of death, whereas *destroy* points to the *finality* of it. *Sinners committing suicide are attempting to escape unbearable conditions; not realizing the finality of their fateful decision. Or that, even though their circumstances do change they will NOT BE for the better—for the spirits of the unsaved descend into hell.* As bad as it gets on earth, *painful conditions will not last FOREVER;* whereas, *eternal punishment means no breaks from suffering—EVER!*

God certainly wants us to take *seriously* His warnings of the *seriousness* of death: "I [Jehovah] call heaven and earth to record this day against you, that I have set before you life and death, blessing and cursing. Therefore, *choose life, that both you and your seed may live* (Deuteronomy 30:19)." God even told His people which choice to choose; *as though they had not the good sense to choose life!* And therein is another deception of our enemy regarding death. *Why would anyone be so dense that they would have to be told that life is better than death?* Because: "*There is a way that SEEMS right unto a man* [suggesting that that deceptive way seems to promise life], *but at the end of* [that seem-right way] *are the ways of death* (Proverbs 14:12)." Proverbs 16:25 is a repeat.

The warning in Deuteronomy 30:19 was to the Hebrews; *suggesting that God's people were CONFUSED as to whether life is preferable to death!* But, in Romans 1:32, we find that *humanity in general is plagued with the very same stupidity!* "Who knowing the judgment of God, that, *those who commit such things are worthy of DEATH, not only DO the same, but EVEN TAKE PLEASURE in others committing the same sins!*" What sins? Romans 1:18-32 catalogs *all sorts of sins, which sinners commit, and EVEN REVEL IN;* mentioning everything from worshipping bugs and snakes, to committing all kinds of sexual perversion, murder, lying, and *MANY other actions that are contrary to God's original purpose for mankind. And, although sinners generally KNOW the truth of Romans 1:32, that everyone who commits those ungodly things is worthy of death, not only do them, but PRAISE others who do them!* (?)

Now, back to God's own people: "Because you have said, 'We have made a covenant with death, and with hell are we in agreement; when the overflowing scourge passes through, *it will not come unto us*: For we have *MADE LIES* our refuge; and under falsehood have we *HID* ourselves (Isaiah 28:15).'" Those people surely did not think they were trusting in lies; but were doing exactly that! *A LIE HAVING NO SUBSTANCE, they were trusting in something that had no substance—that did not even exist! FOR*, there is *NO WAY* anybody can make a covenant with death; and make a pact with hell! *That was one of the devil's deceptions that worked on the Jews of that day.* And apparently still works on many sinners today.

*What was the divine response to their foolish plan?* "Your covenant with death will be *ANNULLED*; and your agreement with hell will *NOT STAND*. So, when the overflowing scourge does pass through, you *WILL BE* trodden down by it (Isaiah 28:18)." *While no one can bypass God's unchangeable rules, the devil sells many on the HOPE that they just might be an exception to those rules. But, if just one sinner could defy His rules and get away with it, every sinner would follow suit.* If the rules (God's Word) could be altered, this universe would fall apart. Look at Colossians 1:17 and Hebrews 1:3.

Rather than any sinner getting away with sin, Scripture says: "As righteousness tends to life, so he who pursues evil *pursues it to his own death* (Proverbs 11:19)." Surely no one would deliberately pursue their own death; if they knew the seriousness and finality of it. But, many who do realize that death is serious, are still deceived into thinking that maybe they can somehow trick death into staying away from them; just as did those Jews whom God rebuked in Isaiah 28:15.

Peter also had something to say about deceived sinners: "But these, *as natural brute beasts*, [animals that are] *made to be taken and destroyed, speak evil of those things they do not understand. And they will UTTERLY PERISH in their own corruption* (2 Peter 2:12)." But sinners do not think so. *They are unaware of the destruction that is sneaking up on them; which they themselves have carelessly opened the door to.*

Paul also wrote: *"To be carnally-minded is DEATH*; but to be spiritually-minded is life, and peace. Because, the carnal mind is *ENMITY* against God: For it is not subject to the law [the rules] of God, neither indeed can it [the carnal mind] be (Romans 8:6-7)." *Those who think they can get around God's rules are definitely carnally minded—are grossly deceived!*

And not only do sinners do things to destroy themselves; they are often *used by the devil to destroy others* who do not deserve to be destroyed. Ezekiel 13:19 reports that religious leaders in Ezekiel's day were *"killing people who ought not to die, and keeping people alive who ought not to live."* Leaders! *Religion is more cruel than the secular world.*

But, that was in the Old Testament some might say. Yet, Jesus, in John 16:2, a New Testament passage, *pointed out that that same depraved mentality and activity still prevailed in that religious system during His days on earth*: "They [the religious leaders] will *PUT YOU OUT* of the synagogues: Yes, the time will come that *whosoever KILLS YOU will think that he does God service."* Jesus obviously had Saul of Tarsus in mind: *Who after becoming the apostle Paul, admitted that he through unbelief had approved of people being killed because of the religious lies that had deceived him—making him think that killing those opposed to HIS RELIGIOUS VIEWS was the right thing to do—Saul was doing God service.* The devil was hiding behind that deceptive view of *the supposed rightness of killing Christian believers.* First Timothy 1:13—Ignorantly, in unbelief. *WHO is behind both ignorance and unbelief?* The devil! *And what was involved in that ignorance and unbelief?* Killing believers! *Satan hides behind religious ignorance and unbelief; making the murder of opposers seem right.* Also,...

Satanic lies lie behind *infanticide* (abortion—the murder of *INNOCENT UNBORN BABIES*—Jeremiah 2:33-35), *suicide* (taking one's *OWN* life), *genocide* (the destruction of *ENTIRE ETHNIC GROUPS*, based upon a *distorted view* of who ought to live and who ought not to live), *and other false reasons to kill other human beings, who are made in the IMAGE of God. Hating God as he does, the devil wants to destroy everything made in God's image.* So he motivates one God-image to put to death other God-images; until no God-images are left.

Now, this Bible Truth about death: "By one man [Adam,] sin entered the world, and death by sin. Thus, death passed upon *ALL*, for all have sinned (Romans 5:12)." Death having originated with sin, neither sin nor death can be God's will; for *NEITHER WAS HIS ORIGINAL PURPOSE FOR CREATION.*

*Death is separation from God.* And *LUCIFER* was the very first being to separate himself from God. Therefore, death is organically tied to Satan—the fallen Lucifer. *Death being the opposite of life, death surely cannot be God's original will for anybody. That truth being so obvious, the devil has to distort people's view of death, in order to get them to ACCEPT death as the will of God for them;* or others. Remember, *Christ said He had come to give abundant life to humanity* (John 10:10). *Death NOT being abundant life, then death cannot be Deity's will for: His faithful followers, innocent unborn babies, entire ethnic groups, or people taking their very own life.* Life is life, and death is death—no middle ground. *Choose life!*

And now, this Bible Truth about death: The devil tempts people with lust: And, "When lust has conceived [is taken in by the tempted one, *so that it becomes the idea and purpose of that tempted one*], it brings forth sin. Then sin, when it is finished [reaches its full course and the one sinning has not repented of that sin, it] *brings forth death* (James 1:15)." My reason for posting this passage is to reveal that: MANY SINS DO NOT HAVE TO END IN DEATH. *Though sin does pull the sinner in that direction, Deity always gives the sinner time to repent, and be delivered from that DEATH PATH.* It is called mercy! Although that does not mean that one may get away with sin, *it does mean that sin and its eventual result, death, need not be the demise of the sinner.* Sin can be repented of; which alters the future of the one having sinned! That is the very Gospel message! And also concerning Christians:

"If any man sees his brother [or sister] *sin a sin which is not unto death, he can ask* [God], *and* [God] *will give him life for those who sin not unto death.* There is a sin unto death. I do not say that he should pray for that. All unrighteousness is sin. But, *there is a sin NOT unto death* (1 John 5:16-17)." The truth of this passage: Some sins have death attached to them and some do not. The Greek word rendered sin means *to miss the mark. That means to veer away from the purpose for which God created mankind.* Murder, adultery, theft, and lying seriously miss the mark of God's purpose for man, and deserve to be punished. *Some other words and actions miss the mark as well, but do not have ETERNAL DEATH attached to them*—Unintended offenses toward both men and God.

Another *religious misconception* about the death of God's people comes from a *misunderstanding* of this one passage: *"Precious in the sight of the LORD is the DEATH of His saints* (Psalms 116:15)." Satan has talked many into believing that that psalmist meant that Deity *ENJOYS* seeing His very own people die. I myself have heard that lie repeated repeatedly: *"God desired a bouquet of beautiful flowers* [made up of His saints], *and so HE PLUCKED so-and-so by death, in order to complete His bouquet." Even little children! What blasphemy!* Seeing Psalms 116:15 in the light of many other Scriptures, we understand that the psalmist meant that Deity takes the death of His people seriously. He does not treat it lightly. *He certainly meant not that God enjoys seeing believers suffer!*

In fact, *the Bible proves that God enjoys NOT the death of ANYONE: "'I HAVE NO PLEASURE IN THE DEATH OF THOSE WHO DIE,'* says the Lord. 'Therefore, *TURN* yourselves [from your evil way] and *LIVE* (Ezekiel 18:32).'" And, once again in Ezekiel 33:11: "'As I live,' [serious oath] says the Lord *GOD, 'I HAVE NO PLEASURE IN THE DEATH OF THE WICKED*; but [rather, I am pleased] that the wicked turn from his evil way and live. So turn you, turn you from your evil ways; for why will you die, O house of Israel?'" God wants *ALL* to live. That is why Jesus Christ came to earth: "That they may have life, and have it abundantly (John 10:10)!" Satan is the one who steals, kills and destroys. He just loves to see people die.

One other *death-deception* is the worn out cliche: "*Sticks and stones may break my bones, but WORDS will never hurt me.*" Proverbs 18:21 *debunks that deception*: "Death and life are in the power of the tongue [words]: And, they who love it will [reap and] *eat [experience]* the fruit thereof [the power of their tongue—words]." *From WORDS coming out of their own mouths, people partake of either life-fruit or death-fruit.* That is additional *Bible evidence* that *death-cliches* release death into the spirits, souls, bodies, finances and families of those who constantly speak them. *The opposite is just as true; but people who speak life-producing words are often RIDICULED by those who are in the habit of talking death morning, noon, and night.* Who would you think talked that *negative-talking* bunch into *talking negatively*; then *sneering* at all who dare to speak life-words? You guessed it: The lifeless devil!

One even worse demonic lie: John Calvin contended that the Christian life is one of *MISERY*; and God planned it that way for our benefit. (???) *And death was involved in Calvin's doctrine; saying that the day of one's death is better than the day of his birth.* I have heard denominational people say the same thing. And after studying Calvinism (and by the way, *I have written three books that expose John Calvin's heresies*), I now know where those people got that error—John Calvin. Moreover, years ago one of my friends informed me that the Christian life is *HARD (difficult and painful)*. *I reminded him that* Proverbs 13:14-15 *says conversely that: "the way of the transgressor is HARD."* I know the devil does *HIS* upmost to make our lives miserable; *but that is his idea, not God's.* On the cross, our Savior took upon Himself every pain the devil wants to put on us, in order to deliver us from those pains. See Isaiah 53:4-5, 10, Matthew 8:16-17, Galatians 3:13-14, Hebrews 2:14, 1 Peter 2:24, 1 John 5:4, etc., etc., etc.

One problematic verse for some is Matthew 8:22: "Christ said to him [one of His would-be followers]: 'Follow Me; and *let the dead bury their dead.'"* What could Jesus have meant here? *A man wanted to travel with Christ, but his father was close to dying, and that disciple wanted to be around to bury his father when that time would come.* So, he wanted to stay home for now and join Jesus later. That is when Christ said what He said. *Dead bodies do not bury other dead bodies, so Jesus was obviously telling that man to let his SPIRITUALLY DEAD family members bury that man's father when he died. There were people who needed to hear the Gospel right then! Preaching that Good News was MORE IMPORTANT than that disciple staying at home awaiting the death of his father.*

*Another religious error is that we Christians are supposed to DIE TO SELF every day.* After all, the apostle Paul himself did say: "*I die daily* (1 Corinthians 15:31)." Now, if the great apostle Paul *died to self every day,* then who are we to deny that we are to do the same? *In that Corinthian passage, Paul was referring to facing possible physical death every day. He said nothing about dying to himself there, or anywhere.* Paul faced wild beasts at Ephesus (verse 32). *The constant threat of physical death was his obvious meaning; not dying to self!*

211

In fact, Paul actually said in Romans 14:7: *"No man lives to himself, and no man dies to himself."* That should forever settle that issue. IF NO MAN DIES TO HIMSELF, THEN PAUL DID NOT DIE TO HIMSELF; AND, NEITHER MUST WE! Many, however, *had rather hold onto their RELIGIOUS TRADITIONS than believe God's Word about that or any other subject.*

At this writing, one very popular TV show is about *dead people walking around.* Of course, *they make the actors look like corpses that have been exhumed from the grave.* But, in reality, *many people today actually are the WALKING DEAD.* They are *SPIRITUALLY DEAD,* although still walking around in the flesh. Many people are fascinated with that TV series, but most of those very same people are totally unaware that the lost are actually more dead than those TV actors appear to be. Consider this Bible example: "This my son was *DEAD,* and is *ALIVE* again; he was lost, and is found (Luke 15:24)." Alive *AGAIN* must mean he was once alive before he became dead. What sort of dead? Spiritually dead! Just as many are today. Most people on this planet today are spiritually dead; for *THE WHOLE WORLD* lies under the *SWAY* of the Wicked One (1 John 5:19). *They are lost because of their separation from God, and connection to the devil:* "You are of your father the devil, and [for that reason,] *his lusts you will to do* (John 8:44)." That means the Prodigal Son was *DEAD IN SIN,* until he repented and went home—Which is when he became alive once again. Had he NOT repented and gone home, he would have remained dead in sin—And upon his physical death, he would have descended into Hades. God's Word is quite clear about that. To the Pharisees, Christ said: *"If you believe not that I am He* [your Messiah,] *you will die in your sins* (John 8:24)." And people who die in their sins descend into Hades; and Hades is a place of perpetual suffering. See Luke 16:23. And, that truth helps us understand the supreme price our Savior paid for us by His sacrifice. Matthew 12:40: "The Son of Man will be in the heart of the earth three days and three nights." Hades is obviously located in the heart of the earth, where the Lord's spirit was during that time. Acts 2:31 says *He was NOT LEFT in Hades,* but *"God raised Him up, having loosed the pains of death* (Acts 2:24)." *Death-pains had to be in the Savior's spirit; not in His lifeless body in the grave.*

In both Ephesians 2:1 and Colossians 2:13, Paul taught that every lost person is dead in sin—*meaning their spirit is dead; NOT their body.* Which proves that the *Prodigal Son* of Luke 15:24 had died in his spirit. Spiritual death is *NOT* the cessation of existence, but separation from God, the Source of life. *So, ONE CAN BE OUTWARDLY ALIVE BUT INWARDLY DEAD at the same time. Spiritual death eventually produces physical death—Which is proven in* Genesis 2:17; *where God warned Adam that on the day he ate of the forbidden fruit he would SURELY die.* The literal Hebrew: *"Dying, you will die." "Your spirit will die on the day you eat; and your spirit-death will eventually produce death in your physical body."* Adam's spirit *DIED* in Eden. Nine hundred and thirty years later his body died and returned to the dust (Genesis 3:19, 5:5).

Remember, we are discussing many of the ways the devil *HIDES* behind death. *He cannot hide behind the actual Bible Truth regarding death, so he relies on the lies and distortions about death he persuades people to believe about death.*

One such lie: *Death is earned; so life can also be earned.* However, *although the WAGES OF SIN is death,* according to Romans 6:23, death is *MORE* than something sinners earn. Death has been part of the human experience since Adam's fall. *That should be obvious, because even those who live the BEST lives still die physically—just like sinners do.* Scripture also solves that death-mystery: "Nevertheless, death reigned from Adam, to Moses, *EVEN over people who had not sinned after the similitude of Adam's transgression* (Romans 5:14)." *Adam's death was the result of his violation of one command to NOT EAT of one tree. When the Mosaic law was instituted, breakers of that LAW incurred death.* However, *Paul pointed out that those BETWEEN Adam and Moses died the same as before and after; even though NO LAW was given during that time for them to VIOLATE. That means DEATH IS LODGED IN THE HUMAN SPIRIT; and affects the physical body more and more, until it finally dies.* Death even takes its toll on infants, who have NOT SINNED! By means of ONLY ONE SIN, death, both spiritual and physical, came upon the human race; and will plague every generation until death is finally defeated (1 Corinthians 15:26, Revelation 21:4). *And the Bible definitely rejects the satanic lie that life can be earned by good deeds.*

Death-doctrine errors affect the way we Christians *VIEW OUR STANDING WITH OUR CREATOR AND REDEEMER*. And *MOST death-doctrine errors in the modern church are based on the heresies of Augustine and John Calvin*. I have written three books that expose John Calvin's *MANY* errors. Surely, you will want to read all three. *ONE* of Calvin's *BIG ERRORS* in his theology—*Even Christians are sinners!* I hear that *LIE* preached in almost every denominational setting. But, what does God's Word say about us believers? A bunch! I will not duplicate what I have written in those books. *But, I do want to point out that IT IS IMPOSSIBLE for one who has DIED TO SIN to still be a sinner. When a person gets born again, he or she is no longer a sinner; for he or she is A NEW CREATURE in Christ* (2 Corinthians 5:17). *All things of their old life have PASSED AWAY; AND ALL THINGS HAVE BECOME NEW.* So, where does *Christians-are-still-sinners* fit in Scripture? Why is the *NEW CREATURE* not a sinner? *Because the old sinner DIED and exists NO MORE.* Romans 6:2: "*How will we, who died to sin, live any longer in it?*" Who died to sin? Believers! Romans 6:11: "*JESUS CHRIST DIED TO SIN! Likewise, count yourselves to be DEAD to sin, but alive to God, through Jesus Christ.*" Who is commanded to count that we are dead to sin because the Bible says we are? We believers! However, John Calvin defied God's Word, *contending that Christians are yet sinners, EVEN AFTER being born again*. Will we believe John Calvin, or Scripture? The way we see our standing with God goes a long way in determining our lifestyle! *How can we be dead to sin, BUT still be sinners at the same time? If we ARE sinners, then we need to get BORN AGAIN, and become new creatures in Christ. If we HAVE BEEN BORN AGAIN, we ARE no longer sinners* (sin producers), *BUT children of God*. That is the *PROPER* biblical view of death and life in Christ. If we died to sin, we must *SEE OURSELVES* dead to sin, and alive to God. *If we ARE SINNERS, we are NOT NEW CREATURES. If we ARE NEW CREATURES, we are NOT SINNERS. It is one way or the other. Sinners serve Satan; Christians serve God!* Nobody can serve *TWO* different masters—both God and the devil (Matthew 6:24). So, it is time to *DUMP* Calvinism, and hook up with God's Word concerning our spiritual condition before our Maker and Redeemer. I am doing all I know to do to get this Gospel Truth out to everyone. What will you do?

One more Calvinist lie is that Christian believers *ARE TO BE PITIED*, because Romans 8:36 states: "As it is written [in Psalms 44:22], 'For Your sake, [*Oh LORD,*] we are killed all the day long; we are accounted as sheep for the slaughter.'"

*But look at the context* of both Psalms 44 and Romans 8. *The VICTIMS in that Psalms quote were REBELLIOUS JEWS.* So, Romans 8:36 *ought to have ended with a question mark.* Those translators disregarded the obvious contrast between Psalms 44:22 and what Paul penned in 8:37. It should have been translated: *"Is it with us believers, as it is written? No!" That is much more true to the context,* because Romans 8:37 says: *"Nay, in all these things we are more than conquerors."* NAY CONTRADICTS THAT QUOTE in verse 36—*The obvious truth Paul was attempting to get across*—No it is not with us *AS* it was written about those Jews in Psalms 44. Read the contexts of *BOTH* passages; then think about it. God's Word plainly teaches that born-again Christians are *MORE THAN CONQUERERS! GOD ALWAYS CAUSES US TO TRIUMPH* (2 Corinthians 2:14)! *OUR FAITH OVERCOMES THE WORLD* (1 John 5:4), etc. In Christ, we are *VICTORS; NOT VICTIMS!*

Another informative Scripture passage on that subject of death is 2 Corinthians 7:10; telling us: *"Godly sorrow works repentance to salvation; not to be repented of. But the sorrow of the world works* [or produces] *death."* The world says that if we are caught in wrong-doing, our apology should rectify any problem. *The Bible DEMANDS repentance! An apology is no more than an attempt to vindicate one's words or actions.* "IF I HAVE OFFENDED YOU, I APOLOGIZE." "IF I HAVE!" *The PRIMARY DEFINITION of apology is to make a DEFENSE. So, apologies are NOT repentance!* They are a very *SUBTLE WAY* of worming one out of taking responsibility. *And what is the result of such worldly sorrow? Death! Godly sorrow produces real repentance, which changes one's attitude, and direction, and destiny!* Worldly sorrow is *hypocritical,* because it offers ONLY words—*NO actual change in either the offender, or any problem that offender has caused. Those who get caught are only SORRY FOR GETTING CAUGHT. They ARE NOT SORRY FOR ANY WORD OR ACTION*—Which is *WHY* worldly sorrow works death. *There is NO change within the offender; or ANY rectification of circumstances the offender has brought about.*

Still another *subtle deception* of Satan is to deceive God's people about how they are to relate to this fallen world. *The Christian has been translated from the devil's dark kingdom into God's Kingdom of light* (Colossians 1:13). *That demands that the new Christian's perspective on everything in life be reversed; just as day is the opposite of night, and light is the opposite of darkness: Which illustrates both the direction and degree of the demanded change of perspective. Being part of the fallen world system, we USED TO have to depend on this fallen world for all of the answers to all of our questions and needs. But, NOW that we belong to a totally different family, and kingdom, we are to look in a totally different direction for all the answers to all our needs—UP!* That does not mean we are to want to die and go to heaven right now, but rather, to look to heaven for all we need while we are still living in this dark world. *But, because of religious doctrine, most believers maintain that same worldly perspective they had before they got born again and became new creatures in Christ.* But how does that *RELATE* to the subject-matter of death? Paul said, "*If you be DEAD with Christ from the rudiments of the world, why, as though* [you are still] *in the world*['s system] *are you still SUBJECT TO world principles* (Colossians 2:20)?" "*If you were RAISED WITH Christ, SEEK THOSE THINGS THAT ARE ABOVE, where Christ sits on the right hand of God. Set your affection on THINGS ABOVE, not on things of earth. For you HAVE DIED* [to both sin and this world], *and your life is hid with Christ in God* (Colossians 3:1-3)." So we *Christians ARE COMMANDED to live from heaven's perspective; not from the world's perspective. Just as dead people are NOT dominated by the world they USED TO BE PART OF, believers are not to be dominated by this fallen world system* (Galatians 6:14).

*More light on another passage that has been darkened by theological mishandling*: Paul wrote: "That I may know Him, and the power of His resurrection, and the fellowship of His sufferings; *being made conformable UNTO HIS DEATH: IF by any means, I may ATTAIN UNTO the resurrection of the dead* (Philippians 3:10-11)." At first glance, *this passage seems to suggest that Paul longed for the resurrection of his body.* But the context itself trashes that view; because, in verse twelve Paul wrote: "*Not that I have already attained that goal, but I press on, that I may lay hold of that for which I was laid hold of!" Paul was expressing his desire to get the MOST out of his Christian life; wanting to experience EVERY BLESSING Jesus purchased for us in His sacrifice.* "Being conformed unto His death" means *being FULLY IDENTIFIED with Jesus Christ in His death, burial, and resurrection, in order to obtain the full benefit of His sacrifice.* Theologians turn Paul's statement in this passage into a sadistic lamentation. *Paul himself would rebuke them for teaching that his words expressed desire to die and go to heaven.* Paul did not mention going to heaven. Moreover, the resurrection of our body is in the future. That does not occur when we die and go to heaven. No; *Paul was expressing his desire to experience the fulness of his new life in Christ in his spirit, soul and body THIS SIDE OF HEAVEN.*

Another Scripture passage many people misunderstand: "*Jesus Christ has ABOLISHED DEATH, and brought life and immortality to light through the Gospel* (2 Timothy 1:10)." Not *physical* death, but *spiritual* death. Jesus Himself said: "*The one who lives in Me will NEVER DIE* (John 11:26)." The Lord has *abolished death* in the Christian's spirit. *Physical death will continue to prevail until the New Heaven and New Earth.* But abolished means abolished—*RENDERED INEFFECTIVE*; or *SHUT DOWN. Death has been abolished in the Christian's re-born spirit.* But Satan and religion lie to us about that.

Just a few more essential passages on the death subject: "Forasmuch then as the children are partakers of flesh and blood, He Himself likewise took part of the same [flesh and blood]; *that through* [His very own] *DEATH, He might destroy him who had the power of DEATH; that is the devil* (Hebrews 2:14)." Satan certainly attempts to keep that truth from the believer! The word translated destroy in that verse means *to render ineffective*; or as I say it: "*to shut down.*" *Whereas the devil has turned death into a weapon, and lies about it to the world and the church*; on the cross, Jesus both redeemed us from death in all its forms, and rendered Satan powerless to *PUSH* death on Christian believers. *Church leaders ought to use that passage every time they serve communion; and the congregation then ought to release their faith in that passage to render ineffective every form of death—including sickness.*

Connect Hebrews 2:14 with 1 Corinthians 11:26: "For as often as you eat this bread and drink this cup, you do show *the Lord's death* until He comes." What did our Lord's death accomplish? Many wonderful things; *including rendering the devil ineffective! So every time we partake of the communion, we need to remind BOTH ourselves and the devil that he has been rendered ineffective to us who are in Christ. Jesus shut down his ability to put upon us ANY form or degree of death;* and that includes sickness and disease. Sickness being one form and degree of death, and Christ having shut down him who had the power of death, then the devil's ability to strike us Christians with *ANY* form or degree of sickness has been destroyed—rendered inoperative—shut down. Hallelujah!

Since Adam sinned, bringing both spiritual and physical death on the entire human race, Hebrews 9:27 has been *an unrelenting law which each and every generation has had to face*: "It is appointed unto men *ONCE* to die, and after that, the judgment." *Even Enoch and Elijah, both of whom did not die before they ascended to heaven, and so must be the two witnesses of* Revelation 11, *will have to die; which they do in* Revelation 11. *Then they will be resurrected just like the rest of us.* Enoch and Elijah were caught up to heaven, and kept alive and preserved for their ministry as the two witnesses.

One passage in Revelation reveals that God both knows, and may expose, *the spiritual condition of Christians* in local churches: "To the angel [messenger] of the church in Sardis write: 'These things says He, Who has those seven Spirits of God, and the seven stars: "I know your works; and that you have the *NAME* [reputation] that you live, but [instead,] are dead (Revelation 3:1).""" That is the *WRONG* kind of dead for believers. And sadly, *many today are in the same condition.*

*The death which Deity inflicts upon unrepentant sinners is punishment for their connection to the devil; a murderer, thief and destroyer of God's creation. But, for believers in the New Heaven and the New Earth, death will not exist* (Isaiah 25:8, 1 Corinthians 15:26, Revelation 21:4); *because the Creator's original plan for both angels and men was not death, but life; and Deity will see to it that abundant life reigns once again!*

# Conclusion

*Remember that the devil never approaches human beings as his diabolical self. Satan cannot afford to divulge his real character to those he seeks to destroy, so he bluffs both men and angels with his lies. But, lies themselves being empty of any real substance, therefore, being easily detected as false, the devil has to cover his lies with deceptive camouflages. He hides behind untruths by presenting them as truths; so that, both angels and men will accept his lies as truths.* I included angels in my comment because one third of the angels were obviously fooled by Lucifer—now the devil—long before man came on the scene. Had the angels known they were getting themselves into eternal trouble, surely they would not have let Lucifer talk them into rebelling with him against God.

The devil's most widespread deception has to be political correctness, seeing that it dominates everyone who is lost in the world; *as well as a significant portion of the church.* As a matter of fact, political correctness has not only *invaded* the modern church, but *within the church has taken on an even more subtle form known as RELIGIOUS CORRECTNESS. It is even more subtle than the world's deceptive version, because it lies about God and even accuses God of lying.* Through his theology, John Calvin brought religious correctness into the church; *although he would surely not call it such, or concede that his theology is a pack lies, or that the devil is behind his falsehoods.* John Calvin was TOTALLY deceived by the devil!

Yet, according to God's Word, *we Christians ought not be surprised that such evil has found its place within the church today.* Remember that *our Savior warned us about wolves in sheep's clothing* (Matthew 7:15). Sheep's clothing would fool church people before it would fool anybody else, so our Lord had to be referring to deceivers within the church itself. The apostle Paul addressed that same problem in 2 Corinthians 11:13-15, where he stated plainly that many ministers, *who had been accepted by the church as genuine ministers, were actually false apostles.* And Paul linked them with the devil. *Jude also pointed out that FALSE believers had sneaked into some congregations,* and were mingling with real Christians in their love feasts—*their true identity still being undetected!*

So, be not deceived into believing that Christ's and Paul's warnings were to the first-century believers only. *Wolves did not disappear after the first century.* Grievous WOLVES have not only survived nineteen centuries since, but, are actually *far greater in number today than ever before; because, today there are thousands of denominations, whereas first-century Christians knew only one church.* Today there is lots of room for foul play. *And you can bet the devil is in the middle of it!*

And, even more disturbing: MODERN CHURCH WOLVES are propagating more disgusting heresies than the wolves of early days. I pointed out that tragic truth in the chapters on the *forbidden practice of private Bible interpretation.* The list includes the blasphemous claim that Eve had *SEX* with the devil; resulting in Cain's birth—*making Cain HALF MAN and HALF ANGEL.* Such being blatant blasphemy, the absurdity of the claim is that Eve was pregnant with Abel at the same time as a result of her intimacy with Adam. The heresy goes on to claim that Cain's offspring boarded the ark with Noah, survived the flood, were involved in repopulating earth, and remain with us to this day. *We Christians who believe in the pre-tribulation rapture of the church are Cain's descendants.* (??) And so are the Russian Communists. (??) See why I say modern sheep/wolves are propagating even more disgusting heresies than those wolves of the church's early days?

*And that is just one of many heresies spawned by private Bible interpretation. We will not REVISIT all of that here, so I recommend that you REVISIT the Private-Bible-Interpretation chapters. I will mention the HERESY that there is NO present hell-fire, and that sinners will be CONSUMED in an end-time fire; and then that fire will just go out. ALL SATANIC LIES!*

When John wrote in Revelation 21:4 that someday in the future God is going to *"wipe away ALL tears from their eyes; that there will BE NO MORE DEATH, SORROW, OR CRYING; NEITHER WILL THERE BE ANY MORE PAIN; for those former things have passed away,"* John and Deity *were referring to people who are SAVED; not to people who will spend eternity in that Lake of Fire.* That ought to be obvious, for Revelation 21:8 says "The fearful and unbelieving and abominable and murderers and whoremongers and sorcerers and idolaters, and all liars, *will have their PART in the lake that burns with fire and brimstone* [eternally]: Which is the second death."

In Mark 9:44, 46 and 48, Christ quoted verbatim Isaiah 66:24, which plainly says: "Where their worm dies not, and *the fire is NOT quenched." That fire is eternal, and will not go out; and those who are immersed in it will suffer for eternity.* Sinners will be tormented without being consumed. *If saved people have ETERNAL life, then those who are doomed to the Lake of Fire will suffer FOR ETERNITY.* If one is eternal then both are eternal, for the same wording is used of both.

Of course, Satan hides behind his lies about money, sex, fear and death. However, some may question whether Satan can hide behind prayer. But again, *it is his distortions about prayer that Satan hides behind*. Yet, even more disturbing is the fact that few believers can detect the difference between real prayer and Satan's powerless, deceptive substitutes.

One final enlightening truth: *Although the devil wants to be worshipped, and will do most anything to get worshipped, his greater desire is to remain unexposed. So, Satan must be behind the teaching that there is no devil! That allows him to steal, kill and destroy without being noticed. HIS DECEPTIVE NATURE forces him to hide in deceptive shadows.* This book dispels those shadowy deceptions with the Gospel light!

*In my own personal library I keep ONLY those books I call keepers.* I believe all of the books I have written are keepers. Surely, you will want to keep this and all of my other books in your library. If my books are helpful to you, they will help others too! So please tell others about them. Thank you!